IMPRISONED $

An Inquiry into Prisons and Academe

Carol A. Mullen

University Press of America, Inc.
Lanham • New York • London

Copyright © 1997 by
University Press of America,® Inc.
4720 Boston Way
Lanham, Maryland 20706

3 Henrietta Street
London, WC2E 8LU England

Library of Congress Cataloging-in-Publication Data

Mullen, Carol A.
Imprisoned selves : an inquiry ilnto prisons and academe / Carol A.
Mullen
p. cm.
Includes bibliographical references and index.
1. Prisoners--Education--United States. 2. Action research in
education--United States. 3. Teachers--United States. 4. Education--
Social aspects--United States. 5. Educational anthropology--United
States. politics. I. Title.
HV8883.3U5M85 1996   365'.66--dc20   96-43222 CIP

ISBN 0-7618-0552-4 (cloth: alk. ppr.)
ISBN 0-7618-0553-2 (pbk: alk. ppr.)

Dedicated to Dr. William A. Kealy, my husband and best friend, for the magic he brings into my life and for the many special ways in which he supports my professional development.

Contents

List of Tables and Figures

Figure 1

Narrative Researchers and Prisoners as Carousel-Riders

Prelude

The Go-Girl's Escape
from Academic Tradition

The five hundred yards stretched away in front of us like five hundred miles as we steeled ourselves for the break. . . . Two swift forms broke from the marching ranks, ran straight ahead, and smashed into the human barrier. Behind us sounded the shrill blast of whistles and loud shouts of 'GO BOYS! GO BOYS!' shattered the stillness of the night (Caron 1978, 29).

Prisoners typically shout "Go boy!" to those escaping from jail. I am adopting this tradition for my own purposes. I see myself as a "go-girl" who is breaking away from conventional studies of classrooms in teacher education and research. My text offers a narrative inquiry about a non-school site, a jail, as an alternative educational and research site. I also provide alternative viewpoints using my experience of this fieldsite. I interpret my experience as a story of teaching and learning in narrative inquiry terms. Sharing, writing and growing were all essential to my encounter with the inmates. So too were experiences of abandonment, loss and suffering as well as intellectual forms of constraint. I am using a metaphor of multiple imprisoned selves to tell my research story and to reveal how I configure my relationship to others.

The first convict I ever talked with is a well-known, Canadian writer. He is Roger Caron, a notorious, long-time federal offender. Caron is prolific: a bank robber, prison-autobiographer and lecturer on prison reform. He tells his story to people in secondary schools and universities where I have heard him speak. I wrote to Roger on October 15, 1990 about his autobiographical novel, *Go-Boy!* (1978). I told him how his story had deeply moved me. I revealed how he had caused me to think about the assumptions I hold, and covert judgments I make, about prisoners and other imprisoned selves. He had been very effective in relating to someone whose life seemed very different from his own. I felt that his story of a life led mis-educatively had brought meaning to teacher education in the areas of autobiography, teacher development and curriculum-making. I shared some of my personal mythology and history with him. I related these dimensions to my creative writing practices, life experiences and family. I described myself as a "vicarious participant" in their story and his. I was later to position myself as a "marginal-insider" not only actually inside a correctional facility for men only but also within the larger world of corrections itself.

Roger telephoned me in the fall of 1990. I was surprised and delighted. I had hoped that his reaching out was a positive sign that the world of corrections would make room for me to listen and to document other inmates' stories of experience. As Glesne and Peshkin (1992) write, the "gift of personal presence is being able to tell the stories of our others" (8). I wanted to adopt an alternative approach to studying teaching and teacher development within higher education. By *alternative* I mean the multiple, non-school contexts in which teaching and learning can be pursued and that still provide opportunities for transformation. I mean research sites other than regular classrooms. Those teacher educators who value a broadening of our constructs of education and research and who include but do not limit inquiry to schools include Connelly and Clandinin 1988b; Diamond 1991; Glesne and Peshkin 1992; Rose 1990; Van Maanen 1988. By alternative I also mean the process of searching for new ways of telling our stories in education. These include narrative inquiry, dream texts, literary images and myths as relevant to my study.

Narrativists approach the self as a story to be constructed and reconstructed through the research process and in educational studies.

Such narrative studies give meaning to human actors and their life experiences (see Clandinin 1986; Clandinin and Connelly 1994; Mishler 1986; Mullen, Blake, Ford, Furlong, Li, and Young 1992c; Polkinghorne 1988). Ethnographic studies that are close to narrative inquiries also probe human lives. These tend to focus on the conditions that give rise to both the construction and possible transformation of human lives (Anderson 1989; Clifford 1988; Geertz 1988; Rose 1990).

Qualitative research inquiry is strongly influenced by the anthropological tradition, but is becoming more open to alternative modes known as narrative inquiry, action research, collaborative inquiry, feminist methodology and participatory research. Researchers' lives become entwined with people in their fieldsites as they interact with them so as to learn from and about them (Glesne and Peshkin 1992, 10). I believe that researchers' experiences are entwined with their participants' in both lived and imagined ways within groups, in community, and in society itself.

Narrative inquiry itself is a process that makes meaning of the self in relation to the people and events under study. As human actors and characters in our own stories, we study, interpret and create human experience (Connelly and Clandinin 1994). By narrative inquiry I also mean the use of story as a self-reflexive method that engages one's artistic sensibilities. Narrative involves others and the reporting self as its participants. The emphasis is typically on the participants' own stories, but it can also be on those of the researcher writer in the forms of self-study and shared or collaborative practice (Diamond, Mullen, and Beattie 1996). Through self-reflexive writing, researchers can discover the personal images, metaphors and myths that determine universal, communal and intersubjective experiences, and that direct their own research (Mullen 1994).

I am also drawn to narrative inquiry as an approach to inmates' stories as it is intellectually open, favoring artistic strokes that are constructive, sensory and imaginative. Researchers have a significant role to play in the creation of experiences and in the production of studies and knowledge (Eisner 1991, 1993). I want to become reflexively self-conscious about how I interpret and represent my own story in relation to others' stories. My portrait, which includes others also living in captivity, is written inter-subjectively. It is about the literal confinement of lives; about imprisoned selves that struggle for articulation and voice; and about the phenomenon of imprisonment itself as linked to education.

My perspective on teacher development is situated within the personal and cultural traditions of narrative inquiry and ethnography. Both orientations allow the researcher to be present in others' lives as the way to learn about another culture and the self. For me, teacher development consists of a personal and professional account (and field within teacher education) that concerns itself with the transformation of teachers and learners in alternative schooling sites (Feuerverger and Mullen 1995). I am aware of academics who have created their own understanding of, and perspective on, narrative inquiry. The graduate students/researchers who contributed to *Stories We Are: Narrative Enactments of Inquiry* (Mullen, et al. 1992c) used autobiography and narrative to make sense of their own inquiries. For example, Bell used her personal experiences as a literacy learner of Chinese; Chapman used her mathematical teaching experiences; Lees focused on the personal practical knowledge of a teacher's computer use; and, I created a mythology of my personal and professional dreams.

As I look back on my conversations with Roger prior to my work in the jail, I realize how much he had inspired me and on many levels. In terms of perspective, at times I strongly identified with him, especially in his self-portrait. I see him now as a writer-outlaw who, unlike the inmate, is not imprisoned in passivity. The *writer-outlaw* speaks back and speaks out. By telling stories of such experiences, s/he tests boundaries and breaks through barriers. The outlaw is born. But, even the outlaw viewpoint is imprisoning. As Diamond (1992) writes, "no code is easily broken . . . but we can seek to become present to ourselves and more capable of referring what we take to be real to our own subjective points of view" (74).

I sought to become more fully present to myself by acting out my perspectives. I played multiple roles in the jail as a curriculum maker, learner, teacher, co-facilitator, Creative Writing coordinator and researcher. I was influenced by Clandinin and Connelly's (1992) concept of teacher as curriculum maker. This helped me to re-envision and then re-write the script of my researcher-inmate-institution relations. The multitude of restrictions, procedures and pressures in the jail minimized opportunities for action, but they did not altogether prevent them. I came to conceive of action itself as consisting of curricular innovations, collaboration and negotiation, and growth.

My actions were also strongly motivated by my goals and visions. I wanted to become a coordinator of a Creative Writing program not then established and an official educational researcher with the

Ministry of Correctional Services. I wanted to connect this domain of teacher education experience to produce, in Bruner's (1979) terms, a form of "effective surprise" that is the "hallmark of a creative enterprise" (18). I considered how a jail might be constructed as a real school and its inhabitants as real curriculum-makers. I knew the possibility of connection between corrections and teacher education in my personal life. I have written, lived and dreamed images of imprisonment and education. A dream that predates this study is about my incarceration in an attic along with my siblings (Mullen 1990). In it, I write to make sense of an unexpected turn of events. I knew that this dream would find its way into my dissertation, only the discovery of the "how" had yet to be lived. I have since guided this feeling to write poetry and stories about the images of my youth, development and personal family history—all called to account in the jail.

In his writing, Roger Caron is a tough but sensitive character. He has a raw but powerful style that he draws upon to write from experience, not just about it. This is what I was to learn about the hundreds of inmates whom I was soon to meet over an eighteen month period. I would work with some of them intensively. Roger had stopped talking for several years during his incarceration but continued writing. He made it the subject of his inquiry to understand why he was trying to "destroy [him]self in such a painfully slow manner" (Caron 1978, 276). Some of the inmates I came to know seemed scared. Many inmate-writers in the Creative Writing program wrote about their sensibilities. Sear Robinson, for example, depicts his life as controlled by "Mr. Jones," a cocaine lord, and the "carousel" of "painted pon[ies] bound for hell" (see Appendix B: "Correctional newsletter," "Mr. Jones (to the moon)"). Another student, Black Hawk, writes about the vision of immortality that is essential to easing the pain of a "diminishing reality" (see Appendix B, "Diminishing reality" and "Dream duration").

How Roger perceived one of his admissions into a federal penitentiary is deeply ironic. He typically despised this ritual. But this time, he re-scripted it as a journey into a "strange new world of self-discovery" that he would make a "compulsive effort" to understand. He chose writing as his means for self-exploration and expression, or, rather, it chose him:

> Jotting down my mercurial inner thoughts on paper was totally alien
> because I hated writing and could barely spell dog and cat; but within

me was a compelling force that drove me to scribble and scribble on
scraps of paper like a drowning man hanging on to a buoy. I was totally
unaware that this early, primitive effort would eventually evolve into
thousands of pages of a manuscript" (Caron 1978, 276).

Roger helped me to see that other inmates could also write. I did
not allow the reports of low literacy levels for prisoners to unnerve me.
One such report, *When Words are Bars*, refers to statistics compiled by
Correctional Services Canada: "approximately 65% of those entering
the prison system for the first time are functionally illiterate" (Paul
1991, 19). Federal prisoners are more functionally illiterate than
provincial inmates. This distinction is probably irrelevant for those
provincial-level volunteers who work directly with inmates and
acknowledge a "noticeable lack of functional literacy skills" among
this "socially-disadvantaged" group (Paul, 19-20) .

I thought that Roger and I would share over the telephone our
individual processes of writing. This did occur, but only haphazardly. I
sensed that something was amiss. Roger sounded incoherent and
listless, and I felt disappointed. My own jottings did not help much
either. They did not reflect the quality of his mumbling speech,
rambling tales, and broken narrative sequences. I tried not to judge
him. Instead, I strove to understand how he was making sense of his
life through writing. I already knew that he used images of drowning
and pacing in his books, but it was as though they had become literal
experiences taken from his life:

> Roger talked about drowning and wanting to be thrown a stick. He said
> that his girlfriend, who is much older than himself, had thrown him a stick
> long ago. He almost drowned, but she saved him. He said that he has
> stayed with her all of these years because she has continued saving him.
> After pausing, he added that he should have stayed in the lake because
> otherwise he is stuck reading and writing, and he still hates these
> activities. When I asked him how he gets himself in the mood to write he
> said "pacing, just a whole lot of pacing in my Ottawa flat. I'm getting ready
> to write a new book, so I have to pace it out first." He then said that he
> also has to do a great deal of strenuous exercise just to keep the shakes
> under control (*Daily Reflections Journal*, November 1, 1990).

I learned that Parkinson's disease has interfered with much of his
mental functioning and life as Roger envisioned living it. He still
writes, but as a medicated storyteller who has since re-offended and

ended up once again behind bars. In societal terms, Roger's cost of rebellion might be "being seen as a no-goodnik, a criminal, an evil-doer" (Lessing 1986, 24). In his relapse he is seen as hopeless and therefore beyond rehabilitation. This is the common reaction that people voice to me on this subject. In narrative terms, Roger has become a prisoner of his old story and his actions predictably and unfortunately follow it. He had attempted armed robbery, but not exactly in the spirit of his criminal record and as his history would have therefore predicted. The gun was unloaded and the holdups took place at a Bi-Way and Zeller's department store. He had apparently been using cocaine to "ease the symptoms of Parkinson's disease and to help him concentrate while writing" ("Jailhouse author Roger Caron gets eight years for two robberies," 1993). Roger spent ten years of his life being straight. I see him as someone who seriously attempted to reconstruct himself and his life through writing, but the "invisible chains," "prison cell," and "bloody phantoms" that were his keepers remain in their various forms (*Bingo!,* 1985, xii) to imprison him.

We *are* our stories. It is difficult, in other words, to refashion the self and its "invisible chains" without sufficient storying and restorying, living and reliving (Connelly and Clandinin 1990). This is a very challenging process to try to gauge but it must be attempted. The sad irony is that Roger, as a re-scripted self, may have been serving as an inspiring example to other inmates (but not all, I learned!). Inmates can learn to tell and live their own deeper life texts through a spirit of re-education. Given the opportunity for growth, inmates can become curriculum-makers, teachers and learners, and creative writers. What emerges from this promising relationship with themselves are new stories to tell. The living out of these stories can also occur should situations that are conducive to self-transformation be fostered in our society. We represent the world to ourselves and we react to others' representations of us (Bruner 1979). If one is locked in a prison, this process of internalization continues. In other words, even prisoners cannot really be cut-off from influences and from being influenced. It is best that we adopt a pro-active stance with regard to prisoners and their process of re-education. We can participate in shaping their journeys, but not without some critical involvement with the penal system itself.

The experience of prisons is discontinuous and interrupted for inmates, staff and visitors alike. I see many inmates as medicated storytellers whose broken dreams disturb the surface of narrative concepts of continuity, growth and transformation. The majority of my participants were either recovering from substance abuse or were taking prescribed drugs for various health reasons. These "health reasons" seemed to function also as measures of control for their anger, insomnia and depression. I too come from a family of medicated storytellers. My growing up experiences have, in part, inspired me to seek the educational value of concepts and experiences of imprisonment and captivity. My poem, "Imprisoned selves," is about my personal history in its relationship to my family (see chapter 3, "My Story of the Jail: Inside the Manila Prison"). My study of the jail has evolved from a nested web of images that seem mis-educative on the surface but, through inquiry, they release promising forms. Much of myself is written into the following pages. For this reason, I require even more courage in telling of my story than in researching the jail.

During courses at my former Institute of graduate studies, a few colleagues noted a critical difference between Roger and me. My own account of life inside correctional institutions was much more enthusiastic and idealistic, they would say. This is precisely the version that I offer. It is authored out of my experience in the correctional scene. I constructed it in the very pit of me. I experienced a wondrous world of contact and communication with inmates despite the physical obstruction of "tightly knitted cells" and "concrete slabs" (Appendix A: "Personal dream text," July 6, 1991). I conjured up this interaction even in my dreaming imagination. The jail that I dream is an amphitheater filled with honeycombs that open up expansively.

My dreams inspire me to write impressionistically. Literary and personal ethnographic narratives encourage me in this direction (Geertz 1988; Rose 1990; Van Maanen 1988). I wish to draw my audience into the "unfamiliar story world" (Van Maanen 1988, 103) of my fieldsite that reflects my curriculum-making in a jail setting. I view *curriculum-making* on a number of levels: as the unexpected positioning of a jail as an educational site; as the self-conscious voice of a learner in unfamiliar corridors; as my negotiated meaning making with inmates and coordinators alike; and, finally, as the production of work and ideas. The curricular areas represented are: literacy and education, creative writing and drug awareness. The curriculum-making sources are: journals, stories, poetry, creative writing portraits, newsletter, proposal submissions, prison media scrapbook, letters, formal interviews, inmate contact sheets, literacy materials, and more.

If we, as teachers and learners, should position ourselves as *inmates* (or at least entertain the possibility of so being), we can then focus on our struggle for voice and selfhood. Institutional pressures and traditional academic paradigms can function as our "keepers". In this enterprise we participate in an educational process. The point is to dignify the spirit and produce alternative perspectives: "Education must, then, be not only a process that transmits culture but also one that provides *alternative* views of the world and strengthens the will to explore them" (my emphasis, Bruner 1979, 117). In narrative terms, I conceive of *education* as a detailed, interactive and participatory narrative that frees marginal and imprisoned selves. Education is also a retelling of the master narrative of teacher education and research that opens up prescribed spaces and transforms traditional concepts, constructs and meanings (Mullen and Diamond 1996).

I am positioning my reader alongside of me. I invite other stories of imprisonment in a variety of settings and situations. Together we shall relocate ourselves on the fringes in order to experiment with perspective taking. We also find ourselves on the margins in another sense: We will share the discovery of what it feels like to walk the corridors of a maximum security prison.

In the following chapter, I elaborate on my alternative schooling study in greater detail. I develop my perspectives, constructs and experiential links. Included is the creation and positioning of my study within teacher education. I cover my reasons and justifications for doing a study of prison education and my accomplishments and "findings". Also outlined is the organization of my text and intentions for how it can be read.

Table 1

Strategies Employed to Ensure Confidentiality of Sources

Strategy	Application
Pseudonyms	used for all prison participants and curriculum-makers—inmates, correctional staff, supervisors and decision-makers, and informants. Only Roger Caron, published author-convict, is identified as a personal contact (see Table 2).
Non-identifiers	used for the *jail*, my fieldsite; its affiliated *board of education*; and the *agency* that supervised my training periods. Cities are identified as geographic locations only.
Self-anonymity	used to protect researchers' anonymity in the prisons. Official identification badge simply read "Carol." Information shared in rehabilitative programs and writings in Corrections did not specify the names of people, places or institutions.

Table 2

Introduction to Key Characters in the Study

Inmates

    Black Hawk, poet/drug group client
    Sammy, student/letter writer
    Sear, poet/creative writer
    Mark, drug group client/letter writer
    Roger Caron, published author

Supervisors/Decision-makers

    Elizabeth, Superintendent of the jail
    Kim, Director of the community-based agency
    Pam, Drug Awareness counselor
    Paul, first agency supervisor
    Rita, second agency supervisor
    Sally, senior Education Coordinator/teacher

Informants

    Jenny, teacher educator/prison researcher
    John, co-facilitator of drug group/ex-convict

Table 3

Chronicle of Critical Research Dates and Events

1988
June   dream of imprisonment in the family attic

1990
November - December   communication with Roger Caron, writer
November 15   agency orientation (to the jail)
December 4   orientation at the jail (lecture only)
December 19   first correctional event (holiday party)

1991
January 2   dream of roses sent from agency
January 3   first visit to the jail
January 16   interviewed Jenny, researcher-professor
January - March   client contact volunteer (Paul, Rita)
March 18   volunteer in Drug Awareness program
March   training sessions/institutional teacher
May 26   literacy conference with coordinators
July 6   dream of prison-amphitheater
August 14   ethical entanglement with Mark/Pam
August 29   interviewed John, ex-convict & addict
September 13   sought clearance of proposal (agency)
October 25   dream of stolen manuscript
November 12   sought clearance of proposal (jail)
November 17   acceptance of proposal (jail)
November 17   official institutional/educational researcher
November   Creative Writing program coordinator

1992
June   publication of *The creative writer*
July 3   final visit to jail/fieldsite
September 19   dream of vicarious-drug use
December   ethical entanglement with Sammy (letters)

Table 4

Lexicon of Inmates' and Educators' Specialized Terms and Meanings

Legend:	• critical terms arranged alphabetically
	• ( ) = sources of meanings
	• no parenthesis indicates non-specific origins

bars, prison	in cells; made of words (Paul)
B&E	Break-and-Entry into private spaces
blue button	emergency mechanism for staff only
blue murder	an injustice against others (inmate)
bookish	academic without life-experience (inmates)
brownie points	participation in programs (inmates)
busted	arrested for an offense (inmates)
butts	cigarettes
buzzed out	high on drugs/medication (inmates)
carousel	painted ponies bound for hell (Sear, inmate)
cell	inmates' individual living spaces
client	inmates and ex-convicts (agencies)
coke/blow	cocaine, also known as "White Goddess"
coming clean	recovery from drugs/telling one's story (inmates)
concrete slabs	limits visibility & communication (mine)
cons/pros	convicts (inmates)
corrections	Ministry of Corrections (provincial); federal
count	institutional check to verify numbers/bodies
court cells	overnight spaces where inmates await court
cover story	aesthetic of self-presentation (Crites/mine)
crack pushers	drug dealers
day area	common area; inmates' ranges
deadtime	wasted time spent on remand (inmates)
de-briefing	time spent exchanging views (agencies)
detention bucket	provincial jail (inmates)
diddler	child molester (inmates)

Table 4 (cont.)

disappeared, the	inmates who are suddenly relocated (mine)
do-gooders	correctional volunteers/humanists (inmates)
doing time	incarceration for offenses (inmates/Yates)
drug group	Drug Awareness program
dry-out	recovery from substance abuse (inmates)
fellows/guys	reference to inmates (teachers and some staff)
fish	newcomers—inmates & volunteers (inmates)
foreign	struggling to comprehend fragments (mine)
frisked	physically checked for drugs & weapons (inmates)
gargoyles	statues; prison gatekeepers (mine)
gatekeeper	decision-makers & censors (mine)
go-boy!	inmate escaping from prison (Roger Caron)
go-girl!	researcher escaping from tradition (mine)
goon squad	inmates' organized violence
gravy	privileged status of programs (Sally)
guards	correctional officers (C.O.s) (staff)
hack	female guard
haven	Millhaven Institution/federal (inmates)
hole, the	isolation for internal misconduct (inmates)
honeycomb cells	spaces inside prison-amphitheater (mine)
hookers	prostitutes
inside	lived experience of prisons & stories (mine)
Institute, the	OISE (pre-existing acronym)
jail	correctional facility
jonesing	the shakes; overwhelming need for drugs
junkie	drug addict (inmates)
keepers	permanent addiction to drugs-of-choice (inmates)
lifer	inmate serving a life sentence (inmates)
lock and key	contained bodies; undisclosed stories (mine)
lock-down	movement brought to a halt in prisons
misted catacombs	prison as diminishing reality/death (Black Hawk)

Table 4 (cont.)

mousetrap	isolation of staff in place of identification
NA	Narcotics/Narrative Anonymous (mine)
narc	undercover narcotic's officer
orphans	outcasts of society; outsiders (mine)
outlaw	inmate who speaks back and speaks out (mine)
pack	inmates who travel in groups (mine)
PC	protective custody segregation
pens	federal penitentiaries (inmates)
piece	gun or revolver
pimps	drug dealers; prostitutes' gatekeepers
receiving dock	Millhaven, assesses & relocates (inmates)
remand	inmates held in custody
rock	addictive form of cocaine
sandpiper	she who focuses on particulars (mine)
screws	guards (inmates)
shackle	unexamined perspectives of marginality (mine)
shoot up	inject narcotics intravenously (inmates)
shrink	psychiatrists (inmates)
signature	the mark of one's personal story (mine/Eisner)
sleeping tombs	cell (Black Hawk, inmate)
snorting	inhaling cocaine (inmates)
straw people	inmates (teacher trainers)
street smart	insider's knowledge of street life (inmates)
tough guy	cover story of some inmates & guards (mine)
undesirables/rats	violators of women &/or children (inmates)
using/user	use of drugs/drug user (inmates)
using dream	dream of using drugs (inmates)
vermin	inmates (guard)
warrior	risk-takers; defiant power-seekers (mine)
war stories	tales of crime and action (inmates/staff)

Acknowledgments

The inmates who participated in this book taught me that the *heart* is the source of not only empowering relationships but also research. Through their actions they also teach that storytelling can be the wellspring of human caring, renewal and re-education.

Chapter 1

Introducing an Alternative Study of Research and Schooling

In this chapter I present the major questions that guide my inquiry. I then provide the contexts of my study and develop the reasons for undertaking it. In this section, I include the opportunity that I had for reformulating key educational terms and for suggesting new ones. I present my findings and accomplishments. My metaphor of the researcher as marginal-insider is illustrated along with other experiential constructs. I also present the organization of the text as well as a guide to how it may be read.

Creating an Understanding of My Inquiry and its Questions

Even the prison guards liked Sammy. This is unusual. Sammy was a convict "doing time" in protective custody for murder. He was no "friend" to the general inmate population and his life was at risk. Outwardly, Sammy was a clown. He knew how to make the guards laugh. One of them told me that Sammy was his favorite inmate because he always made an effort to be upbeat and cheerful. Sammy was never "frisked" or checked over in the official manner to which other prisoners were subjected to. He was the only student I had who managed to use humor to escape the humiliation of such a ritual, sparing both himself and me.

Sammy was sloppy and smelled bad but he had no qualms about being in the "company of a woman," as he put it. He was a Native American in his early thirties. We met on July 11, 1991, six months after I had been working in the jail as a volunteer. I was his teacher, assigned to him because his usual tutor, the math and science coordinator, was overloaded. I had already seen many tattoos in the Drug Awareness program, but I had never had the opportunity to examine one so close up. Sammy's tattoo was of a grinning woman, naked and voluptuous. It covered his left arm from shoulder to elbow. I was more than distracted by it. It took time to get past the tattoo to see the person. He never got past seeing me as an object of desire.

The first exercise we ever worked on involved a decision-making ladder in a secondary-level sociology textbook. The situation required that he think about a married couple's dilemma. They wanted to have children but they did not know if the time was right for them. Their situation was explained in some detail. Sammy's task was to indicate the advantages and disadvantages of this couple having children. I encouraged him to further the problem using his own imagination and life-experience. With each attempt I assisted him. He seemed very pleased and told me so. I chuckled when alone that evening writing in my *Prison Journal.* I find it odd that Sammy and I, two very different people and in such a place, had tackled the same problem regarding an imaginary couple's dilemma over whether or not to have a baby!

When I first met Sammy, I was struggling with my research question, "What are the inmates' stories of experience and imprisonment that offer possibilities in education?" As I encountered the inmates, I, too, was restricted. I was limited by the cycles and rhythms of such a place: its programmatic philosophies; curricular objectives and procedures, as well as institutional security regulations.

My focus began to shift. I began paying closer attention to my own experience and asked, "What is my teacher development story in the context of the prison site?" This was not a surprise. I had been developing my own narrative of experience and education during my graduate studies. Sammy was one of the personal influences that introduced me to new dimensions of my teacher development story. For example, I became aware of specific ethical issues that re-shaped my inquiry. The letters that he later sent from a federal penitentiary challenged our agreement that we were to write only about educational themes. He was asking me personal questions. I responded first by creating clear boundaries; later by consulting with the Senior Education Coordinator; and then by dissolving our correspondence altogether. The consensus was that my safety was more important than any educational inquiry into his life. Sammy's conduct had, inadvertently, helped me better to understand the existential condition of imprisonment.

I began to consider another meaning of inmate. Anyone who feels seized and held captive is an inmate. Educators, for example, may feel restricted by research traditions and paradigms, and institutional regulations and practices. I recognized my own experience of being an inmate myself. This led me to construct portraits of imprisonment as a lived phenomenon for institutionalized selves. My text is about the inmate experience inside a prison. It also resonates more widely within academe, other institutions and society itself.

In summary, my focus shifted from attention to the inmates' stories, through my own story, to stories of imprisonment. This development blends biographical and autobiographical story-lines. I list the three questions raised above in order to facilitate my discussion of them throughout my text:

1. What are the inmates' stories of experience and imprisonment that offer possibilities in education?

2. What is my teacher development story in the context of the prison site?

3. What is the experience of captivity and education for imprisoned selves?

The opening words and above questions sketch the development of my inquiry into a prison site. This story-line is about inmates' literal captivity and imprisonment within established regulations and procedures, paradigms and fields of inquiry, and an institutional setting. My narrative inquiry extends to other metaphorical inmates who struggle in academe to be active and self-conscious. They can re-write the script of teacher education to produce alternative notions of education, schooling and classroom, and teacher development. My evolving questions reflect my complex relationship to the concepts of inmate, story, imprisonment and inquiry itself.

As I write, think and talk about my study of the jail, I focus on imprisoned selves as my primary story. In a course paper, "Spaces of inquiry" (1991b), I wrote about the advice for doctoral thesis writing that was often extended to me: it is essential to develop a clear focus early on and to judge, as peripheral, emerging ideas. This was the very basis of the tension that was propelling my inquiry. I discovered how the act of de-focusing my study kept me open to its many possibilities; living and thinking spaces; rifts and shifts; and feelings of wonder, surprise, and amazement. Through my own story, I wrote about how staying de-focused can stimulate a creative, multifocal process. It can also function as a phenomenon of inquiry itself.

In connecting my inquiry with my internal experience I became alert to institutional pressure to develop premature tightness. Resistance helped to convert my impulses into art. This process is described by Bruner (1979) who demonstrates faith in the fringes of association that may require expression: "The conversion of impulse into the experience of art comes from the creation of a stream of metaphoric activity and the restraining of any direct striving for ends" (72). Such an impulse might move the writer away from constructing a traditional text to a narrative inquiry, one that "teaches you about yourself as a researcher . . . . We cannot be sure of what we will find, but we invariably get caught up in the search" (Glesne and Peshkin 1992, 178-179).

The portrait of how my questions evolved reflects my complex relationship to the inmates and the correctional institution itself. The multifaceted character of my narrative and the interweaving of many different voices produces an ambiguity in my focus. My initial attempt was to observe and understand the "ongoing experiential text" of my students' lives as they told their stories to me in words that "reflect upon life and explain themselves" (Connelly and Clandinin 1990, 4).

My impulse is now to understand inmates' lives as being shaped principally by my own autobiographical purposes and intentions. In other words, I am attending to my educational autobiography as the meaningful curricular construct (Pinar 1988) that helps me to create links between inmates' stories and my own. I use my own frame of reference to make sense of others' subjectivities; others' subjectivities, in turn, help me to construct new perspectives on imprisoned selves. In terms of the way I have shaped my text, my own stories and those of the inmates are successively pivotal in importance. As one becomes central, the other becomes marginal. I do not predetermine this turn-taking. Nor does any one voice nor story dominate. What leads, if anything, is the metaphor of multiple imprisoned selves that my inquiry has produced.

One of my colleagues asked whose story is primary, the inmates' or my own. He felt that one must be central. I answer that a primary story that promotes inmates' stories is academic and distant. It is lifeless without the researcher's own narrative of experience. I explore voice itself as a frame of reference that is internal, partial, interpretive, particular and situated. Voice can be shaped in inquiry to become multiple. Each voice, in my writing, represents different opportunities in and perspectives on teacher development. This position reflects the space that I wish to create for multiple voices: the student-inmate's voice, the researcher's voice, and the jail as a social institution. In chapter 3 on my story of the jail, I narrate using all three voices. In it, I view the jail as a somewhat rigid institution but also as a place within which an interplay is experienced among the curriculum making energies of its teachers and learners.

Providing the Contexts of this Study

This book is about my research on prison education in a correctional facility for men only. I am treating inmates' life stories and histories as a significant part of schooling practices and of education in a wider sense. Correctional institutions are a hidden if significant part of the social fabric and may be investigated with the tools similar to those that have been developed to do research in schools, literacy and autobiographical writing contexts, and in counseling situations. By studying prisons as significant schooling sites, broader sense can be made of experience and education. Incarcerated individuals need to be seen as human beings and, more than this, as creative writers and thinkers, marginal-insiders, and imprisoned selves. By studying the inmate experience, whether in a prison site or in our own lives, we can re-examine ourselves and our wider educational and social relationships. I have learned that inmates' life stories represent a legitimate and necessary tool for re-examining our individual and institutional narratives.

My emphasis is on incarceration as education, jails as schools, inmates as curriculum-makers, and on the self as autobiographer. This text pursues the links among these themes. I focused on the experience of the self in my master's thesis on narrative, autobiographical inquiry entitled *The Self I Dream: A Narrative Reconstruction of a Personal Mythology* (1990). Other contexts that shape my inquiry include a manuscript on women's narrative research entitled, *Stories We Are:*

Narrative Enactments of Inquiry (Mullen 1992c); papers (later published) on dream and prison research (e.g., Feuerverger and Mullen 1995; Mullen 1994); and coursework on teacher education, curriculum and narrative studies, and the writing self. In my study, I connect narrative theory and inquiry to life stories and histories, teacher development, and dream discourse. I am using the metaphor of imprisoned selves to create a teacher development study of an alternative schooling site. Images of my imprisoned selves include marginal-insider, vicarious participant, literacy teacher, and even creative writer and curriculum maker.

I have been involved in narrative ethnographic studies since 1988. As a former doctoral student in the JCTD (Joint Centre for Teacher Development) within the Department of Curriculum at OISE (The Ontario Institute for Studies in Education) in Canada, I pursued personal and professional approaches to teacher development. I am part of a community that values education as a life-long process of teaching and learning (Dewey 1938), and that sees narratives of life-experiences as contexts for making sense of educational situations (Connelly and Clandinin 1990). I understand narrative inquiry as a process that challenges me to create and re-create my self and others. I am using writing and storytelling as my vehicles for development.

A jail provides the context of my study which I am constructing narratively and educationally. I have been learning about the world of corrections for five years. A community-based agency introduced me to the jail and sponsored my visits within it. This agency assists convicts who are incarcerated and also released. Corrections itself cooperates with agencies that guide the re-entry process of inmates in society.

While it would be useful to research the phases of an inmate's life with regard to incarceration, release and community life, I study the story of my own development as a researcher, teacher, learner, coordinator, co-facilitator, and woman in the context of inmates' lives *and* in an unusual schooling site (instead of a "regular" classroom situation). *My primary story-line is that the jail is a legitimate schooling site which functions as a community of curriculum-makers.* This is an alternative perspective to existing notions and stereotypes.

The jail also represents a web of curriculum realities and possibilities worthy of sustained inquiry. I experienced three correctional programs: Drug Awareness, Literacy/Education and Creative Writing. These contribute to the teacher-learner schooling context of the jail and to the study of human lives. My narrative inquiry approach is well suited to this context and to such a study. I wish to tell the story of my narrative inquiry into a single "school" as an educational narrative. Yates (1993), correctional officer (guard), tells his own story as a "picaresque journey through three very different corrections institutions and twelve very educational years" (21). I feel challenged by his goal to write a book instead of a "vapid doctoral dissertation with all the humanity footnoted out of it" (21).

In preparing this study I had envisioned it as a narrative that would free me from the prescribed curricula of thesis writing. As a creative writer, I strive to resist institutional control in favor of my own self-motivated, artistic endeavors. I wished to work beyond the "forms of instrumental knowing that comprise the center of our awareness" to "see the possibility of connection in internal experience" which I "strive to recreate . . . and to live . . ." (Bruner 1979, 73).

My struggle was to shape a text that reflected what I saw, heard and felt in the jail *and* that invited my reader to walk the corridors of my fieldsite for him or herself. Many of the inmates followed a similar artistic course: they, too, resisted the conforming pressure of formal and prescribed curricula, and of institutional censorship and story-ownership. They produced enviably rich material whenever they were given the freedom and support to do so. They also initiated or responded well to writing about their own life-experiences and feelings through poetry, musical lyrics, drawings and art, short stories, novelistic segments, journals and letters, and conversations. In the spirit of joint effort, I generated, with students' input, the title for our correctional newsletter. Such a process constitutes a struggle for the inmate who functions within the jurisdiction of governing bodies.

Reasons for Doing this Inquiry

I am charting this course for myself because of my interest in exploring a correctional institution as a humanly significant landscape of teaching and learning. I felt compelled to discover and re-discover new dimensions of the teacher education concepts that had been informing my research over time. The concepts and accompanying definitions below are an elaboration of those found in the prelude.

I understand *teaching* to be a social relationship that occurs among people and that transcends school-related contexts and settings. Alternative studies within the fields of teacher development and curriculum are becoming more acceptable, but I wondered how the academic community might respond to a study of lives in detention. By *autobiography* I mean self-story, or the experience of self, as a meaningful curricular construct (Pinar 1975, 1981, 1988). I understand *classroom* as a situation, or set of circumstances, that brings together people whose sharing of stories and ideas is educative. I interpret *curriculum* as both text and situation for exploring educational experiences and events that can be experienced from without or invented within (Mullen 1994).

The *margins* are a place where the teacher self challenges its institutionalization (Mullen and Diamond 1996). I use *marginality* to confront the paradox of being forced onto the outside or periphery by a complex web both of images of institutional control and restraint, and of prescribed curricula, denied selfhood, and by limiting educative relationships. As a theoretical story-line, I wondered how marginality could be developed as a model of inquiry. I wanted to discover something about the essential continuity of all social, educative and interpersonal experiences. I had confidence that these links could be constructed though my own educative process. I was challenging myself to succeed in an environment that placed great strain on the continuity of experience as a criterion of growth (Dewey 1938).

By *self* I mean a multifaceted configuration of personal knowledge, professional knowledge, significant educational events, and broader life-experiences. As a key term, the *prisoner* is seen as an icon of oppression, and as one who is seized, confined and held captive in the restrictive and/or expansive spaces of a surveillant community.

Research on drug awareness, addiction and substance abuse is crucial to social reform. So too is research into literacy problems, interpersonal abuse, and other criminal offenses. Less obvious is the relationship of inmates' life stories to social reform. Educators can use these stories as a tool for re-examining ourselves and our wider educational and social relationships. So far there has been little research on inmates' life stories. Narratives of marginality can present us with powerful educational phenomena. Moreover, even little has been done to contextualize this narrative perspective as teacher development and autobiographical inquiry. What makes my study potentially significant, then, is its focus on stories in captivity as a way of re-discovering and re-covering the meaning of education. My approach has prepared me to offer connections between teacher education and corrections, and between myself and inmates.

By recounting the development of my own teaching story in a jail, I can explore the possibilities entailed in doing a narrative, autobiographical study. In addition to recounting my teaching story, I will provide reflection on the process of doing narrative. My reflective meta-text will be about how I engage a schooling site as material for a personal knowledge study and narrative inquiry. Finally, I am doing this inquiry so that I can tell my own stories of experience in the context of captivity (literal confinement) and imprisonment (metaphorical constraint). I worked with incarcerated men as a way of un-covering and re-constructing certain aspects of my own childhood, teaching years and ongoing inquiry.

Findings through Sharing and Learning

In retrospect, I believe that my most noteworthy "finding" is that inmates—my prison participants and partners in curriculum making—embody the message that the *heart* is the source of empowering, educative relationships. The inmates' gifts of pedagogic storytelling taught me about caring, connecting and creating in the starkest and most dangerous of institutions. Storytelling also exposed me to the paradox of feeling inspired in a place of strict bounds, staff-inmate barriers, and lock-and-key rituals. Their sharings and my own learnings have taught me that the story of these men as criminals, prisoners, inmates, convicts and cons is limiting. A more intricate and human story can be told about what it means to encounter, interact with and listen to such men in an institutional setting. We can learn to recover what we need to know:

> We forget much too easily that media people, corrections brass, and, quite simply, people have the same social problems as guards and inmates. Usually it is a matter of degree and of who gets caught. And, these days, how the information is packaged for the rest of society. Corrections has proved itself inept at informing the public, and yet it despises the impression the public has of what goes on in prisons (Yates 1993, 11-12).

Humanity and violence exist on both sides of the bars and walls, and in all our human experience. It is not the uniform we wear but what is inside of it. We are imprisoned in our stories. Our perceptions are regimented. We live in our chains, rarely finding ways to break out of them, let alone learning to sing in them.

In academe, we need to question also how we are imprisoned in our own perceptions of ourselves and others, and teacher-oriented research. The current approach to curriculum development and school reform, for example, involves "significant changes at the classroom level" as teachers reflect on "what classroom change means for them, from their own perspective and criteria" (Butt, Raymond, and Yamagishi 1988, 88-92). I believe that this perspective includes an epistemological contradiction: on the one hand, teachers' biographies count as a legitimate form of knowledge and appropriation, but, on the other hand, researchers' own stories are ignored and protected. This omission of the researcher's story, which is commonplace in the literature on teachers' biographies, may be an out-growth of the empiricist tradition that values an "objective understanding of the events and objects under study" over researchers' own signatures (Eisner 1991). Even when Peshkin (1988), a reflexive example, engages in his self-story through the use of a "subjectivity audit," there are vaguely empirical hints. Nonetheless, his attempt to monitor how he was feeling throughout the research process can be viewed as a researcher's "coming clean" (Guba 1990).

When I began to trust the impulses of the heart, I heard the inmates' stories differently and my own more meaningfully. Until then, I lived the ethnographic life, studying men in uniform who shared "butts" and rolling papers, and who swapped "war stories" about their lives of crime. If Crites (1979) had been present in the chapel-turned-addiction meeting room, he would, no doubt, have noted my "cover story," or artfully rendered aesthetic, of being in control, quasi-street-wise, and non-judgmental. He would have noted, too, the change in my own institutional "uniform" from heavily cloaked professional to open and exposed storyteller. My own uniform changed as I began to think less about how to protect myself from others and more about how to connect with others through story. I transformed from wearing black layers to bright colors. As Eisner (1991) asks, and as I am confirming, "Why take the heart out of the situations we are trying to help readers understand?" (37).

I believe that an educational approach that is conceived in narrative ethnographic terms is best suited to the human dimensions of my transactional story-line of "self" and "other." It is in this context of "self" and "other" (Eisner 1991; Rose 1990) that I aim to "let the reader in" on my own reality, if only vicariously, and the inmates' realities, if only interpretively. I believe that ethnography and narrative both have a contribution to make to this transactional context. I think that it is a mistake to see the two research traditions as being somehow in conflict with one another. Both cross ideological borders. Their writers recognize the role of human values and interests in the construction and investigation of self, schools and society. They also view knowledge as both constructed and situated within positions and frames of reference. Banks (1993) writes of the changing field of teacher education that "transformative academic scholars assume that knowledge is not neutral but is influenced by human interests, that all knowledge reflects the power and social relationships within society, and that an important purpose of knowledge construction is to help people improve society" (9). The chapter on narrative ethnography called, "A Story of the Jail: Inside the Manila Prison," is the heart of my narrative text. In it, I show how narrative and ethnography complement one another within live contexts or grounded experiences. In chapter 4, "Narrative Methodology: A Personal Account," I discuss the relationship between these two approaches.

I am developing a narrative ethnographic approach in order to better understand my teaching-learning practices and the meaning of narrative inquiry itself. Connelly and Clandinin (1985) assert that tension exists in educational inquiry and within the researcher him or herself: it is between the "theoretician of modes of knowing [and] the practitioner of teaching and learning" (175). In my study I adopted their perspective of:

> . . . teaching and learning [as] one in which teacher and student actors are subjects of interest. Because of this attitude to teaching and learning, actions are not merely performances; they are minded, knowing actions. Accordingly, for us, knowing is an experience. Action and knowledge are united in the actor, and our account of knowing is, therefore, of the actor with her personal narratives, intentions, and passions. This practical knowing of teachers and students is complex because it embodies in a history, in the moment and in an act, all modes of knowing aimed at the particular event that called forth the teaching and learning act (178).

I took into account the wider storytelling landscape in the correctional field as it made sense to me within the context of education. This was my general approach to teaching and learning in my new fieldsite. I focused on gathering case-study accounts of inmates' inquiry processes. Through group discussion, one-on-one literacy sessions, letter-writing exchanges, and creative writings, I learned just how powerful are inmates' stories about life, teaching and learning, and education to narrative conceptions of knowledge and experience. My storytelling landscape is configured not only in these terms—the various teaching/learning situations in the jail—but also in personal biographical terms.

My narrative perspective includes the elements of mythology, story and dream as embedded in my ongoing research story and the educational literature. Personal dream narrative provides me with an invaluable resource for understanding educational phenomena, and teaching and schooling theories and practices. Narrative practice can be conceived of as a teacher innovation that allows me to understand the process of narrative inquiry on my own terms and in my own voice. In other words, I have attended to the process of narrative inquiry in the context of prison education, and personal and professional development.

This book presents incarcerated/involuntary inmates as teachers, learners, curriculum participants and writers in the context of my experience of, and intensive involvement in, the *inside.* My autobiographical approach to inmates' stories and lives is told as an encounter of multiple imprisoned selves. My primary story of multiple imprisoned selves began as an awareness within myself and what I saw in the inmates and others in corrections. But, more significant than just corrections, we are all prisoners of our cultural stories, and wear personal and professional chains. Just as we are imprisoned by culture, we are created by culture. We live in a matrix of story, culture, institution and society. Self-conscious storytelling about our own positionality offers the possibility of transformation.

My direct experience is a paradox that I refined through writing and rewriting: As an imprisoned self, I am learning about other selves who are also imprisoned in story, culture, institutions and society, but my life text, or set of experiences and how I construe it, is also different. In the jail, I was unique. My life-experiences do not include expertise in, or a keen understanding of, criminology and law. Nor do my experiences include first-hand knowledge of drug use and substance abuse, crime and the criminal network, anti-social behavior, mental illness, or weak life skills and literacy difficulties.

The concepts of myself as a vicarious participant and marginal-insider were born in the above context. Eisner (1991) has contributed richly to this concept of the "vicarious experience" as a feature of qualitative research, but its autobiographical possibilities have not been fully explored. I make vicarious experience a vital part of my own self-story. In the context of my study, the vicarious experience is, at the level of teacher development and dream narrative, a problematic. For, the closer I got to the people, and the educational phenomena and processes that I was studying, the more deeply I was living my story of them. I provide a dream of vicarious needle use as a dramatic metaphor for my close involvement during the study (see Appendix A, "Street Researcher").

We need more examples of deeply mythologized, personal accounts of educational experiences in which the teller has a full-bodied presence in his or her text (Mullen 1994). Driven by eclectic impulses, I am drawn to many sources and several fields of study. In addition to narrative literature, I also make use of ethnographic studies that provide, in their more progressive spirit, narrative portrayals of lived experiences in field settings and "off-beat" sites such as the streets (Goffman 1961; Marcus and Fischer 1986; Rose 1990).

I am using the narrative inquiry approach to develop a perspective on the jail as a legitimate schooling site and, moreover, to explore my journey as a valuable teaching and learning experience. My metaphors of *jails as schools* and *selves as imprisoned* will help to convey a broader picture of the complex world of people and how we relate to one another. The key questions of inquiry are: "How is the cultural self like a prison? How is the jail like a school, and how is school like a jail? How is society like a jail? What is my primary story of prisons in relation to society, school and the self?" And finally, "What does a study of the jail contribute to teacher education theories and practices and, moreover, what will be its unique contribution to other studies conducted in correctional sites?" These questions help me to probe both how corrections is linked to teacher education and what education means within the scope of addiction, imprisonment and incarceration.

I hope to make sense of how, in my involvement in these two spheres, I have been living on their experiential, amorphous margins. By this I mean that I shaped my world to empower me to do research beyond the bounds of convention to pursue my own research impulses and interests in teacher education *and* corrections. A narrative inquiry approach to research in *both* fields is somewhat atypical and unconventional, exploratory and risk-taking. The study of the self in teacher education and corrections is doubly so. Personal narrative is an area of research where discoveries do not stop with ourselves but can lead us to probe deep narrative structures and relevant educational phenomena, perspectives and issues. Coles (1981) speaks of dreams letting us "dip into ourselves as deeply as we know how" and also into stories of existence and culture (29). I view this image of "dipping" into the self as a metaphor for understanding narrative inquiry and the autobiographical enterprise. Polkinghorne (1988), too, views narrative as "one of our fundamental structures of comprehension [that] shapes the character of our existence in a particular way" and that makes a significant contribution to the experience of being human (15).

Primary autobiographical questions that complement my set of narrative inquiry questions include: "What are my images of the jail as reflected in my journal accounts, creative writings, dream recordings, and community involvements?" Also, "How does the image of myself as a 'marginal-insider' and 'prisoner' help configure a wider set of experiences?" And finally, "How has this study re-shaped my thinking and contributed to my new understandings of 'imprisoned selves'?"

Contributions to Teacher Education and Research Practice

As a study of the lived experience at the level of engagement of inmates in a maximum security institution, this inquiry potentially contributes to the fields of qualitative and narrative research, and to the world of teacher education. My expression at this level of engagement is mythological: Through dream analysis and journal writing I am capturing this feeling of the vicarious experience of others' lives as an expression of myself as a marginal-insider. In my exposure to a new culture and social environment I felt like a stranger (marginal) at certain times and a prisoner (insider) at other times. The notion of the stranger has been explored in the educational literature as an image of historical development and personal biography (Schutz 1971; Shabatay 1991). As Schutz (1971) comments, "the stranger starts to interpret his new social environment in terms of his thinking as usual" (97) but will make adjustments as his or her frame of reference begins to shift. I develop the image of stranger (or "fish") as "marginal-insider" in the context of the prison culture.

The image of myself as marginal-insider in corrections is accentuated by my overlapping experience in education. As researcher in corrections and teacher education, I am marginal in the sense that I function on the fringes. My orientation moves me along adjoining edges of two worlds. But, it is along the adjoining edges that my insider's perspective developed, that I connected with others, and that my personal mythology, narrative and self became re-shaped.

As a fully authorized researcher, my directed "covert inquiry" (Rose 1990) of the jail led me to new and exciting research practices, some of which required a great deal of adjustment. My weekly rounds of participant-observation (an inside-out image), for example, demonstrated my ability to connect in unforeseen capacities as a teacher, co-facilitator and coordinator without calling attention to myself as a researcher. In chapter 4, I address my covert research practice in some detail. In chapter 3, I tell the story of my covert practice as it emerged within the folds of a prison site. I will now provide only a few examples of restrictions which, once made apparent to me, created a shift in my taken-for-granted world of education:

(a) I was not allowed to refer to my multiple roles in the various programs of the jail or to make announcements, to this effect, to inmates;

(b) I was not permitted to use a tape recorder or any other research materials, tools, surveys and instruments;

(c) I was discouraged from note-taking, except in the case of institutional forms, namely inmate intake sheets and teaching progress reports, and

(d) Although I work autobiographically to tell my own story, I was encouraged to protect my anonymity (and the inmates' anonymity) by observing certain rules of conduct, guidelines of interaction, and written accounts of non-identifiability.

In subsequent chapters I treat my participant-observation experiences in the jail in relation to this theme of the covert research practice. I found the bureaucratic restrictions to be neither simply innocuous nor oppressive. However, they usually added to burdensome institutional pressures, regulations and procedures. Imprisoned in a mechanized space, I did not feel incarcerated in community among inmates. However, I did feel confined whenever my rhythms were uncomfortably regulated. I also felt imprisoned at certain times and in certain moments. These included when officers ("guards") were not visible from the meeting rooms; when I was locked up with a hostile and angry inmate(s); when electrical black-outs occurred and other failures that disrupted elevator use; when inmates moved in packs through the corridors making sexist comments or just "hungry" momentary connections; when inmates, working one-on-one, made sexual and emotional advances (which did not occur any more frequently than with the guards); and when I embarrassed myself by making interpersonal blunders. Like the inmates, I had to learn the rules of the institution and to carry them out if I wished to avoid incident. Also like the inmates, I had additional pressures but only some of mine were different. As researcher I had certain rules to follow; as volunteer, other rules; as coordinator, still other rules; and other rules yet as teacher and woman.

This study about multiple imprisoned selves in part explores how my own voice and story developed in the jail. My account of researcher/teacher development overlapped with and reshaped my ongoing dream mythology. My inquiry in the jail is in keeping with my personal interpretation of qualitative inquiry research and with the tradition of narrative autobiographical research. I argue that, through storytelling, narrative autobiographical research provides a significant and worthwhile vehicle for exploring a personal-and social-relevance orientation to educational studies, sites and settings. A personal-and social-relevance orientation exposes, for example, the social story of inmates as told by the media (see chapter 4).

As I collected newspaper articles for my *Prison Media Scrapbook,* I saw a pattern. We are imprisoned by our social meanings of criminals; we rarely create room for their versions of their own lives; and, when contact with inmates is established, potential exists to re-create our presuppositions. These presuppositions *are* our stereotypes. I am "letting go" of the taken-for-granted world that is being portrayed for me. This gives me a feeling of control over society's capacity to shape itself in its own best interests. I experience inmates as partners in curriculum making; jails as complex educational sites; and incarceration as mythology, narrative and dream. I experience how my learning is valuable for "non-prison" situations.

Mapping Personal Experiential Constructs

In November 1990 I connected with an agency that oriented me to work in a jail. I gained access in January 1991 to a prison site as a client contact volunteer. After several weeks I became a co-facilitator of a Drug Awareness program; teacher in the Education/Literacy program; official educational/institutional researcher; and finally coordinator of the Creative Writing program. During an eighteen month period, all of my roles or functions overlapped. Officially cleared as an educational/institutional researcher by appropriate authorities, I was formally enabled in my work. Yet, I remained marginal in my study of the jail as a study in teacher development and as a study of (personal and professional) curriculum.

As marginal-insider, my thinking about the inmates in relation to innovative possibilities in education and even the field of narrative inquiry has shifted. Initially, I imagined the inmates as an untapped resource whose stories were probably rich in learning and teaching. Now I can look back and see that my frame of reference shifted to viewing inmates as inspired pedagogic storytellers; as connected knowers; as invaluable resources for curriculum making; and as multidimensional storytellers, family members, writers, teachers and learners, and curriculum participants. My thinking about myself has also changed: The metaphor of imprisoned selves is used, in my narrative mapping, to capture this paradox of curriculum makers as prisoners, and prisoners as partners in curriculum making. I, too, am caught in this paradox. How is it that we can learn to "sing in our chains" to the somber tune of imprisonment?

My study of writers in captivity has led me to use a diverse literature. I address various perspectives of writers whose stories of experience, education and imprisonment illuminate my own: *convicts' autobiographies and writings* (Abbott 1981; Caron 1978, 1985; Dostoevsky 1965, 1982; Grossman 1990; Harris 1986; Karpis 1971; MacDonald (with Gould) 1988; Morrison 1989; Sharansky 1988; Wilde 1986); *biographies of convicts* (Callwood 1990; Radish 1992; Scott 1982; Yates 1993) and *academics' prison accounts* (Davies 1990; Feuerverger and Mullen 1995; Harlow 1987; Hospital 1986; Lessing 1986; Lovitt 1992; McClane 1988; Mullen 1992b), *editors' collections of prison writings* (Horsburgh 1969; Katz 1970; Livesey 1980; Marken 1974), and *penological literature and essays* (Birnie 1990; Correctional Service of Canada 1983). All five categories overlap: for instance, some convicts who have written their self-narratives, such as Dostoevsky and Wilde, are 'academics'. Some writings by academics, involving direct contact with inmates, are suggestively autobiographical/biographical, and the collections of convict's writings are autobiographical.

The Organization of this Text and Guide to its Reading

Cycles of Inquiry

Throughout the study I gave the inmates space as well as myself. I revisited both of our meanings in a cyclic fashion, depending on the context at hand. I see this spiral shape as integral not only to my text but also to the nature of narrative inquiry itself. Cycles of inquiry are central to the structure of this book. For example, I was struck by certain dilemmas, sometimes ethical, that evolved for me. I visited and revisited my ethical entanglements with particular inmates, especially Sammy and Mark. I was also drawn to significant events and particular dreams. I used dreams as a way of both getting in touch with my inquiry and constructing it. Pivotal dreams include: my incarceration in an attic; life within a prison-amphitheater; and immobility within prison corridors. As new contexts arose I often re-visited salient events. In this way, I could attribute new, or modified, meaning to them.

Even the linear presentation of this text is to be read in the context of its cycles of inquiry. It has a beginning, middle and end: I introduce my study; develop it in the context of my prison fieldsite; and conclude with its significance and implications. The chapters themselves also reflect a linear pattern. For example, chapter 3 is organized temporally through the narrative structure of "Going in," "Being there" and "Going out." However, I overlap each of these time-frames with others. I did this while in certain situations by either anticipating what would happen or by reflecting on what had already occurred. An example of this temporal overlap is the anxiety I experienced over whether or not I would be cleared as an official educational researcher in corrections. In this book I rethink and reformulate constructs that offer possibilities in education. I hope that my reader will understand my revisiting in the spirit that was intended.

Summaries

Each of the five chapters, including the prelude, conveys an analytical representation of narrative with descriptive and anecdotal passages. Chapter summaries are provided. The summaries appear at the beginning of each chapter, together constituting an overview of this book.

Pseudonyms

Pseudonyms are used in my study for the following participant groups: inmates; correctional staff, supervisors and decision-makers; and informants (see Table 2 for a list). The only exception among those with whom I have had contact is Roger Caron, published author-convict. I have used non-identifiers for the jail; its affiliated board of education; and the agency that supervised my training periods.

Indented Passages

Inmates' longer writings are indented throughout this book. Emphasis is placed on their own voices, sharings and writings. This includes the writings of my own student-inmates and the published accounts of prisoners. My intention is to foreground the voices of inmates and ex-prisoners.

Italics

Italics are used to underscore points of emphasis, such definitions of key terms.

Reduced Print

Reduced print is used for longer passages, such as excerpts from research journal records, inmates' poetry, and educators' perspectives.

Tenses

This text is generally written in the past tense. I wanted to convey the sense that my fieldwork study is complete. I also used shifts in tense to reflect my current and ongoing thinking, and the analysis of my study. For example, I used present tense verbs for the major questions of my inquiry (listed at the beginning of this chapter); for self-reflexive commentary on the correctional and educational literature; and for meta-level analysis of my various story-lines.

The Researcher's Signature

Ultimately, I, too, will be captive of my own institutional setting and milieu. The paradox for me is that I had also been encouraged to learn by discovery. Part of this discovery led me to create a set of unique relations among personal knowledge, teacher development, and prison education. The teacher educators of my former doctoral committee repeatedly expressed faith "in the powerful effects that come from permitting the student to put things together for [her]self, to be [her] own discoverer" (Bruner 1979, 82). They showed sensitivity to my desire to generate alternatives to the traditional study that often camouflages the writer and his/her heart. I felt much supported as I displayed my own "signature" (Eisner 1991; Geertz 1988). Signature is a "matter of the construction of a writerly identity . . . [and] the establishment of an authorial presence within a text" (Geertz 1988, 9). The realm of the aesthetic belongs to anyone who participates in creating form, whether this be a theoretical framework, taxonomy or novel (Eisner 1985).

My study of a jail is an integral part of my creative writing practice as a researcher of dreams. Reflecting on narrative inquiry in studies of classrooms, researchers need to learn to represent their own voices. First-person accounts of personal educational change in academics' lives are to be encouraged. The perspective of the artist can help us to understand how researchers and participants live out an aesthetic approach to curriculum situations. I share the view that "impressionalistic, postmodern ways may still need to be found of bringing the sensibility of the artist more fully into ethnographic observations. . . . This enlargening process involves not only awareness of how one observes and how one thinks about the observations but also engagement in self-reflexive analysis" (Diamond 1991, 6). My student-inmates explored their artistic voices on their own and with me as we interactively developed our creative writing practices.

Reader as Artist

In my creative writing practice, I view my student-inmates and myself as artists and, potentially, all "qualitative educational inquirers" as artists (Barone 1992). I would like to be read for the sensibilities through which my own consciousness shaped a particular setting with a particular set of people that opened to an exploration of a particular researcher with a particular life history. I include, in this portrait of qualitative researcher as artist, my readers. I encourage these co-creators of my meanings, and co-participants in my inquiry, to reflect on their own lives in captivity. What are my readers' stories of experience and how might they be shared with the wider academic community?

Chapter 2

Background and Context:
Unlocking the Inquiry

> While leaning against a beige prison wall, dressed in my blue uniform, I'm chatting with the young woman next to me. We are sitting cross-legged. As we busily chat, I'm aware of deserving to be here because of a crime I've committed. This feels like a scene from a high school gym class, I chuckle privately. The lot of us are lined up against the wall, waiting to be "picked" for something. I chat with a male guard who is especially warm and polite, feeling struck by his humanity. It doesn't feel so bad in here after all, I think, as I watch him move down the right-hand side of the corridor (Mullen, Appendix B, July 21, 1991).

This chapter unlocks my inquiry of the jail site as a human story and curricular site. I provide the background of, and context for, my study in relation to the various interrelated conceptions that drive my inquiry. These include: marginality, aesthetics, teacher development, narrative, story, dream and text. My method of presentation is to both describe and situate my multifocal lens in a series of brief vignettes. A fuller account of these portraits follows in chapter 3.

My aim is to develop an evocative story-line to link prison education to teacher education in this writing. I explore constructs, such as of prisoner/inmate, voice, self, personal knowledge and surveillance, to connect corrections to education. I also explore my personal and professional experiences in the context of these two unlikely but related worlds.

Marginality as Aesthetic in Teacher Education

Spaces need to be opened up in teacher education for research previously thought unreliable or irrelevant. Marginality is a theme that merits more attention in current teacher education (see, for example, Davies 1990; Mullen and Diamond 1996; Foucault 1977; Haraway 1988; Harlow 1987; Kirby and McKenna 1989; Van Maanen 1988). A jail provides an "ideal" in which to study marginality. I invite marginality by writing on the fringes of educational research. I have deliberately positioned myself to study *margins* as a place where the teacher self challenges its institutionalization. Narrative inquiry provides with me with the opportunity to recompose myself differently on the margins in a prison setting. I therefore understand *marginality* to mean positionality of the researcher self as marginal-insider. I write from the unfolding colonized perspectives of learner, person, woman, researcher and creative writer.

I also use *marginality* to mean resistance. I confront being forced onto the outside or periphery by a complex web of images of institutional control and restraint, and by prescribed curricula, denied selfhood, and by limiting educative relationships. I am experimenting on the outside so as to become closer to my participants and to temporarily distance myself from the center of teacher education and research. In moving away from the center, one can imagine education and research in new forms. Marginality is a multi-faceted concept that underscores my paradoxical stance. I both invite and resist it. I invite marginality as the successive transformation of perspective. I resist it as the entrenchment of institutional control and restraint. The paradox of expanding the margins of teacher education by using the jail as a research site is that ever more confined spaces are encountered. Once in the jail, the researcher has then to free up the prescribed curricula.

In my research, I mainly explore the educational question of what it means to live in detention as an inmate in jail. I also explore what it means to live like an inmate in academe. To be an *inmate* is to live a daily performance within accumulating meanings and practices of captivity. Inmates are those marginalized and subjugated others whose stories are traditionally told by outsiders who lack personal knowledge of their condition. Yet, inmates can also be active and self-conscious people. Inmates struggle, whether in jail or academe, to find their voices and to express selfhood, countering institutional pressures and traditional research paradigms.

My text represents the development of one perspective on a socially marginalized group and this in the context of schooling, education and teacher education. I acknowledge the diverse perspectives of prisoners, immigrants, students, teachers and researchers. I use narrative as an approach to marginalized aspects of my imprisoned selves. I do this by linking the metaphorical worlds of education and corrections. I also broaden the concepts of jail, prisoner and detention to include teacher educators, researchers and students.

As a young female researcher/learner in a world of imprisoned men, social workers, discharge planners and counselors, correctional officers and administrators, I "lived" in maximum security for eighteen months throughout 1991 and 1992. In my attempt to relate the world of corrections to education, I became marginalized in both teacher education and corrections. In the stories I tell, my experience of *marginality* is in tension with *connection*. As I struggled in my inquiry to relate these two domains of experience, I came to realize their interrelatedness. As I struggled to relate to the inmates both conceptually and emotionally, I came to re-envision my own narrative. I explain the methodology developed for exploring the relationship between marginality and connection in chapter 4 (see sub-section, "On Writing to Connect").

My identification with inmates enhanced my awareness and knowledge of my own marginality. In living on the margins of a culture of maximum security, I paradoxically connected to inmates as they sought educational opportunities and struggled with minimal resources, waiting lists and charge sheets. Pinar (1988) recognizes identification with marginalized social groups as a key educational, autobiographical and curricular issue. Consistent with Pinar's position, my narrative ethnographic research on margins is central to teacher education. My research is, contradictorily, responsive to critical perspectives on education, teacher development and inquiry.

My perspective on narrative ethnographic research focuses on myself and inmates in a relational context that I understand through personal, institutional and social narratives. Diamond (1992) describes this interactive narrative process as autoethnography. It provides teachers with the opportunity to engage in mutual collaborative inquiry. In the context of my own study, as female teacher, researcher, co-facilitator and co-ordinator, I functioned in three rehabilitative programs alongside my inmate-students as partners in curriculum making. I am assuming that marginalized others, including immigrants, students, teachers and researchers, can benefit from an inquiry that narratively promotes the construction and reconstruction of their meanings.

The notion of researcher as marginal-insider and curriculum maker disturbs personal and professional boundaries and challenges pressures to conform to existing research conventions, methods and paradigms, even those of narrative inquiry itself. All of these images help me to contextualize a matrix of self, story, culture, institutions and society that inspires transformation. To this end, I moved along the adjoining edges of two worlds. It is along these adjoining edges that my insider's perspective developed, that I connected with others in a new culture, and that my teacher development story became re-shaped.

My Narrative Inquiry Approach to the Jail as Text

As an approach to self, story, and curriculum, narrative is recognized as a "species of qualitative research" (Eisner 1991, 1993) and, more particularly, as a view of schooling. A narrative view of schooling involves personal and professional accounts of teachers', and possibly students', lives and this lens constitutes a valuable area of educational study. Narrative refers to the process of making meaning of experience by telling stories of personal and social relevance (Connelly and Clandinin 1988a). Curriculum is a useful vehicle for exploring a personal-and social-relevance orientation to educational settings. Reflection on curriculum is therefore central to a narrative inquiry approach that provides interpretative accounts of schooling experiences in the larger context of life. Some writers in curriculum theory and in other fields, such as Carr (1986), Connelly and

Clandinin (1988a, 1990), Crites (1971), Hardy (1975), and Polkinghorne (1988), agree that human beings interpret the self, and its configurational elements, through story. Moreover, they argue that narrative is the primary form in which we construct and formalize meaning based on our experiences. Researchers embed this perspective in educational research by engaging teachers' lives, collecting stories of them, and writing interpretative accounts. The approach to narrative as method includes reflection on its complex relationship to phenomenon and inquiry (Connelly and Clandinin 1990).

I write personally in order to gain a sense of inmates and their educational experiences as well as of my own. By *personal* I mean something that is interactive and social rather than something that is idiosyncratic and private (Clandinin and Connelly 1989; Eisner 1991; Polanyi 1962). By *teacher development* I also mean growth that is interactive and social as well as being mythologically-and narratively-oriented. My teacher development story is situated in a detailed contextual narrative about the education and re-education of teachers and students. This means that my development involves the recovery, construction and reconstruction, of my teaching experience of self in community.

I view my own autobiography as a meaningful curricular construct (Pinar 1988). Narrative research into my own autobiography embraces the four commonplaces: teacher, student, subject and milieu. This is not meant to be a discussion of the commonplaces at work in my study; rather, there is a particular view that I wish to relay here. It is the sense that the commonplaces are filled with meaning only as our own story or "life text" encounters them interactively in teaching situations (Connelly and Clandinin 1988b). I view curriculum as an inquiry into this narrative process. For me, an interactive context involves my own autobiographical voice and its educative mythology. Curriculum can be viewed as a vehicle for inquiring into both of these processes in schooling contexts. The jail is one such environment.

As a way of getting at my own voice to monitor "experienced phenomena" (Barone 1992), I use images from my dream-world that reflect on my life in the jail. My images represent an interactive mix of the four commonplaces in a variety of imaginative classroom settings. Accordingly, my story of the jail is rooted, in part, in the teaching mythology which my dream-world fosters. In one dream I perform as a beginning teacher of water-aerobics in a community-college setting (Mullen 1990, 142-143). As a beginning teacher I struggle with an unfamiliar subject which causes me a great deal of stress. I only assume leadership by trusting my own artistic improvisations. In retrospect, as I make meaning of this dream, I interpret it as strangely distorted, although familiar enough, in its schooling and educative dimensions. I have provided this brief account of a personal dream to show how imagination may contribute to an educational understanding of life-experience. I am also showing how my study of the jail, and my use of relevant dreams, constitutes for qualitative researchers both a strange but yet familiar perspective on educational processes and phenomena.

My Teacher Development Study as Text

My teacher development story in action treats "real things" in an imaginative, interactive context. My story in writing treats these "real things" as material for my personal knowledge study. Late 1991, I established a Creative Writing program in the jail as an adjunct of the Education/Literacy program. In it, I focused on the artistic sensibilities of inmates and encouraged perspectives on creative writing within the Education/Literacy program. It was my aim to bring inmates' subjectivities into full view while struggling to represent my own subjectivity (Mullen 1992a, b). I used creative writing as a way of tapping the practical in my curriculum. Specifically, I aimed to meet the creative needs of inmates and myself by encouraging an exchange of writing. Just as inmates shared their poetry, short stories, musical lyrics, novelistic segments, letters and journals, and drawings and art with me, I shared some of my own writing that was shaped by our interactions. For example, the correctional letters and journals I wrote to inmates provided them with a context within which to continue writing. Moreover, I developed portraits of prisoner-artists based on their life-experiences and our interactions.

A commonplace perspective in the educational literature is that researchers need to learn to represent teachers' voices and that a narrative account builds on this process of growth (Clandinin and Connelly, 1994; Glesne and Peshkin 1992). Although my target group is prisoners rather than school teachers, I, too, believe that their voice and story need to be represented by narratives of experience. These accounts equip me with the perspective and insights that shape the other aspects of my inquiry, such as the focusing and de-focusing of my research topic. This process is seen as "virtuous" from the point of view that "subjectivity is something to capitalize on rather than to exorcise" (Glesne and Peshkin 1992, 104; Peshkin 1985, 1988). My own voice as creative writer is the subjective basis for the story that I am telling. The voice of the artist permeates an understanding of researchers and participants in various curriculum situations (Diamond 1991, 1993). Participants and researchers can be treated as artists in the act of curriculum-making. My student-inmates explored their artistic voices on their own and with me as we developed our creative writing practices, even within confined time frames and problematic working spaces. My own creative writing practice views them and me and, potentially, all curriculum makers as artists.

Teacher-initiated research, which is a focus in the curriculum literature, is a reaction to prescriptive models that generalize classroom problems and solutions (Butt et al. 1988). This approach to curriculum development and school reform involves "significant changes at the classroom level" as teachers reflect on "what classroom change means for them, from their own perspective and criteria" (Butt et al. 1988, 88-92). I believe that this perspective embraces an epistemological contradiction: on the one hand, teachers' biographies count as a legitimate form of knowledge, but, on the other hand, researchers' own stories are ignored. This negation of the researcher's story is commonplace in the literature on teachers' biographies. It is probably an outgrowth of the empiricist tradition that values an "objective understanding of the events and objects under study" over researchers' own signatures (Eisner 1991). Even Peshkin (1988), a positive example, engages his self-story through the use of a "subjectivity audit" which hints at being vaguely empirical. Nonetheless, his attempt to monitor how he was feeling throughout the research process can be viewed as "coming clean" (Guba 1990). As artists, researchers need to tell their own stories. I give more attention to this concept in chapter 4 (see *"Telling Your Own Story"* as a strategy for future researchers).

My focus is on a mode of qualitative knowing or expression referred to as *aesthetics* and *art* by curriculum thinkers (Barone 1992; Connelly and Clandinin 1985; Dewey 1934; Diamond 1991; Grumet 1988; Eisner 1985, 1991, 1993; Schwab 1969, 1971) who reflect on the value of educational experiences in classrooms and schools.

Moreover, an *aesthetics of narrative inquiry* (my term) is gaining currency in the curriculum literature. This area of educational research is being used to re-envision the nature of the curriculum field and to re-evaluate school curriculum. It is within this emerging tradition of which I am making sense of my own study.

I entered my fieldsite to investigate imprisoned lives in an unconventional schooling setting. I had in mind Schwab's (1969) concept of the practical: "the stuff of theory is abstract or idealized representations of real things. But curriculum in action treats real things: real acts, real teachers, real children, things richer and different from their theoretical representations" (35). When I ask what constitutes "real things" in my work, I can pinpoint diverse writings, including a newsletter, journal recordings, conference papers and presentations, and academic publications. Nevertheless, what primarily comes to mind is the artistic process involved in shaping a story of my fieldsite. I view "interaction" and "situation" as meaningful curricular notions that shape experience (Connelly and Clandinin 1988b; Dewey 1938) and that give substance to story. What is "real" to me are those perspectives and viewpoints that enabled me to interpret educational situations in prison and to relate intra-psychically to marginalized groups (Pinar 1988).

The teaching-learning dimensions of my own experience as inmate are also "real" to me. As I view the jail in educational terms I feel both enlarged and confined. Like the inmates, I am defining who I am and what I am becoming by virtue of my constructs, strengths and limitations. Like the inmates who experienced me, I felt their impact on my own learning. Through storytelling and writing exchanges with the inmates, they revealed to me that narrative is an integral part of their own living. My narrative inquiry orientation was therefore shaped and validated in context.

Personal Confinement as Text

My work with Sammy (see chapters 3 and 4) is an example of a teacher-student relationship of mine in the jail. It illustrates one dimension of the 'practical' in my curriculum. I also tell more of his story in a later sub-section, "Prisoners as Marginalized."

The correctional authorities approved *The creative writer* after its second draft. I had compiled the newsletter not knowing whether or not it would be accepted. Once cleared, the newsletter was then circulated to the student-inmates only within the Creative Writing program. I was relieved that we were given the administration's signature of approval and that our synergy would appear in print. I felt strapped by the system. I was told that the administration would make a decision without consulting me or the Coordinators, and without referring to my intentions as stated in my official institutional proposal. I had doubted that the administration, which excluded the Superintendent in this case, would react sympathetically to my request to tell the human story of my experience of the jail.

I had also doubted that the administration would take pride in my representation of their rehabilitative programs as valuable teaching-learning experiences. I had remembered the words of Lisa Birnie (1990), National Parole Board member and writer, that humanitarian concerns are critical ". . . because unfair treatment greatly reduces the chance of an inmate's rehabilitation" (33). With a few notable exceptions, fair treatment of inmates, along with protection of their rights and suitable life-skills training, seems to represent the best of humanitarian feelings towards inmates in the prison world.

In some ways, I felt confined by a system that does not appear to realize its own limitations. On a macro level, its limitations can be attributed to the history of academic criminology and of corrections itself. Both attend almost exclusively to the offender in the criminal process without sufficient coverage of victim, police and community. Revisionists in critical criminology write that the "logic of positivism suggests that intervention be aimed at correcting the offender. Such a one-sided focus on the offender then is not a dynamic approach and, therefore, can be viewed as correctionalism" (MacLean and Milovanovic 1991, 2). I grapple with the possible criticism of my book that it, too, exclusively focuses on inmates in chapter 5 (see sub-section, "Re-inventing Corrections: The Future"). Elsewhere the balance is redressed.

Paradoxically, imprisonment has an expansive quality for me. My dream research conveys this sense on the theme of self-imprisonment and what it means to me. In one dream that I had of honeycomb cells (Appendix B: July 6, 1991), I felt connected to inmates and their "beehive of activity." In this dream, as in real life, imprisonment is not a strictly restrictive phenomenon for me or the inmates. Contrary to expectation, an inmate's journalistic account, "Notes from a cell," includes an image of 'cell' as it lives in the outside world *and* to a world that is open and expansive. More typically in jail, I encountered sleeping tombs, misted catacombs and entrapment as images of imprisonment (Appendix B). Black Hawk related his own "diminishing reality" to the dreadful quality of inmates' mental cages.

Personal connection with inmates was reflected in our shared narrative themes. Our imprisoned selves were expressed in the forms of death, dream and desire. Certain scenarios of mine reveal the image of imprisonment as a potent metaphor of self. My own education in the jail deepened this possibility for me. I saw new opportunities as my students configured and reconfigured their life-experiences together with me in various narrative forms and through growth situations.

This sharing of our multiple imprisoned selves emerged from my interactions with the inmates. One ethical aspect of this educative process paradoxically involved my own imprisonment. I tell a story about how I felt confined by Sammy and our interpersonal and writing relationship. Mark, another inmate, also illustrates this theme, but in its reversal. Our writing relationship was terminated by an outside agent. Pam felt that my unofficial status as researcher at that time was probably sending confusing signals to Mark. This decision had been communicated to me after it was finalized. Neither Mark nor I had been consulted. Mark evidently felt cheated. As an institutional volunteer, I had no rights in this case. I too felt like a prisoner. Marginalized, I identified with what I imagined to be Mark's feelings. I wrote in my journal that we had both been relegated to the same status as marginal-insiders. At least one difference remained. The experience gave me more material for my thoughts on voice, violation and termination.

My treatment by the correctional system during this time was played out in my dreams. In one, my intellectual faculties as a teacher had become dry. I lost confidence in myself and blurted out something unintelligible to the rather "bookish" teacher who planned to discuss Dostoyevsky's *Crime and Punishment* (1982) with Mark ("Sam" in the dream). The image of crime and punishment has its parallels in reality. The bookish teacher is suggestive of the facilitator who followed procedures ("the book") in terminating our relationship, but only after bypassing procedures in the first place to put us in writing contact. The student could be Mark and the fretting teacher, me (Appendix B, September 15, 1991). In a later dream, my manuscript—my story, my life—is stolen from me by an attacker and I react in horror as I pursue him, through a residential area, in high heels (Appendix B, October 25, 1991). Dreams of myself as a prisoner in jail also recur. I am "leaning against a beige prison wall, dressed in my blue uniform, . . . sitting cross-legged . . . [and] deserving to be here because of a crime I've committed" (see the opening of this chapter). More of this story about the politics of voice and institutional control is uncovered in chapter 4.

I use my creative writing practice to construct portraits of situations encountered in the jail.   Images from my dream-world, journal recording and writing convey the ethics of voice, violation and institutional control. They include: stolen manuscripts, dry intellectual faculties, "bookish" teachers, blue uniforms, and beige prison walls. In a teacher education context, Mark is like the teachers that Diamond (1991) represents and engages narratively. They were "reduced unintentionally to being ventriloquated" by the school system (5). This can happen in both the research and writing process. As I think about the self as a text, I ask who is interpreting my own text and which experiences and conceptual frameworks are being drawn upon to re-constitute it. The reader's representation of my text is an implicit level of my inquiry.   As I unlock a human story of prisons, I am resourcing personal experience to guide my representation of others and their stories. If self can indeed be seen as a representation of metaphorical relationships and possibilities, then my story of others can be read in the same constructivist spirit.

Self as Text

My concept of *multiple imprisoned selves* is the primary metaphor that I am developing for interpreting not only the jail and my orientation to it, but also for narrating myself contextually. I agree with Bruner (1986, 1990) and Polkinghorne (1988) that the self is a construct, or representation of metaphorical relationships and possibilities, one that is subject to change over time. My inquiry into the jail as a schooling site and myself as a prisoner are examples of how I am creating metaphorical relationships and possibilities. Self, as a text, is about how we "situate" and "distribute" (Bruner 1990) ourselves in relation to others and the world, and how these experiences will be interpreted. My emphasis is on a text that consists of narrative ethnography rather than classical ethnography. I want to tell the story of how I lived in the jail in relation to others rather than merely describing how other people lived there. I interpret experiences of self as deeply mythologized, personal accounts of educational moments and events in which I have a full-bodied presence (Mullen 1994). Problematics involving narrative ethnographic representation are presented in chapter 4.

In my master's thesis (1990), I relied heavily on my representation of self through personal dreams to create a narrative text. I interpreted this narrative dream text as a resource for personal knowledge studies, teacher development, and educational inquiry. I also experienced my narrative dream text as a living representation of my self. This accounted for my varying emotional reactions to going public with privately held dreams. I wrote about this experience in a manuscript that I coordinated and contributed to on narrative inquiry (Mullen et al. 1992c). I wrote about how my nervousness had become theatrical even in my own mind as I formalized my experiences and impressions as a dreaming researcher. I felt challenged by the spread of welts that this occasioned all over my body. But, in conversation during a seminar with colleagues, I was set free. My colleagues warmly grappled with notions of dream, sharing their own profound questions, stories and experiences, and connecting them with each others' narratives. I felt empowered. I promised myself that I would never hesitate to be marginal again.

I am telling the human story that my inquiry is shaping, and I feel strongly that this story must be told as sensitively and meaningfully as possible. I chose to tell this human story with respect to my understanding in relation to the inmates, decision-makers, teachers and teacher-educators. I am therefore inquiring into the self as a prisoner in relation to others, society, systems (cycles and rhythms), and curriculum. I use various images, such as marginal-insider and curriculum maker, to configure the dimensions of my metaphor of imprisoned selves. The dimensions of myself include learner, researcher, woman and teacher; those of the inmates are teachers, learners and men.

Prisoners as Marginalized

Prisoners are the orphaned children of our society and the outcasts of our educational system. We banish a part of ourselves when we label prisoners. The very term, *prisoners*, encourages our social narrative of inmates as captive misfits, anti-heroic convicts, and misanthropic wrong-doers. We need to see that prisoners are people who, like ourselves, are capable of tenderness and understanding, recovery and creativity. Instead of looking to see what the prisoners are actually like, we accept others' representations, stereotyping prisoners as unredeemably wicked and wanton (Jones 1992). In this way, we help perpetuate a marginality that is mis-educative for both prisoners and ourselves.

Empirical researchers typically construct perspectives on prisoners without reference to personally lived accounts of the inside. Abstract accounts of ordinary prisoners distance us from the humanity of inmates (see, for example, Davies 1990; Harlow 1987, and Lovitt 1992). Without having experienced either incarceration or classroom teaching, some writers appropriate the authority of prisoners and teachers. They authorize themselves to construct "prison knowledge . . . in the context of mechanized space" (Davies 1990, 26, 229). Such accounts would be more meaningful if writers had tried to understand the lived experience of *the inside*. Too little of the correctional and pedagogical literature deals with the human dimension of research with inmates. I find the "traumabiographies" of prisoners, such as Caron (1978, 1985), Harris (1986), MacDonald (1988) and Sharansky (1988), educative because of their insider's perspective.

As teacher-educators, we also need to consider the meanings that we invent about marginalized others. In this way, we can take responsibility for re-inventing our meanings through sustained, narrative ethnographic inquiry. In a single creative writing visit to Auburn Correctional Facility, McClane (1988), an American writer-professor, sensed the humanity of his banished "brothers." What draws me to his perspective is the depth of his own humanity and the recognition that

> Whatever these inmates were—and all of them were sentenced to Auburn for corporal crimes—they would not permit me to view them merely as maniacs, psychopaths, or what have you. They were people,

cussed and joy-filled: people capable of tenderness and murder: people like me and yet unlike me, because I haven't yet, thank goodness, killed anyone (230).

Biographies that are written by researchers who rely on prisoners to write or tell their own stories (Padel and Stevenson 1988) can be treated as teacher development texts. Such full-bodied accounts by inmate-insiders are rare and privileged. Jean Harris (1986), for example, had been a teacher for thirty-six years. She was headmistress of an exclusive school when she was imprisoned for second degree murder. She became a stranger in both worlds. However, she could not just sit in her cell and let others write about her life. It was her life. She had lived it. She concluded that so much of what she saw in prison had to do with education or the lack of it: the "hardest part of teaching [women prisoners] is unteaching what they have already learned" (338). "Little is done here," continues Harris, "to try to develop a woman's power of moral reasoning . . . Mind-numbing drugs are the main 'therapy'" (524, 488). Foucault agrees that prisoners are "the victims of a social system which, having produced them, refuses to re-educate them and is content to degrade and reject them" (Macey 1993, 259).

Like Harris (1986) and Cleaver (1968), my inmate-students often wrote as castaways, estranged from themselves and the world in which they live. As an instance, Black Hawk, a Native American, wrote "Cast away beyond the reach/Pretend to be was made of me" (poem, "Diminishing reality," 1992). Sear Robinson wrote that he was "charging forth without proceeding/on [his] painted pony bound for hell" (poem, "Mr. Jones (to the moon)," 1992). And Adrian Sands wrote: "Lashing us one final series of welts, he released us. In continuing episodes with Norman [employer/supervisor] we were told to write one thousand lines to the effect that we would be good work boys in future. My respect for authority was diminished greatly as a result of my exposure to Norman and, subsequently, my entire early teens were wracked with learning problems in school" (short story, "An all too common experience," 1992). As educators, we are also struggling for authentic expressions of ourselves and our experiences. We inadvertently draw attention to ourselves caught as inmates, subjugated by the ways in which we both create and define knowledge.

Narratives of Marginality

I wish to contribute to the re-invention of the idea of prisoner. My approach is to negotiate new possibilities in how we construe life behind bars, metaphors of self, the educative process and relationships. I also work with the critical perspectives of devalued and neglected lives. Educators need to learn how to work with such perspectives. I attempt to do this here by giving a sense of the "ongoing experiential text" of my inmate-students' lives whose experiences of imprisonment and marginality "reflect upon life and explain themselves" (Connelly and Clandinin 1990, 4). In chapter 3, I provide an enlarged perspective on such vignettes.

It is my intention that no voice or story should dominate. But, as I focus and re-focus my perspectives, my images of imprisoned selves do dominate. This is a reflection of my role both as an authority figure *and* restricted researcher. I was most often prevented from negotiating, at some length and over time, inmates' representation of themselves. I therefore question to what extent I, too, am responsible for re-producing aspects of the "surveillant community" (Foucault 1977) in my representation of inmates. I also question to what extent I am creating a text that restricts the dimensions of an interactive and participatory narrative that might otherwise free marginal and imprisoned selves. I am uncertain as to whether my efforts are translating into reclaiming inmates' silenced voices. But, then the reality of my surveillant community is that it is simultaneously struggling to restrict aspects of my work exactly in this direction.

A number of my inmate-students exemplify the theme of prisoner as marginalized. A theme of prisoner disempowerment probably seems odd or even paradoxical. In both chapter 3 and a paper called, "Prisoner as artist: A narrative account of a Creative Writing program" (Mullen 1992b), I develop portraits of my inmate-students that convey a fuller sense of my interactions with them than I can hope to illustrate. I have selected three of my inmate-portraits from my journal writing. I developed two of them, vignettes one and three, in chapter 3. A later section, "Researcher as Marginalized," in this present chapter provides a fourth example of marginality in a correctional setting.

Vignette One: Black Hawk, the Poet

Black Hawk, a Native American, lives without hope. I wrote that

> Black Hawk had difficulty locating a poem of hope in his impressive
> file. After many long moments, he found nuances of hope in a long
> poem. Now I wonder: Was I imposing hope and healing on him? Or,
> was I possibly moving him towards hope and healing in his life beyond
> his written text? Or, was I in fact clued in to a sub-text of his poetry?
> (*Prison Journal*, December 16, 1991).

Black Hawk and I connected, and yet I had possibly marginalized him
upon again pressing for a poem of hope. The orphaned child in
"Diminishing reality" (1992) may be himself and his own child:

> Oh come to me won't you please
> Listen to what I feel
> Many many nights alone
> Locked within a sleeping tomb.
> Memories of a child in time
> The boy still cries inside
> Dreamt of many things so grand . . .
> No one loved a child, it's late
> Cast away beyond the reach
> Pretend to be was made of me.
> Silent tears came to me
> Memories they are so clear
> Hurt the child, mentally
> Full life would never come to be.
> Bleeding, it hurts to know
> Crying, my pain it shows
> Lonely in this world so scared
> Not knowing where to go, betrayed.
> Keep your dreams inside the heart
> I know you lost a bigger part
> Someday you'll find the missing spot
> Someday someone will come to heal your heart. . . .

Black Hawk, as a homeless Native American and inmate, is doubly
orphaned while spending "many many nights alone/Locked within a
sleeping tomb" ("Diminishing reality"). When pressed, he nodded
saying that his little girl *is* Hope to him. Black Hawk expresses his

own feeling of marginality in powerful images of abandonment, aloneness, violence and heroin use, death, and creative struggle in his many poems. A sample of his poetry was published in *The creative writer,* the correctional newsletter that I initiated and coordinated as part of the Creative Writing program.

Black Hawk teaches me about the image of child as inmate. He is held captive within the autobiographical memory of a personal family history and mythology. This is suggested by: "Memories they are so clear/Hurt the child, mentally/Full life would never come to be" (third stanza). With the aid of a narrative inquiry process, such images can play a significant role in reconstructing the self, and re-awakening to one's deeper creativity. I too am seeking to rescue the children in my dreams and within me.

Vignette Two: Alec, the Beginning English Literacy Student

Alec was a Polish immigrant. With his downtrodden white face and glazed eyes he looked lost. Mid-way through our conversation to clarify Alec's requests and answers to my questions, I called for his cell-mate, a Polish-English translator.

Alec arrived in Canada in December 1991. Two days later he was arrested on a spouse battery charge. He was found guilty. The consequences were grave for him; for two years he was not permitted to have any access to his partner or children. While his partner worked in a professional capacity in the city of my study, he had raised the children for two years on his own in Poland. Alec had been an engineer. He and his partner had been drinking one cold, nasty night. His partner became vituperative. Alec warned her of what he might do; she ignored him; he blackened both her eyes. He was arrested, handcuffed and taken to jail in a housecoat and slippers. Alec's Polish-English cell-mate translated this story for me. This young man, who had fought with a different inmate, was parading two black eyes and a broken nose.

After that session I never saw Alec again, even though he had requested a Polish-English dictionary and the possibility of being tutored by me on a weekly basis. I could identify with Alec as he swung his arms around to indicate his desperate need to be understood. I, too, felt "foreign" as I struggled to comprehend broken fragments. As in Black Hawk's case, I was left with a few incomplete insights into his life. Fragments. Beginnings. No sophisticated story-line. No sense-making of particulars. No text. No polish. Only the raw experience.

Although an insider, Alec returned to his cell marginalized with respect to the language barrier within the institution. I was marginalized in a different way in the institution. To exit, I had to wait for a correctional officer (guard) to key the electronically controlled elevator. Next I signed out and then moved to the electronically controlled airless room (the "mousetrap") to be identified, signing out again. The guard in the control room watched: one set, and then another set, of front doors shut behind me as my image exited on the monitor.

Vignette Three: Sammy, a Student of Letter Writing

Sammy, my heavily tattooed Native American student, quickly moved through many formal high school courses with me. He was my most devoted student. Over a one-year period we together accomplished Basic and Advanced English, Family Studies, Canadian Law and Accounting. (Sammy tutored me on the basic principles underlying accounting so that I could be authorized to continue to teach him.) Sammy showed no particular interest in creative writing *per se* but he did want to write letters to his estranged daughter as well as to me. We began writing back-and-forth once he was transferred from protective custody to a maximum security federal prison. When I discovered that he was reflecting on his childhood and inviting me to do the same, I thought about conducting an inquiry into the educational life and pursuits of one inmate. I included a sample of our letter-writing exchanges in the correctional newsletter.

This story of connection with Sammy has another side. He wrote persistently, even asking the other Education Coordinators to encourage me to respond more frequently. He sometimes asked me personal questions, challenging my request-turned-stipulation that we were to write only about educational themes. The inappropriateness of Sammy's demands and my inability to deal with them made me feel like his prisoner. The more aware I became of Sammy's feelings, the stronger I felt compelled to create boundaries in order to protect my safety. During class time, I began wearing my grandmother's wedding ring to jail. When Sammy and others asked about it, I referred to an imaginary fiancé. Sally, my favorite Education Coordinator, chuckled that the ring was a good idea but that it would probably fail to protect me. Sammy's conduct had, inadvertently, helped me understand more about imprisonment. While working with him, I felt both connected and confined.

Researcher as Marginalized

Institutional Cycles and Rhythms

Anyone who works or lives in a correctional system soon learns to adjust his or her own rhythms to its constraints: for instance, the rotational cycle places great pressure on the continuity and success of rehabilitative programs and working relationships. Inmates, remanded until their court dates, are detained in the jail, which functions as a "holding cell." On rotation, inmates move through various cell blocks of the jail to await court trials and sentencing, transfer to other detention centers (maximum or medium/minimum security depending on the outcome of the trial), or release on bail. Often, the inmates I met with were rotated after a single session or only a few sessions. Our interpersonal rhythms were disrupted and our curricular objectives were seemingly unfulfilled.

The marginality I experienced in the jail also came partly from the way I responded to the institutional cycles and rhythms, procedures and regulations that define the jail as mechanized space. When I met with the inmates on a weekly basis, I never quite knew what to expect, whom I was going to see, or what we were going to do. Sally, the Education Coordinator, kindly warned me in a letter not to expect too much from my inmate-students in terms of productivity, given such a challenging and unpredictable place. Her concern was that I was "over working" with respect to the copiousness of my stories. They had been written in the form of journal entries and circulated to inmate-students. She probably sensed my frustration with some of the constraints and regulations of the jail, especially as they impacted on my creative writing students. I also initiated a system of regulation and documentation that involved Sally and me in dialogue about the new Creative Writing program and its scheduling, rhythms and developments. I develop this story-line of the cycles and rhythms in my fieldsite in chapter 3 and with respect to methodology in chapter 4.

Dreams as Poetic Insight and Meaning-Based Data

I use dreams and dream recordings to connect me to my creative writing process. My dreams give me insight into how I construct and reconstruct my setting and the world of my research. To date, I have organized two formal dream texts (see Mullen 1990 and Appendix A) using emerging themes. I created these texts from my daily dream recordings. My jail-related dream text features themes on education, literacy and writing; the marginal-insider; prisoner as criminal; researcher as prisoner, and storytelling in correctional settings. In studying a culture we study ourselves (Geertz 1988; Van Maanen 1988). We also study the text that the self creates and the self that is created by the text (Geertz 1988). I develop an inquiry into these almost indistinguishable processes that provide an aesthetic challenge to the storywriter in chapter 4. The qualitative researcher makes use of her subjectivities, their origins and influences, to aid in her understanding of the culture that she is studying.

Prescribed Curricula

The inmates and I responded to the prescribed curricula with far less enthusiasm than to our own creative writing. Some of my inmate-students resisted their formal coursework. They favored instead their own self-directed, often artistic, writing. Indeed, at times, my inmate-students performed impressively, if not magically, when they had greater control of their own curricula. Birney (1966) asserted years ago that creative talent should be encouraged, acknowledging that it is potentially defiant of "school curriculum and pedagogical doctrine" (49). Some inmate-writers, with less than high school education, produced, for their personal satisfaction, poetry, musical lyrics, drawings and art, short stories, novelistic segments, journals and letters.

They wrote despite the censorship they encountered through my own awkward interpretation of institutional expectations. The effort I displayed in our creative writing newsletter does not tell the story of how curricula can be negotiated as a surveillance tactic. Thus, the newsletter, on one level, marginalizes writers in prison. On a public level, it represents their experience of marginality in the forms of drug addiction and recovery, lost love, abandonment and abuse, and failed and fleeting dreams.

We were connected in our efforts to support a Creative Writing program and the institution itself permitted us to work in this way. I contributed anonymously as editor and journal writer to the newsletter for reasons that included my own safety and protection. For the same reasons, the inmates contributed as anonymous writers. If our identity had been publicly exposed, we would have been both collectively and individually recognized as drug addicts; victims of childhood abuse; orphans of society; romantic/despairing figures; humanitarian peacemakers; mythologizers, writers and poets. We showed that images of marginality and connection can be interwoven to reflect a complex educational narrative.

Female on a Carousel

As volunteer in a variety of capacities, my visits never took me directly to the ranges and cells but only to the interview rooms on a number of floors. I often spent hours on a merry-go-round, searching for an available room in which to meet the inmates on my list. Men in protective custody, for example, could not be moved to an interview room on another floor. This set-up suited me during those times when I felt frustrated with certain inmates. This included those inmates who yelled obscenities out to me from their cages. While traveling in packs, they made inappropriate comments and lewd gestures. While on the elevators jammed up against one another and carts filled with supplies, they leered at me. Yet, once alone, these same men acted very respectfully and appreciatively towards volunteers whom they mythologized as saints and "do-gooders".

When I worked with Sear one afternoon, inmates from his range continually poked their heads into our interview room. The signaling of 'thumbs-up' to him referred to me. Eyes flashed suggestively to my legs. I felt caged. The guards were nowhere to be seen. While sitting, blushing, and sitting, I quickly calculated that the guards were being deliberately detained on the ranges. Sear, my musician-student, assured me that he, too, took exception to such offensive behavior. The image of the carousel in his rock lyrics portrayed him as an object on a merry-go-round in prison and within himself. He put into words how I felt. Did he know how I felt? Sear's image of imprisonment connected me both to myself and to him. We sat in that stuffy and abandoned room like two frozen ponies on a carousel, halted in mid-gallop.

Teacher Educators as Marginalized

Teacher educators are also marginalized in many if less explicit ways. Goffman (1961) discusses the concept of "total institutions" (hospitals, prisons) where the imprisoned self is rendered anonymous as further punishment for challenging or endangering society. But, in doing so, the self is also regulated and violated. Such symbolic activities as wearing a specific color force inmates to "take on a disidentifying role" (23) which is incompatible with their conceptions of self. The concept of total institutions can be applied to academe with its surveillance and elimination of the personal. Antiphonal accounts by teacher educator-researchers reflect on personal induction to the professoriate and continuing struggles within academia (e.g., Diamond and Mullen 1996; Mullen and Dalton 1996). Mutual feelings of isolation and the need for expressive opportunities are sometimes explored against a backdrop of institutional relations of power and inequality. The challenge for teacher educators may be to explore creative enterprises that enhance awareness of personal knowledge and intersubjectivity, and that facilitate political stories about community.

How can we open up spaces for ourselves in academe? We may need to live on the margins of educational research and practice in order to create spaces within the constraints of our individual, institutional, and social narratives. We may even need to re-think ourselves in order to provide fresh perspectives on how the world of teacher education can be re-imagined and recast. Rose (1990) had to alter his taken-for-granted methodology during his research inquiry into the lives of working-class black men. As he attempted to live alongside his participants, he changed his thinking as an ethnographer, altering the received practices and traditions of his research paradigm in order to create anew. As another example, spaces in higher education can be expanded through interpersonal experiences of positive chumming. These can help to counter shark training. Shark training in academe breeds a culture of negative chumming that enables human qualities and behaviors to exist which are steeped in exploitation, abandonment and competition (Mullen and Dalton 1996).

Teacher Educators as Inmates

Are we, as teacher educators, teachers and students, forced to live in maximum security? Are we also inmates, marginalized by powerful narratives about what constitutes legitimate research, teaching, and selfhood? However, we may be able to learn how to move gracefully on the periphery of metaphoric worlds and within the hearts of the oppressed. As I draw from my own experience of maneuvering between and within the world of teacher education and corrections, I am struggling to understand how we can broaden conventional, if not restrictive, understandings of schooling and research. Constructs of education needs to be questioned, deepened and broadened, and finally transformed. They also need to be re-lived in the context of their formulations of possibility.

As I write within the prison cell of my own being, I associate researching the margins with living more deeply and expansively. I am, simultaneously, the prisoner in blue leaning against a beige wall (see opening of this chapter) and the street-researcher with an insatiable need for experiences that are first-hand, concrete and immediate. As the prisoner in blue, I felt like an inmate when my relationship with Mark, the letter-writer, was abruptly terminated. I identified with what I imagined to be Mark's feelings. The paradox was that, whether I moved to the inside or functioned on the periphery of the jail, I still felt enclosed and constrained.

I write to expand. I feel inspired to do this within the prison cells of myself and others to encourage innovation in teacher education and research. We need to sweep out some of the conventional ideas within teacher education. If we stimulate a transformative approach to inmates, for instance, we may view them as partners in curriculum-making and as creative writers. More research needs to be done on inmates in jails as well as on the professional development experience of educators inside sites. More research also needs to be done about the different contexts in which teacher educators in general and students work. We need to give ourselves permission to set the scene for our own educational narratives.

We can challenge our taken-for-granted assumptions in teacher education by moving to the margins to conduct research in alternative settings and by adopting a personal approach. Soren (1992) accepted both of these challenges in her study of museums as curricular sites to be experienced and understood in personal terms. We can accept the challenge to look again by creating links in different educational communities. My narrative themes connect to the creation of self and transformation of knowledge in alternative settings. The next chapter situates this conception inside the "manila" prison where I construct an account of my fieldwork.

Chapter 3

A Story of the Jail:
Inside the Manila Prison

This narrative follows chapter 2 in which I provide the background and context of my study. I use a narrative framework based on the passage of time. This establishes a sequence of temporal vantage points which provide a context for immediate impressions, and which also allow me to look both backwards and forwards in time.

In this chapter, I tell the story of my experience of corrections. My focus here is on the jail itself. My aim is to narrate my novelistic ethnography of that "unfamiliar story world" (Van Maanen 1988, 103). I invite my reader to re-live my experience as a fieldworker, not to interpret or analyze it. I reconstruct or re-visit my journal recordings, known as "data sources" in the social sciences, here. My story is therefore a "field text" based on journal notes. It is about my relationship to participants' stories and their lives (see Connelly and Clandinin, 1994). The story that I tell is, nevertheless, told in real, concrete terms as a "curriculum in action" (Schwab 1969) that includes what I did, felt, thought and observed (Schwab 1954). As I represent it, then, my experience is both directly apprehended and mind-forged. As I investigated my research site, I simultaneously created it, dreamt it, and re-imagined it.

Just as "manila" is made from strong fibers, I chose this image in my title to evoke an association with construction (as on paper). This chapter, and the book itself, can be read as an "experience of reconstruction" of actual events. I interpret "reconstruction of experience," to mean reflective inquiry/practice and autobiographical memory (Mullen 1990). This phrase has a history as I have encountered it in Dewey (1938) and then in Connelly and Clandinin's (1988b) narrative writings. I include "prison" in my title to mean both an actual place and my experience of it.

The manila prison image has implications for the themes of this chapter. For example, I use this image to create the sense that my mother lived her life blocked by "four edges marked by the wall, ceiling, floor and banister" (illustrated in sub-section, "Unnegotiated closures: The disappeared"). I also develop the manila prison image by referring to other events in my story. Sear, Black Hawk and Adrian are inmates who attempted to reconstruct themselves through writing. Prison writing provides the means of regeneration for inmates, but writing is itself a prison. Prison writers contend with the constraints of censorship and termination imposed both on their writing and writing relationships with others. The manila image is not restricted to prison. Academics also cope with the constraints imposed on their research and inquiring selves. Van Maanen (1988) writes about his own human frailties, mistakes and blunders, in fieldsites. In doing so, he tackles the prison of perfection that compels traditional ethnographers to eliminate "troublesome worries [and]. . . self-reflection and doubt" in favor of "interpretive omnipotence" and "feelings of ownership" over cultural others (51). My connection to academic life as a prison completes the circle of incarceration and confirms the usefulness of the manila image.

Going In

The First Visit: Gargoyles Bid Welcome

It was January 3, 1991, two months since my being oriented to a new culture of institutionalized others. I had finally been cleared to begin work in the jail as a client contact volunteer. I had been introduced to this provincial correctional facility, both on-site in its administrative section and in one of its community-based agencies. I was aiming to be cleared in two interrelated capacities: as a teacher in the Education/Literacy department of the jail and as an official researcher from the Institute documenting my teacher development experiences. I had discussed my hopes with two representatives from the agency: Paul, the Volunteer Coordinator, and Kim, the Executive Director. Over the months, I struggled with uncertainty and eventually received clearance on these levels and on others that evolved situationally.

In narrative terms, I was beginning to learn about an unfamiliar storytelling milieu. I would be provided with a stage for exploring education, life-experiences, and imprisoned selves. I anticipated that this new research community would help me to re-educate myself. I wanted to shape alternative perspectives on, and directions for, my own teacher development narrative. One of the ways in which I would accomplish this was to study a population that was, in turn, studying me. The inmates were part of an hierarchical structure of guards, supervisors, coordinators, teachers, counselors, discharge planners and administrators. Everyone performed implicitly as anthropological fieldworkers. I, too, had a role to play in rigorously studying others within an enclosed hierarchy of observation. I was there to perform narratively and therapeutically in a conversational mode. My personal emphasis was two-fold: I wanted to learn about the inmates and their experience of education and re-education in their lives and within the penitentiary itself. I also wanted to learn about myself in such a challenging place and how I might come to be re-educated in it. Even though I was a learner, I anticipated co-constructing a new set of meanings for education with the inmates.

I would soon discover that, while everyone had a great deal of "objective" knowledge about inmates and their official and social lives, they knew very little about inmates' expressive and emotional selves. Rehabilitation ignores the personal except as a step-by-step forging of the self in programs that predetermine desirable outcomes. I was to learn this critical lesson in the three jail programs that I participated in as well as in the community they represented. In my work, I would explore the established programs in the jail. I would also explore the inmates and myself. In our partnership of curriculum-making, I would learn about our stories of experience as imprisoned selves. I stood out as a young female volunteer interested in the stories of men in prison that could be enhanced through a responsive curriculum.

On that cold, frosty evening, I absorbed the look of the building again and again on the way in. It was the first time that I had actually been inside the prison. It looked eerie with its tiny barred windows. Gargoyles stood watch like prison gatekeepers. I produced my identification badge within view of the monitor. It contained my picture (that had been previously taken in the administrative building), as well as my first and last name. I would later turn my name inside out to establish anonymity. I was ostensibly being screened by security personnel in the monitor, yet all I could see were the gargoyles peering down. I waited. I could not simply knock to gain entry. After ten minutes, the heavy steel door clicked. I stood inside the door not knowing where to go. I felt lost. The orientations had not prepared me for this feeling. I could "clear" security only with Paul, my immediate supervisor, so I entered the designated waiting area on my left.

Two women sat talking and drinking Coke. This room contained a vending machine, public telephone and washroom along with wooden benches. One black woman (origin unknown to me) was telling how her "old man" had been "nabbed again with the blow and a piece". She said that he had been "thrown in the bucket" until she "milked granddaddy for coin". I squirmed. Her colloquialisms may have been spoken in English but they were alien to me! I wondered how I could make sense of a research site that was probably populated with people who talked a foreign language and yet understood one another. Over time I learned to decipher the speech of the hundreds of people with whom I made contact: She meant that her boyfriend, a recidivist or habitual offender, had been arrested on a cocaine and weapons charge. He was being detained until her father produced bail money for them. I was a visitor here too, but in a different sense. Paul was now one hour late.

Paul arrived, apologizing that he had just gotten back from holidays. He was rubbing his cold hands. We then went through a second security check at the next heavy steel door. I could see our images in the monitor darkened by tinted glass. Paul moved to front security. Here the bullet proof glass revealed the guards' quick movements. I was to learn that the guards worked in pairs at all stations throughout this institution. Paul produced his identification and then I did. He signed in. I reproduced his line of information on my own. I printed my Irish name; indicated my status (volunteer); the name of the agency I represented; and then signed to the left. I looked at the other occupations on the list. Mostly lawyers. On request, we were passed a heavy lock through a narrow slot. The tiny locker room contained dented, antiquated lockers. It was full. I felt disoriented. Paul asked the guards if we could store our belongings inside their station. They agreed, piling everything on the floor.

Cigarette butts littered the soil of a pot plant mocking the "no-smoking" sign above it. A large, uniformed man holding a bag of fried chicken and a coffee approached us from a corridor leading inside. He told us to move from this "lounge" area. I looked at Paul and knew not to ask why. We paused for security to open the door, then returned to the designated waiting area. This was a twisted game of Monopoly: as players we were being prevented from proceeding directly to "jail," which was our goal. Although cleared by the institution, I felt like an outsider. I identified more strongly with the other women waiting than with Paul, my knowing guide. As I was to learn from the inmates and staff, the women who wait when men are sentenced to prison are under the control of the criminal justice system. As Birnie (1990), a parole board member, writes: "When a man is sentenced to prison there is often a woman in the background who is sentenced along with him. . . . Who are these women? There are over twelve thousand male inmates in Canada's penitentiaries and most of them have a woman who is waiting" (83). As I was to learn for myself, everyone who came into contact with the criminal justice system was under its control. Paul explained that we had to wait to see inmates until the institutional dinner hour was over. From what I gathered, this "lock-up" situation brought contact with inmates, on all units, to a temporary halt.

Again cleared, we moved on. My usual sense of time altered as we waited in the narrow passageway between the front reception and the inside of the jail. This passageway was the "mousetrap" to everyone. It contained mail slots for staff and a video camera. My own form was alert and professional, black cloth rising and falling though there was no breeze to stir it, or me. Paul still appeared relaxed but impatient. I asked what the two Correctional Officers in the corridor ahead of us would expect. Paul pointed to the registration book on the stand to our left and commented, "sign in." He picked up on my use of "Correctional Officers," saying that I should refer to them less formally as guards or even C.O.s. I would hear "screws," too, he said, but from the inmates. I felt pleased that I already knew these terms from my reading. The smell of garbage permeated the air as we crossed over. Coles (1989) writes that when we cross over some lines, it is a different life awaiting us and our lives can be changed forever. Crossing the line changed my own life.

The Correctional Facility: A Detention Bucket

Provincial correctional facilities are known in prison nomenclature as "detention buckets." It is also a maximum security prison, one of four provincial correctional facilities in the location of my study. Twelve federal institutions, which receive some of these inmates, are located throughout Ontario. They exist for both women and men; in conjunction with them, there are twenty-six parole offices and community correctional centers (see Correctional Service of Canada's Facility directory 1991, 17-22) .

This jail, like all other jails in Ontario, is directly governed by the Ministry of Correctional Services (which I refer to as the "Ministry of Corrections" and also sometimes as "Ministry" and "corrections"). This Ministry, a provincial jurisdiction, is responsible to the federal correctional authority. At the federal level, corrections is governed by the Correctional Service of Canada under the authority of the Honorable Pierre Cadieux (1990), Solicitor General of Canada. He was responsible for establishing its mission and document: Mission of the correctional service of Canada covers core values, guiding principles, and strategic objectives. The term "corrections" is itself ambiguously used, even by writers in the criminal justice field. One can, however, attempt to make distinctions by inferring from the context whether the level under discussion is provincial or federal. This information was confirmed for me during a telephone conversation with a researcher at the agency that supervised my visits to the jail. In my own lexicon, "corrections" is sometimes used ambiguously whenever the distinction seemed unimportant. Otherwise, I attempt to make the distinctions in my writing.

Within the particular scope of my study, inmates who are 18 years of age and over are held in custody (in all provincial jails). Accused persons are admitted to this institution for one of three reasons: remand (held in custody) prior to trial or sentencing; held for immigration violations; or to serve a sentence of imprisonment. The majority await trial and sentencing. Some of them, upon being sentenced, actually "do time" in this jail. The majority of inmates who are on remand do "deadtime" at one of the detention centers until their trial or sentence date, or until bail is determined.

During my own stay, I noticed some inmates being re-admitted upon their release for subsequent offenses. I remember one mentally challenged inmate who used to lie on the floor of the chapel to watch videos on recovery and relapse. The rest of us would sit in a semi-circle during these drug awareness sessions. One day Jimmy was released. Later he was back, and then he was gone again. He was one of the disappeared.

Prior to court, inmates are moved from their overcrowded cells to court cells to await trail. They need a lawyer, legal aid assistance, a suit for court, and maybe a translator. If found guilty, they are detained further; or, transferred to another provincial jail; or, shipped out to serve federal time of more than two years. In the latter case, they are assessed at Millhaven ("Haven") Institution, known as the "receiving dock." Inmates are then usually sent elsewhere to an institution appropriate to their offense and criminal case history.

This jail, like others, was organized according to classification of offenses. It contained areas for the mentally ill, physically ill, dangerous offenders, and general population. On the first floor, inmates were detained in *protective custody* (PC) quarters. These inmates were at risk from the general population of inmates for their offenses against women and children. Segregated inmates were therefore restricted from attending rehabilitative programs along with others. All of their routines (eating, sleeping and exercising) were carried out separately and mostly on an individual basis.

The *general population* was detained on the second floor of the institution. The cells are found side-by-side along all units in the building. They are separated by walls and face into the common area (also referred to as the "day area"). Cells have windows and locked barred doors. Although the cells contain a double bunk, along with a few minor provisions, inmates often bunk three to a cell due to overcrowding. The least powerful sleeps on the floor next to the toilet. None of the inmates I met admitted to being this marginal person.

Buggies containing food and medicine were regularly pushed onto ranges located at both ends of the corridor (or interior of the jail). A library cart was also brought around to all of the ranges on a daily basis. I talked with the head librarian at the Annual Awards banquet for volunteers on March 27, 1991. It was sponsored by the Ministry of Correctional Services. This modest woman in her sixties told me that she divides her cart into sections for slow and more advanced readers. The most popular writers are Danielle Steele and Stephen King; genres in demand are fiction, biography and history. Inmates can make special requests for books but these can only be supplied if already on order.

The *kitchen workers* were housed on the third floor. They had much more freedom than others and even worked outside on the premises. One day I saw inmates in uniform taking care of the garbage bins. I was stunned, but gradually saw their activity in the community as commonplace. Workers are the envy of other inmates. They do not participate in programs because they are close to their release dates. As I was to learn first-hand and also read: "Inmates sometimes participate to gain the eye of staff and to earn an early release" (Goffman 1961, 110). The physically ill and injured were also detained on the third floor in segregated hospital quarters. These inmates delighted in showing off their tattoos and waving bandaged limbs.

At one end, on the fourth floor, the *mentally challenged* were detained and, at the other end, *federal offenders*. I was surprised to learn that some federal offenders do serve their sentences, even if only partially, in a number of detention centers until they are properly classified and then transferred. Detention centers that house federal offenders intensify their security regulations and are therefore classified as medium and maximum security prisons. Rape, murder, indecent assault, arson, drug trafficking, bank robbery and fraud constitute the main offenses for federal clients. The majority of offenses for all inmates are drug-related.

Inmates segregated in "the hole" for poor behavior are permitted to read only the Bible. Isolation cells contain solid metal doors with a slat for viewing and a larger slat for passing meals. The experience of such cells in terms of lighting, bunking, and the circumstances surrounding such penalty is documented by inmate-autobiographers (Caron 1978; Conlon 1993; Sharansky 1988). Inmates interacted in the common areas except during "lock up" which froze all movement. Such a state also limited the movement of staff but not the guards. Because the inmates were secluded on ranges, they could not be viewed in their immediate environment. I did glimpse them, however, through partially open doors during traffic flow. Observers must learn to make a quick study of such times if they wish to gather impressions of inmates behind bars. Inmates have access to telephones, but only as "collect" calls. Inmates resourced twelve special telephone operators while competing for available lines.

I learned from inmates, staff and guards that inmates also spent time, in addition to eating and sleeping, playing cards and other games. Communal washrooms contain shower stalls. Other activities include exercising; viewing television; writing letters and poetry; drawing; doing homework; and participating in programs. Various programs are scheduled during the days and evenings throughout the week and on weekends. This institution does not offer a work program unlike some detention centers where inmates work either on site or in the community. Programs available at this facility include anger control, chaplaincy, rituals and customs, and education (school board courses, literacy, correspondence, and community college programs). Additional programs focused on self-help, drug awareness, creative writing, counseling and volunteer contact (for special requests). Inmates attend all programs on a voluntary basis. Also available were courses sponsored by the Quakers (on special topic areas), Alcoholics Anonymous (AA), Cocaine Anonymous (CA), and Narcotics Anonymous (NA).

Developing a sense of this institutional context as a setting for doing fieldwork required that I approach many people to ask questions. This was a confusing place to understand in its more intricate functioning. For instance, some inmates wait a year or more before being sentenced. The story of one accused (anonymous), who was incarcerated in my fieldsite for over one year, was published. (I cannot identify this publication as it reveals the identity of my fieldsite). This particular inmate was found innocent of all charges. I worked for over one year with Sammy, another inmate, on numerous high school courses during his "deadtime." Once he was charged with the first degree murder of his spouse, he was detained for several more months prior to being transferred. As a volunteer, one is offered only a quick sketch of how the prison operates. Not only did I ask questions, but I also listened carefully to everyone's stories; observed patterns of movement wherever I went; and read literature that shed light on organizational aspects of, and social patterns within, penal institutions (Birnie 1990; Caron 1978; Goffman 1961; Harris 1986).

A visitor also has almost no understanding of his or her own "clients" in such a place. First, the inmates' statuses vary within the Ministry of Correctional Services' own infrastructure. This system includes provincial and federal prisons; secure custody for inmates (while awaiting trial and bail or sentencing); and open custody (while on probation or parole in the community). Second, the inmates' offenses range from parking ticket violations, through drug-related crimes, including Break-and-Entry (B&E) and robbery, to bodily assault and murder. Third, some inmates were newcomers in contrast with experienced inmates. Newcomers sometimes knew less than I did about what to expect and how the institution itself functioned. They were labeled "fish," along with the volunteers, by other inmates. On the other hand, those who had served significant time in prison knew a great deal about the criminal justice system, including how to work it to their advantage. They were labeled "pros" and "cons" by staff and inmates alike.

The Education/Literacy Program: School of Hard Knocks

This place was my "school of hard knocks" with metal doors that clanged as visitors wanted in and inmates wanted out. Inmates lived by their wits under the gaze of constant surveillance and in accordance with disciplinary procedures. However, we were all inmates of the system, struggling with the same problems and issues to varying intensities. As Yates (1993), the prison-writer, puts it: "What's tragic about being human is that we must make laws and then strive to observe them. And fail. Hence the birth of the prison where one serves time. It could be said that we all serve time anyway" (12). As inmates serving time, we did not just occupy our space metaphorically. This was a real prison and a real school.

School boards provide educational sites for offenders in our country. In my research site, the Education/Literacy program was in great demand by several hundred inmates. This constituted an impressive percentage of the total population. The inmates in our program ranged from 18 to 73 years of age. Inmate-students (my term) typically had only 22 days to participate in our educational program, but this "average stay" varied greatly. This statistic was cited to me by my Education Coordinators and confirmed in a Health and Welfare report. The researcher (anonymous) states that:

> Approximately 50 percent of admissions to jail are for a 30 day sentence or less. The majority of offenders in the provincial system represent this large group of short-term inmates. Generally, 80 percent of sentenced admissions into the provincial system are for sentences of 120 days or less, giving a high representation for short-term sentences (1992, 4-5).

The motto of our Education Coordinators was "meet-greet-motivate." They generally experienced the inmates as very needy but without motivation. Their pet name for our inmate-students was "straw people."

Students would meet with us individually in one of 11 interview rooms (another cell-like structure) throughout the institution. The tutor/professional would go to the range location specified on the day's agenda. S/he was restricted by the classification of the inmate which determined his range of mobility. In other words, one could look for a room on another floor only if the inmate was classified as other than protective custody, federal or special case. These same rooms were shared with lawyers, chaplains, social workers, discharge planners, and more. Other obstacles existed in addition to insufficient resources and crowding. For example, our waiting list for the Education/Literacy program was very long. We therefore felt constant pressure to evaluate and re-evaluate our progress with particular inmates to determine whether or not they were making good use of tutors' hours. One of my students was warned that he would be withdrawn from our program if he continued coming to sessions without his homework done. We also struggled with the lock-down schedule of eating, clothing changes, and incidents of mischief. Because security was the top priority of the Ministry of Corrections, all else was considered "gravy" (Sally, the Education Coordinator, personal communication, April 18, 1991). Inmate-students had the option of continuing in their courses once they were transferred to other jails. They would send us letters, drawings and cartoons, and general "wish-wells" from wherever they re-located. The educators preferred those on probation and parole to seek assistance from community-based agencies. Fifty to 60 literacy programs exist in the Canadian city of my study.

Our Education department was supervised by two teachers from the public school system. They were both experienced, joyous and positive. Sally was the more senior partner. She is also the one with whom I clicked and with whom I developed a friendship. We showed interest in each other on a personal level even during my training sessions. Sally was an associate teacher for the Ministry of Education with an undergraduate university degree. She was happily married. Her adult children were pursuing university degrees. She had taught English at the secondary level and also assisted mentally challenged students. Sally had been declared an "on site marker" for the jail to monitor its Education/Literacy program to see if and how it contributed to the improvement of inmates' literacy abilities.

Sally implemented three literacy methods through the Ministry to aid her and others in teaching inmates: One, phonics (sounding out consonants and vowels); two, language experience (student as creator and author of his own texts); and three, Blade (formalized step-by step approach to upgrade literacy levels within three months; its lessons include audiotapes). She also implemented formal secondary level courses in a range of subject areas (math, science, English for native and non-native speakers, family studies, accounting, law, and more), as well as life skills methods (individually geared to address specific problems of personal hygiene, how to greet people, and more). Her partner, Anna, was also a skilled and experienced teacher in science and math. They teach as a flourishing partnership at the jail. Team work began for them in 1985 when Anna joined Sally who had been coordinating alone.

Sally and Anna were assisted by a team of tutors/teachers all of whom they trained and supervised. Their tutors came from three streams of life: Qualified and/or certified teachers; academics/graduate students; and ex-convicts successfully pursuing formal education. Sally was responsible for supervising the English and the arts curricula and its tutors, and Anna, for the science and math curricula and its tutors. The Education Coordinators processed volunteers who had already been screened by the institution itself. I spent time with them. They trusted their intuition about people and collaborated with one another to make decisions. They talked openly in front of me about what they valued in others. This included: commitment, formal qualifications and teaching experience and personality (pleasant, respectful and dedicated). They trained us according to our areas of specialization; selected inmate-students for our weekly sessions; designed easy-to-follow agendas; packaged suitable curricular materials; and notified us of key dates and information.

As tutors, we were oriented and trained individually and on-site for a minimum of five sessions/institutional visits. My training period consisted of only three visits. I did not meet or consult with tutors, except by chance in the jail and during in-house seminars and literacy conferences. I saw one tutor from my undergraduate university days. He had become a banker and taught math to inmates to add variety to his life. Although shy, he was effective. Another tutor was much older and her style was traditional and distanced. A third woman was young, pleasant and science-based.

We were given a Volunteer tutor hand guide written by the coordinators. It is about institutional policies, routines and office procedures designed to accommodate the Education/Literacy program. It is mandatory, the guide states, that "tutors adhere to institutional regulations and educational guidelines" (6). This included avoiding wearing the color of the inmate uniform so as to be easily distinguished by the authorities. Quick methods of tutoring are also outlined in this handbook. Everyone worked in relative isolation, guiding formal coursework for some inmates and doing upgrading with many non-English speakers.

In my work in three programs, I met inmates who were born in Canada, the West Indies/Caribbean and in West Europe. These three places of birth constituted a high percentage of the inmate population and were almost equally represented. South or Latin America was also represented. A study (Anonymous 1992) conducted in another, but similar, correctional facility confirmed my own impressions. Given that I was not inclined nor permitted to use survey interviews and questionnaires, it was difficult for me to assess accurately cultural and ethnic backgrounds. Despite the challenge of different cultures, in isolating and demanding, if not potentially dangerous, circumstances, caring relationships still developed. Isolation, not fear, was the major cause of teachers not showing up for work or even dropping out altogether.

I felt proud of students who made good use of their time and who even managed to graduate. In 1992 I was informed that three inmate-students received their secondary level diplomas with us. One had managed to do his entire high school studies inside in just 11 months. This is especially impressive given that, according to the Education Coordinators' familiarity with Stats Canada, 2.9 million Canadian adults cannot read or have difficulties reading. Moreover, 3 of 6.9 million Canadians cannot cope with unfamiliar and complex reading material. In 1990, 50% of inmates scored lower than grade 8 level in their language and mathematical abilities. In a similar institution, it was found that "sixty-eight percent of all inmates had a self-reported education level of Grade 9 to 11. . . Twelve percent graduated from high school at the Grade 12 or 13 level, while nine percent completed some post-secondary education, and one percent graduated from college" (Anonymous 1992, 16). There are more than twice as many functionally illiterate people among the prison population than there are among Canadians as a whole (Paul 1991).

Given all of these statistics, one might expect that we had to "pull teeth" to inspire motivation. Instead, as indicated, our Education department had a waiting list throughout all areas of the institution. The "pulling of teeth" would sometimes occur while working with a particular inmate who may have appeared lazy but whose attention was really on more immediate and pressing matters. These included: phone calls from and to lawyers; terminating lawyers; Legal Aid assistance; sentencing; hostile family relations; news from home; immigration complications; injury, pre-release counseling; drug addiction withdrawl; drowsiness and other side-effects from prescription drugs; insomnia and fear; transfer to penitentiaries ("pens"), and more. The image of "tough guy" is a cover story, in the film, *The other prison*, for inmates with literacy incompetencies who struggle with poor self-esteem. Some of the inmates I knew not only challenged the image of tough guy, but also re-invented themselves as teachers and learners. They worked in sessions with teachers; helped one another with lessons and assignments; struggled with homework in crowded and unsafe areas; fought for new pencils and writing paper; and, despite the odds, created and monitored educational goals for themselves.

The Aims of my Study: A Sandpiper in Unfamiliar Surroundings

On January 3, 1991, my first visit to the jail, I was in a nervous daze. I was preoccupied with the multi-layered story about where I was coming from, and where I was going to, in my professional and academic development. I was not especially focused on my safety even though others constantly warned me. The first time that I went into the jail I attended to being in training. I was essentially geared towards understanding the nature of a professional investment in a new setting. I also wondered about how I might interpret an unfamiliar world. But even then I viewed the jail in storytelling terms; as a context for "doing" education, and as a research site. This spirit persisted for the next 18 months.

I knew that I was going to be observed and evaluated by my first (in a series, as it turned out) supervisor. He would turn out to be only one of the larger forces shaping my destiny. Even though I felt like a fish in foreign waters, I was determined to do well and to put my ambition and qualities to good use. I wanted to prove to myself that I could succeed at such a difficult study. I knew that I was risking not being formally admitted as a researcher in corrections.

The training period itself had weighed heavily on my mind. Paul, my supervisor from the agency, had already told me that for the first few weeks of my training I would observe him interviewing inmates. Then he would observe and evaluate me, setting me free to function on my own. This was the plan that was both fulfilled and yet complicated because of my own goals. I worked with several supervisors, overlapping with Paul, in various capacities until I felt comfortable and useful.

I was also preoccupied with understanding the "big picture" of my study of corrections. I struggled privately with whether my research topic would be considered acceptable in my field of teacher education. I asked myself if I could develop a curricular perspective on the prison as classroom. As a student in the Joint Centre for Teacher Development at the Institute, I was part of a community that sees narratives of life experiences as contexts for making meaning of educational situations. I wanted to extend this community of curriculum makers to include a correctional facility. I therefore puzzled over how a study of prison education would contribute to teacher development and narrative inquiry.

As I tried to make sense of my reasons for selecting the jail as a fieldsite, I furthered earlier inquiries into self-development. One of my links, I felt intuitively, to marginal lives in prison was my own imaginative and life-experiences. I had been resourcing my dreams to construct understandings of educational inquiry. I was also using my dreams as a way of placing my own experiencing consciousness at the center of my narrative. I feature a dream below about this realm of the personal. It inspired me to tell my own story for my master's thesis in education. It also inspired me to work with inmates in a jail setting. The dream reflects aspects of my own family history. I tell it here as a narrative about the role of incarceration in my own educative process:

> Now I am being pushed. . . . For hours upon hours we bang on that door to no avail. No one comes . . . no one hears. Where are we anyway? What time is it?
>
> I don't know this part of the house. The short staircase is unfamiliar and so is the livingroom it leads to. We are checking everything out. The livingroom is pleasantly arranged, with one large sofa, TV and carpeted floors. A small but well equipped washroom is situated to the side of the entrance. The far livingroom wall has a small window and the bluish tinge of the light pouring in registers "dawn" in my mind. To my delight I spot a pad of paper and pen on one of the end-tables. I am wnting down the date and the words, "It's dawn" (Mullen, excerpts, 1990, 1).

I kept this dream in mind as I encountered inmates, believing that it would help me to relate to them. I wanted to resource my own experiential learning and images as a way of connecting with others. My vision was to enact, with the inmates, a shared way of constructing and reconstructing our stories. I needed not only a setting but also suitable conditions to communicate and establish links. My vision was vague without a storytelling milieu. Such a context would permit me to "interact with [my] own personal needs, desires, purposes and capacities to create the experience which is had" (Dewey 1938, 44).

As a further backdrop to the aims of my study, I had felt emotionally affected by a colleague's words at the time. I later reconstructed our exchange, in my journal, as a question about my self-identity. My colleague had asked me, "Why do you feel so compelled to live on the fringes of educational research? Don't you think that what you're doing might be considered blind improvisation since you are not very well informed about the prison system? To be convincing, you will need to emphasize rigor. Why not pursue doing research with classroom teachers like other doctoral students? Aren't you concerned about being hired for a university position once you graduate, or are you changing course to become a social worker?" I was scared. I looked back. I reflected on how, when I did my study of dreams at the master's level, I had initially been told that my creative impulses were getting the better of me. As the study progressed, I was encouraged and even praised. I knew that I had to do another study that reflected my alternative view of education and teacher development. I needed to reflect in it my value of bringing direct perception, which is often in the form of partial and fleeting realizations, to systematic awareness (Huxley 1977).

I was determined to rely again on my creative processes, personal knowledge, and research experience to inform the logic of my inquiry. I felt that even the educational and social significance of my study would evolve along with my exploration of the personal. The worlds of teacher education and corrections would be interconnected through my self-story and knowledge. Even so, I prematurely yearned for rigor in the form of experience not yet lived. In my turmoil, I risked creating a too narrow cognitive portrait of lives in prison.

The sandpiper in me felt challenged to preserve simultaneously her identity and dignity and to raise her head. I re-discovered myself in the image of the sandpiper in Elizabeth Bishop's poem, "The Sandpiper." Her sandpiper, a shorebird, busily focuses on the sand particles of a beach. This image has implicitly guided me as a writer, qualitative researcher, and narrativist over the years. I went into the prison to listen to people talk in their own voices about how they make sense of their lives. This approach is valued by those who focus on narrative and life history in people's lives (Coles 1981; Clandinin and Connelly 1991; Connelly and Clandinin 1986, 1988a, b; Bar-on 1991; Wiener and Rosenwald 1993; Rose 1990). I also went into the prison anticipating being shown how to live and how to rethink education by the inmates themselves. I felt the intensity of the sandpiper, and like it, I wanted to make sense of particles, or rather particulars, in my own landscape. I wanted to make connections among them and to story-lines and meta-themes. Other qualitative researchers (Glesne and Peshkin 1992; Van Maanen 1988) also emphasize the value of close observation of particulars within various cultural domains. Eisner (1993) describes this process of close observation as "get[ting] in touch with the schools and classrooms we care about, to see them, and to use what we see as sources for interpretation and appraisal" (11).

I raised my head to see that my fieldsite is a jail and that its inhabitants are inmates in the strictest sense. Besides prisons, mental hospitals and schools are the other primary examples of "total institutions" (Goffman 1961). The Panopticon itself is a metaphor for hierarchy, power and surveillance in other cultural domains. The Panopticon is also an administrative mechanism or "machine for dissociating the see/being seen dyad; in the peripheric ring, one is totally seen, without ever seeing; in the central tower, one sees everything without ever being seen. . . . It is an important mechanism, for it automatizes and disindividualizes power" (Foucault 1977, 201-202). Panoptic institutions confine the individual to his cell where "he is seen, but does not see; he is the object of information, never a subject in communication" (Foucault 1977, 200). Such institutions house, monitor, reward and discipline inmates. Anywhere that people struggle for selfhood and articulation, as in schools, academe and prisons, they are constrained or imprisoned. In Foucault, the structure re-produces power relations regardless of who occupies it.

Inmates entertain partial and fleeting realizations about how humans function. Lessing (1986) views human development as contradictory: we live inside multiple, overlapping prisons. As groups, nations, members of society, and academics too, we imprison ourselves in "blind loyalties, obedience to slogans, rhetoric, leaders, group emotions . . . and subjection to group pressures" (60). We can re-educate ourselves by reflecting on these patterns in our behavior and by applying what we have learned. We can also re-educate ourselves by constructing narratives of marginality. This process, tackled alone and collaboratively, can help us to envision ways of moving from imprisonment to transformation in our lives, in institutions, and in society itself. I am exploring the unexamined perspectives that shackle the prisoner. I am learning about the personal knowledge of the inmate condition; bringing such otherness to awareness through own my life-experiences; and offering transformative perspectives of marginal, or devalued and neglected, lives.

Being There

Encountering Participants: Meeting the Inmates

Paul and I spent òne hour with Bill, our first client of the evening. "Client" is the term that agencies use for their assigned inmates. Before I met Bill, I learned that I could only record certain information in the presence of the inmate. I could also record in between visits. This recorded information strictly concerned the inmate's circumstances as related to his request, and the volunteer's purpose and function. The notes were to be recorded on a formal institutional sheet (different for each program) and forwarded to the relevant supervisors through mail slots and designated lockers. No additional notes could be recorded for my own use. We were not permitted to leave the premises with anything other than our belongings. The Panopticon forbids unauthorized writing. The reason given for these very rigorous constraints is security of prisoners and staff alike.

During my first visit to the jail, I met two of Paul's clients, neither of whom I saw again. I was being prepared to meet and interact with the inmates. I was also going to learn to dialogue with each as appropriate to the inmate and his circumstances. I would outline the objectives for the meeting and the philosophy of each program. I was also being prepared for a pattern of life-experience and re-education (relapse and recovery) among addicts and offenders who were, simultaneously, citizens, fathers, employers/employees and children themselves. This theme of the multi-faceted inmate narrative would later emerge in inmates' groups, formal coursework and creative writing.

As I interpreted Paul's feedback to Bill, Bill was not prepared to begin his recovery as a substance-free addict. Neither was he prepared to change related life-patterns. Paul intimated that Bill sabotages his relationships with others because he wants to continue his drug use. The fact that he was ill-informed about the services available to him even inside the jail seemed to confirm Paul's impressions. From this interview, I sensed that I would need to find ways of sensitively probing untold stories. I was to learn later that such probing was ethically complex and ambiguous on a number of levels. In the Education/Literacy program it constituted a violation of inmates' rights and jeopardized teachers' rights. Teachers who became familiar with inmates' cases could be subpoenaed to appear in court to testify as witnesses. Inmates could also try to exploit such teachers for their own ends. This was the official story. The institution itself did not condone any practice that was in potential violation of security, but each professional proceeded according to the character of situations and his or her own intuition, experience and personal boundaries.

In order to offer a more in-depth sense of how probing occurs in such a setting, I include some of my field notes. These are from my first visit and relate to these issues of volunteer preparation and training; inmates' stories as revealed in context, and ethics of interviewing:

> The interviews were meant to take care of inmates' legitimate requests for services. The first inmate asked about his clothes. He expressed his desire to have them picked up by Paul's agency and delivered to his new address. The second inmate asked for a suit for court. I will need to understand how the connected social services (of welfare, Street Link, Futures and others) function. This is one point. The other is that I need to learn how to gauge the counseling process which is inevitably involved. I'm no trained counselor. I asked Paul about this and he gave me good advice: Do a more surface interview of their life history the first time you see them, and then go more in-depth with each subsequent visit. I could tell that he was role modeling his own technique for me.
>
> I was amazed that Bill, the first inmate, only 23 years old, outright denied himself the right to emotional comforts and a stable existence. He had gotten busted for cocaine trafficking. He committed a string of other crimes in the past (drug-related, robbery, break-and-entry (B&E), but no violence). Funny that he didn't seem to know of the drug program at the jail. Paul caught on: He made it clear that Bill may not really want to rid himself of his habit in order to take the necessary steps to get on track.
>
> Paul pointed out that Bill relapses with respect to heavy drug use, trafficking, robbery, etc. when things are not going well in his life. It's as though he sabotages himself every time things start to go well, Paul emphasized. His life-pattern is a cruel paradox, I thought. Paul later told me that this pattern prevents recovery for most of the inmates.

Bill turned to me part way through the interview to say: "Don't I know you from somewhere?" I was surprised, but not shaken or threatened. I thought of my sister who had once lived on the streets. We resemble one another. I said, "No."

Paul kept at Bill: He was trying to impress upon him that his problems in life are drug-related, which is why he repeatedly strikes out against others. Bill responded that he only steals from close friends. He does this whenever someone gets too close to him. Apparently his parents used drugs in the home. I was exposed to drug use in my home too. I felt sympathy for him, but I also can't understand why he isn't owning up to his own responsibility. He blamed his brother for attacking him emotionally and deflating his self-esteem. Yet, his Dad has pulled through and supported him. His parents don't know that he's in jail again. He doesn't want to upset his mother who is on medication.

Paul said that his vote was for honesty. Bill could begin his plan for change by being emotionally honest with his parents. (Why wasn't Bill owning up to his responsibility for trafficking cocaine? He claims that he really likes kids, but can't he see that his "profession" contradicts this claim. He could damage kids in the same way that he was damaged by his drug-using parents). Paul ended by saying that it is important for him to acknowledge his mistakes and not to repeat them. Otherwise, he will keep getting into trouble and re-enacting dangerous life-patterns. Bill nodded in agreement.

Later, Paul told me that for the new clients I would need to record basic information, including their criminal charges and places of incarceration in detention centers and penitentiaries. For ongoing clients, this information could be reviewed in order to be updated. Paul said that I would be interviewing clients but with a specialty in literacy teaching, if all goes well. I'm much more interested in the teaching than the interviewing per se although the life history part of it is fascinating. The inmates appear to be reasonable enough . . . (*Prison Journal*, January 3, 1991).

Paul was teaching me techniques for the purpose of providing a service to our clients and also for making meaningful contact with them. The implicit agenda, which pointed to reform, became obvious as I gained experience in other programs. I could see that it was best to be direct and honest with the inmates. I could accomplish this type of interaction, for instance, by detecting and revealing "cover stories" (Crites 1979) that are in tension with real stories. I could critique discrepancies in inmates' self-representation, story-lines and details. I could also spend time reiterating key points; digging to generate a life-history connected to educational patterns; and, eliciting as many responses as possible from the inmate himself. My purpose was to employ myself and my imaginative resources in my work. I was not there just to fill requests like a restaurant employee. I needed to listen and to try to understand what I could do to help and to provide comfort; to use my life-experiences to relate at appropriate times; to become educated about the jail itself and its internal programs; and to accurately report inmates' requests and the outcome of visits. The agency needed this information in order to follow-up.

During the second interview, that same evening, I learned something critical about my own values. I could not simply eliminate them from my interactions with inmates. But I could not allow them to be violated and, in the process, my personal boundaries:

> The second inmate, Tom, was more difficult to swallow. He was a messy-looking 29 year old with wandering eyes (no muscle control). He needed a suit for court. We spent 45 minutes with him. He was being detained for making threats against his wife and friend. Even though he is a native English speaker, he spoke very unclearly. He said that he doesn't see drugs as a problem and that he's never been busted for "using". What upset me was his generalization that he doesn't know what I'm like but that other women are dangerous to men. He said that it's because of his wife that he's behind bars.
>
> He told us a story about how his wife lied in court (perjury) claiming that he threatened violence against her. He also told a story about another inmate in the jail. Apparently this other inmate's arms had been slashed by his wife. Then she hit him in the face. All he had done was to hold her arms so that she couldn't hit him anymore. Then she called the police on him and is now charging him with spousal abuse. He said that this is really unfair and that women of today are getting away with "blue murder." The courts favor their testimonies and the men are all unjustly paying for women's perjury. Paul said, "All I can say is that there are three sides to a story: the inmate's, the wife's, and the truth." Tom insisted that he was telling the truth.
>
> My body reacted to Tom's insistence that he was telling the truth; that all men are behind bars because of women; and that he was therefore absolved from all responsibility. I got out of my chair and moved towards Tom. I glared at him. Tom moved back.
>
> Later Paul told me that he saw me react physically. He said that I had appeared upset. He told me to keep my reactions in check. I said

"okay" and agreed that I would do my best to act appropriately from now on. I was very shaken up. I couldn't help but add my private truth: that the situation was complex and riddled with possibility. It might be a good thing for the inmates to see an honest human response, I stumbled. Paul added that I might have reacted as I did, partly because he was less interactive in the second interview. He said that he had felt "red" by then (*Prison Journal*, July 3, 1991).

Official Educational Researcher: Living as Inmate

The institution had restricted me, for security reasons, to my own mind's capacity for recall, even as an official researcher. My research practice therefore altered in the penal institution. I had been taught in the field of teacher education to record detailed field notes while in interaction with phenomena that included students, teachers and other stakeholders. Things were different here. No on-site field note recording; no taped conversations; no spontaneous sharing or casual interaction; no corresponding with inmates unless approved; no self-disclosure that might violate anonymity; no knowledge of inmates' criminal offenses and related pasts; no photographs; no distribution of questionnaires and surveys; no curricular materials in addition to the institution's; no self-orchestrated curricular activities unless permitted and supervised; no display of wealth or feminine sensuality; no provision of information inside one program about another; and no questioning of regulations or confronting of authorities, or inmates for that matter. Just control.

As a volunteer and then co-facilitator of the Drug Awareness program, I could only jot general impressions, in point form, on relevant hand-outs. Even this proved tricky. Although I was exposed to inmates' names and case history details on-site, I was not permitted to record such details. I left my concentrated writing efforts for home and compiled numerous, detailed prison journals. Yet, I must still have been recording on-site too often. I felt awkward when the facilitator of the drug group told me not to record profusely in the company of inmates. Although no explanation was forthcoming, I guessed that my practice would understandably make others feel guarded. I became self-conscious in a different way: I learned to jot very casually and only periodically when my impressions were solely for my own information. I also learned when and what to record for the institution itself, and this requirement differed from one program to the next. My personal on-site jottings in the drug group also became less frequent as I became more familiar with the patterns in inmates' stories and the events around me. As I had no choice but to commit my recall of vivid sense impressions to later that day or evening, I learned to retain even minor details.

I felt freed up to become thoroughly engaged once I had proven to myself that I could remember a great deal. I had learned the value of self-dependency in relation to project field notes and memory as a Research Officer. During academic meetings, a professor had encouraged us to talk "away" from our notes. This practice required us to rely mostly on our reconstructive memory, not our documentation, of classroom events. In addition, my memory work with daily dream recordings and associative journal writing had done much to prepare me for the task of remembering what I saw and felt in the jail.

Sally, the Education Coordinator, was sensitive to my wish to have a copy of my weekly student-inmate list. This sheet was organized in the following way: inmates to be seen and general interests (coordinator's entries); inmates seen and topics covered (teacher's entries); and additional attachments (teacher's notes). Sally always forwarded me a photocopy the following week which I used to confirm certain details in my notes. I also created a file that allowed me to see at a glance who my regular students were; what curricular content had been mapped out and then accomplished; and what the overall pattern was of my visits. I would slip this sheet from Sally (in my curriculum envelope) into my pocket each week. I did this when the guards weren't looking to avoid unnecessarily alerting them. This gesture of mine would sometimes remind me of a night-time dream wherein I envisioned myself as a prisoner in a jail (Appendix A, July 21, 1991). Although I was a teacher in reality, I still had to obey, without questions and conflict, institutional policies, procedures and regulations. The twist in my dream is that I felt the humanity of the prison, even as an inmate.

Playing Multiple Roles: Entering the Mousetrap Alone

One year later I was waiting in the "mousetrap" alone, that isolated place baptized with this name by keepers and inmates alike. I had already experienced being a client contact volunteer, and was now functioning as a co-facilitator of the drug program; teacher in the Education/Literacy program; and coordinator of the Creative Writing program. I had also successfully undergone four separate training periods in total with experienced staff from both inside and outside the institution.

While stuck there, I drifted and played a mental game. How were my inmate-students describing the "inside" of the prison and themselves in their poetry, journals and lyrics? I listed images that I had been collecting from my student-inmates' writings: "misted catacomb; sleeping tomb; age old time; mid-gallop, frozen carousel/frozen pony; diminishing reality; Mr. Jones, to the moon; sniveling whore; world of pain; insane war; scattered ruins; notes from a cell." I anticipated using these images in a coherent narrative about my experience of the jail. My focus was also on how I understood the inmates' meaning-making processes for myself. In it, I wanted to illustrate how the inmates made sense of their own selves and lives, and culture of the jail and culture more broadly. As Van Maanen (1988) notes, "no longer is the ubiquitous, disembodied voice of the culture to be heard. . . . it is no longer adequate for a fieldworker to tell us what the native does day in and day out. We must now know what the native makes of all of this as well" (my emphasis, 74, 50). My challenge was to cope without recourse to typical research practices and procedures to make sense of the "native's" perspective.

I relied on a variety of other literary and educational methods to complement my narrative inquiry approach to research. I was developing my impressions in three journals (*Prison, Dream,* and *Daily Reflections*), and making use of context-related childhood memories and various teaching and learning episodes. Although I was substantially steeped in personal and unconventional modes of knowing and researching, my narrative of the study was continually resourced by others' perceptions to deepen my own impressions. As I communicated with others, they verified, extended, and informed my understandings.

As biographer, I generated others' perceptions of the inside, but what about my own? I had been co-constructing a new set of meanings in my work with the inmates based on my images of "fleeting piracy; hiding place; addicted doctor; drug lord; seemingly intact front door; honeycomb/amphitheater with a roof; high school gym class; monkeying; challenging environment; meaningful fragments; rusty pens; masculine prison" and "disconnected time." I was resourcing my journals, academic papers and poetry to stimulate this list. I intuitively felt that my own set of images was linked to the inmates' images, but how? I was simultaneously creating my metaphor of imprisoned selves while exploring it. In this chapter, I present this principal metaphor that links teachers and learners to each other and to specific settings. I describe the moments, events and developments in our stories that thematically linked us.

My sub-headings and images, in this chapter, provide snapshots of my joint understanding and collective narrative. Here is a partial list: writing addictively and in captivity; experiencing solitary confinement in cells and in the mousetrap; struggling as the newcomer or "fish"; living untold stories vis-à-vis child molestation, abandonment and abuse; creating cover stories and playing multiple roles; developing professionally and creating new stories; struggling for clearance in corrections; encountering Eros in corrections; (un)negotiating closures and exits; enterprising with others, and waiting for developments. In my fieldsite I discovered what I had in common with other inquiring selves. While writing my text, I had the opportunity to pursue these links and to construct a joint narrative.

I was still waiting. I had already been cleared at the front desk. But what had I been cleared as: Teacher? Co-facilitator? Researcher? Creative Writing coordinator? Institutional volunteer? I was playing multiple roles inside which confounded my question of identity. The staff looked confused, often reacting pleasantly, but with surprise, to having seen me recently in another part of the jail with a different group. I flourished as my self-identity became multi-faceted. I thought of Janette Turner Hospital, another academic seeking identity as a fieldworker. She wrote in *Dislocations* (1986) that "we tragic bloody humanists have problems with our esoteric educations" and so look for real work in real places. She, too, had been a teacher in a prison for men. I adjusted my identification badge, with picture only of yet another humanitarian "hung up" on heroics, to expose it fully within view of the monitor. My schedule, or list of inmates' names with accompanying objectives, was braced against my weekly package of curriculum materials. I glanced at the schedule from the Education Coordinator, quickly devising a strategy for execution. I was alert to the movements, in the bright, white corridor ahead. Let me in! I was ready to perform.

Why were the guards taking so long? I was ready to participate in the theater of my own imagination. I was creating a theater to learn about the inmates' lives. Months earlier I had dreamt of the jail as an amphitheater in which the inmates and myself performed as characters:

> As I turned around in the middle of it, I closely observed its tightly knitted cells positioned one on top of the other. The cells looked like bunk beds with concrete slabs separating one from the other. Am I inside a honeycomb, I wondered, or an amphitheater with a roof?
>
> Once in my cell I realized that lying on the bed gave the place more scope. Standing served only to accentuate its small, comb-like size.
>
> Contact soon began. Male prisoners yelled to me and sent coded messages my way. I could see the prisoners across on the other side. They began waving and certainly making a point of seeing me. So much activity! Are they going to show me how to live? This wasn't going to be so bad after all! (*Dream Journal*, July 6, 1991).

As I speculated on what I was doing, I became tucked inside my theoretical mind. As in my dream, I was communicating with inmates in code, or in their prison jargon, to approach writing, sharing and learning in this new storytelling context. Talking in code is an example of the "genuine re-education" that Foucault (1977) believes needs to occur within the penal system. His vision for transformation is an "artificial and coercive theater" to explore inmates' lives "from top to bottom" (251). This vision promotes a thorough biographical examination of inmates and their lives. Biography is a concept that exists in the history of penality, Foucault (1977) writes, but it functions by virtue of reducing the offender to his criminal actions, thereby confusing causes and effects. Responsible educators must seek understanding of inmates in the stories of their lives in the form of a "sum total existence" (251). In my dream I created a top bottom image of "tightly knitted cells positioned one on top of the other." I also imagined lively contact with inmates across a distance and without the imposition of a hierarchy of gatekeepers. Foucault himself calls for psychiatric discourse to enable us to communicate effectively with inmates. In reality, I was fulfilling my vision, but in very restricted ways. I dreamt Foucault's vision of the theater of open discourse. I have experienced, in my fieldsite, a continuum that ranges from expansiveness to restrictiveness.

Foucault's vision embraces the re-education of inmates. I imagine that my personal involvement in this process of re-education offers a critical dimension. I reached out to people in the collective act of becoming and growing. My openness included being shown how to live by the inmates themselves. I empowered the inmates to perform as partners in curriculum making, teachers and learners, and mentors. In this way, they showed me how to re-think education and lives in prison. I wanted to be re-educated in a new and fresh way and to share the story of my inquiry with the wider educational community. If genuine re-education is to occur, then the researcher must be open to self-development and disclosure if she is exposing another culture or others. Yet, researchers' own stories are largely ignored in the teacher education literature in favor of teachers' and other participants' biographies. The hidden irony of this is that the other" is the "I". We are, in the very least, engaged in the process of representing others' stories (Denzin 1989).

This experiential chapter takes my readers inside the jail to bring them closer to my fieldwork. I am "walking" my reader through the corridors of what I saw, experienced and felt. Readers make keen co-storytellers. They wanted to be engaged about the story behind the study and the one(s) that informs it. I have been asked by colleagues such questions such as: "Was I ever afraid?," "What did I do in the jail?, and "How did the inmates respond to me as a young female visitor?" People seem to be operating with an implicit narrative framework in mind. I find such textual guideposts not only stimulating but also helpful to the act of constructing my inquiry.

I do not offer certainty, but rather ways of thinking about narratives of marginality to make sense of people's lives. I also interpret the multiple meanings that such an inquiry has generated for me. In my narrative inquiry, prisoner means an incarcerated individual and one who experiences confinement. A prisoner is an icon of oppression, but one who is seized, confined and held captive in the restrictive and/or expansive spaces of a surveillant community. Voice and story are also ambiguous in my writing. I understand inmate to mean that we are all struggling to find our voices and to express our selfhood in the context of institutional pressures and traditional academic paradigms. I use my own frame of reference to make sense of others' subjectivities; others' subjectivities, in turn, help me to construct new perspectives on my teacher development story.

Van Maanen (1988) inspires me to write an impressionistic account that tells the story of my coming to terms with a new culture. I understand him to mean that worlds that are "deeply uncertain" can be richly conveyed through narrative inquiry. The ethnographer can experience a "silent disavowal of grand theorizing . . . [in favor of a] radical grasping for the particular, eventful, contextual, and unusual [which] contain[s] an important message" (119). I was grasping to make sense of transactional and transformative stories of experience in context to enhance discoveries about fieldwork, teacher education, and research.

Still in the mousetrap, from behind me, inside, back where I was not looking, I heard inmates trapped between dark sound-proof glass. I felt awkward as they banged and shouted muffled words. Hues of black and gray moved against a canvas of blue and white. Where were these inmates going? There were a number of possibilities or places that I had not directly witnessed myself: Court cells to await trial; solitary confinement for misconduct; visiting quarters to see relatives and loved ones; release, into the community, on bail; transfer to another detention center or even a federal penitentiary to serve time. Two guards paced in front of me, behind glass. They chatted, laughed, and then moved to "key" the elevator for someone. Looked like a lawyer. Lawyers didn't look as natural as the teachers. No time for pleasantries or laughter. Did they permit room for growth in ways unseen by me?

My back stiffened as the inmates continued to bang on the glass to get my attention. Trapped inside this mentally airless pocket, I wanted to vanish. What was the "cheese" that brought me here and to this study? In other words, what were the reasons, justifications, and rationale for my use of a prison as my fieldsite for education? I could only think poetry. The poem, to follow, is about the experiences that take place in my dreams, imagination and life. I make no attempt here to distinguish or categorize my images of experience. All of my experiences, regardless of their individual sources, feel "real" to me.

The poem below is written in the third-person. It provides a third person perspective on my own self and other imprisoned selves. I use shifting time-frames to uncover multiple selves: the self and other; child and adult; researcher and recorder. The children I present are constructions drawn from my personal history, dream world and public (media) stories. One such ambiguous image is the little girl's abduction from the gymnasium. At other times I reflect as an adult on imprisoned selves. I create situations wherein children, who are in grave trouble, are rescued. One such example is the anticipated rescue of the boy in the deserted house. As the adult, I am a researcher of dreams. I have incorporated, into this poem, my dream about the woman who was incarcerated in a beige prison with men. And, at other times, I am the recorder of my family history. I provide images of my present, past and future throughout the poem which culminate in the two concluding stanzas. I view "Imprisoned selves" as a multi-faceted narrative about personal and cultural selves:

> She sang boldly
> that little girl who skipped in and out
> of the dusty, heavy folds
> of velvet drapes
> that hung in the gymnasium
> breathing "No enter"
> against her pretty blue dress.
> Her long white spring coat
> took her there
> to a deserted house
> whereupon she placed her hand
> on the door
> feeling the energy of the boy within
> who sensed her return.
> Consuming chocolate,
> she swelled,
> to become a mare
> strapping a bomb
> underneath her own belly.
> Lilies exploded
> from her grandmother's garden
> as she trampled
> near the ladder
> beside the window
> where inside
> the puzzle of green and blue
> still smelled of dirty socks.
> Who was she exactly,
> that smiling five year old
> equipped with a pixie cut,
> painted Barbie dolls on her briefcase,
> and skipping rope in hand?

She courted herself
with pride, shows the photo,
on the first day of school.
It was her very first day
in jail with men
cradling a daughter not her own,
her younger sister,
left behind in the Charleton house
now cradling baby eyes of blue.
They banged hours upon hours
to no avail on that door
where inside there
they had been pushed
in the attic of some old woman's house.
Three siblings
no longer in their parents' custody
yet still struggling to be free.
The eldest, the writer to be,
recorded, "It's dawn,"
on a notepad
in the blue of the light
of a small window.
In *The Ballad of Reading Gaol*
the very prison walls reeled
for Oscar Wilde who gazed
"Upon that little tent of blue/
Which prisoners call the sky"
inscribing: "each man kills the thing he loves."
She sat cross-legged
against a beige prison wall
with men in custody,
who had prayed to the White Goddess,
to bring no pain with the cocaine.
Morphine Mama
missed her daughter's head each morning
with the alarm clock.
By noon, the dishes flew like saucers
off the balcony,
except for the ones
underneath her own bed.
The neighbor,
a young, close friend,
was shot by a lover.

They pieced together
her pretty porcelain face,
leaving the lid open.
Her baby-sitter
had witnessed the
the carousel of wild ponies
brake, then break.
Her family history merges
with inmates' stories
of a time
"halted in mid gallop,
charging forth without proceeding"
without the thing they love,
yet forever dreaming of
someone connecting them,
creating them anew.

(Mullen, September 17, 1993. The final embedded quote is from "Mr. Jones (to the moon)," see Appendix B).

In the mousetrap, I stared wide-eyed. Was it ignorance or courage that was propelling me to work inside a jail; to live out my personal history and research inquiry on foreign soil; and to function as a perpetual learner grasping for metaphorical connections between myself and others, education and corrections?

Unnegotiated Closures: The Disappeared

I felt relief as the heavy steel door clicked. The weight of it pulled against my sore, lower back. One inmate to my left, detained in an isolated cell for reasons unknown to me, grinned and said, "Hi baby. In for a stroll?" He casually hung his black forearms through the bars as if over a park bench. I pretended not to notice. As I moved towards the register, one guard signaled to me to sign it. I recorded the date, my name, and the purpose for my visit. "Education," I scribbled.

"Purpose for your visit?," one guard asked.

"Education," I responded. "I'm a teacher." I knew, from the orientation and my dozens of visits since, that this was a key question. Guards have the right to ask professionals to declare the purpose of their visit many times during a single visit. One needed to be clear and objective about the institution's policy regarding security.

"This place is a dump heaped high with vermin. Who'd ever want to volunteer here? At least I get paid for it." I could detect no accent.

"Yeah," echoed the other guard. He was juggling coffee in one hand and handcuffs in the other. "What's a pretty girl like you doing in a stinking place like this, and with such a nice smile?"

"I enjoy my work, " I said pleasantly. "Actually, I don't find it depressing in here at all, but then I don't have 12 hour shifts like you guys. My own work might also be lighter, less oppressive somehow."

He noticed me looking at the handcuffs in his hands. "Oh, these babies," he chuckled. "I've got to be ready for anything and everything in this hell-hole. Just watch." A tough guy with a grin.

I scanned for available rooms. As I handed my inmate-list to one of the guards, I searched for human warmth. No warmth meant a longer wait. An inmate was sitting in one of the interview rooms with his lawyer. Both were ill-shaven and hunched over a document in the same uniform color with individual files in hand. Their similarity was exaggerated in this context. Magnified sameness.

As directed, I took shelter in an interview room to await my first "client." Literacy, this is called, even in the chambers of protective custody where guards openly mock inmates, and probably even feel obliged to. What was the goal of the institution regarding my interactions with its visibly marginalized population? That these inmates, incarcerated for crimes mostly against women and children, will become "literate" in moral attitudes and behaviors from me? My progress sheets will be read later by the Education Coordinator and a report will be compiled on programmatic developments and accomplishments within the jail. The Chief Program Coordinator would see me about documenting my Creative Writing program as an example of a prison curriculum. Maybe a guard will even light-heartedly ask my student if he learned anything from our session today. They sometimes did.

I anticipated meeting my students and a few new inmates too. I had to be ready for anything. We would work near the guards whose job it was to be vigilant, in pairs, at their designated stations on every floor. Back and forth. Back and forth. But not always. At times when they were not visible to me, I, too, was a gatekeeper. I also kept watch at other times and in other respects in my fieldsite. I admitted to my own world those visitors and cell-mates who guided me and whom I guided. I had an impact on the feelings of those who were being detained and put on trial for offenses. I felt sensitive to inmates' perceptions of our sessions and to their treatment of me. I also felt sensitive to my perception and treatment of them. Inmates and staff alike often commented on my respect for the inmates. In one of my early college-level teaching days, a student had yelled at me, several times, to shut up during my own lecture:

> I stared at him with my feet firmly planted on the ground, hands clenched, and body trembling under layers of black clothes. I repeated myself one more time over the students' chit-chat. Dan called out, "Do you think we're deaf? Why do you keep repeating yourself? We've all heard you." Red. My head was spinning with embarrassment, now anger. When he approached me to apologize after class, I responded that I will, for now on, speak my mind, within limits, of course. No more tactics to get people's attention. I will just ask for what is rightfully mine. If it is my time to be speaking, then this will need to be generally respected (Mullen excerpt, 1990, 110).

Like the inmates and professionals inside here, I desired to be treated with respect and dignity and to be seen as worthy of investment.

I looked over the familiar, but changing, curriculum materials in my package: *Webster's Dictionary*; *Mastering essential English skills*, *English help handbook: Helpful hints for English language proficiency*; a pad of paper, and a pen and pencil. Five minutes went by. I read over my inmate list, allocating equal times for each student and preparing notes for each visit. I read the notes beside Rick's name for the second time. He was new to me. Ten more minutes went by. Had he been transferred to court cells to await trail? Had he been sent to the "hole" for misconduct? Maybe he was just on the phone with his lawyer or in the exercise yard. The echoes on the ranges sounded like the distortion of human voices in an indoor swimming pool. Only the odd word was distinguishable. Something to do with the "slop" they were eating, probably at their bolted down picnic tables while playing cards. Many spent more time playing cards than reading, writing and doing their homework. The inmates themselves would tell me so.

As I caught the eye of one of the guards, he said that he would check on my student. A poem that I was reading stirred a distant memory. It was written by one of my students. The lines that struck me read: "A shadow dancing on the wall, come to bid/ farewell, make claims on my soul,/ someone I've never met but seem to know so well/

. . . I can't believe what' s happening here,/ Mr. Jones has brought me to my knees " (in Appendix B: Sear Robinson, "Mr. Jones (to the moon)"). I had begun thinking about abuse as a shadow game played by puppets. The "Mr. Jones" in my mother's life had also made claims on her soul. He made claims not only while she was living with him, but also long after she left him. He followed her around town in his yellow vehicle, and then left the Maritimes to stalk her. Years later, we, the adult children, have a healthy communication with my father. This entry focuses on the shadow game itself:

> They looked like overgrown hand-puppets playing a shadow game on our livingroom wall on North Street in Halifax, Nova Scotia. From behind the partially open door of my bedroom, I watched as a wide-eyed, 10-year old. Dad grabbed once, then twice, for Mom's large accounting books. A burst of orange shot-through the air—orange covers held together, very gingerly I knew, with black masking tape. Books toppled to the ground. Mom covered her face with her hand, the one that is missing its baby finger from cancer in adolescence. Blocked, she looked helpless in the manila prison of four edges marked by the wall, ceiling, floor and banister. I picked up the scraps of paper the next day and brought them to her. With heaving breaths I asked her if she would be finishing her business courses. I did not want her to give up, no matter what she'd be risking. She often took my advice seriously. She did continue, but years later in the expansive space of her own life that deteriorated when she again became a "bird in a gilded cage" (*Daily Reflections Journal*, July 2, 1991).

I stood at the entrance-way. I had made a "puppet" connection between Mr. Jones and my father, and step-father. I had watched my mother brought to her knees. I refused to feel helpless as my mother had been forced to in her manila prison. My interview room in the jail was part of a row of five rooms. This, too, was a manila prison but I etched it expansively. Here I could watch traffic from the elevator, stair-well, ranges and adjacent communications area (with wall telephone and desk) for guards only. They could consult their daily lists of inmates and their exact in-house locations. These were printed periodically after each institutional check called a "count." The rest of us had our specific inmate lists and assigned duties that the guards also checked.

It was in this general area of traffic that I could also get a sense of the place on this particular day. One male guard must have finished his duty or switched duty with another. A petite, blond-haired attractive guard emerged from the place they call the "ranges." This is where the inmates live on every floor locked up in overcrowded cages. Because I was not paid staff, I was prohibited from entering the inmates' dormitory. But, whenever the metal door was ajar, I could see the inmates stirring behind bars. With a mixture of curiosity and embarrassment, I always watched.

The female guard, or "hack" in prison slang, was followed by two black inmates. They were cushioned, at the other end, by a bulky white male guard. The woman's large keys dangled against her confident hips. She told the inmates to halt. After "frisking" one in the middle of the corridor, she also checked the other. Her hands moved knowingly to key areas that can conceal contraband. No drugs, weapons or property of any sort.

"Go do your garbage chore," she ordered the first inmate. "Here's Sedley, your guy," she hastened to me. "Teacher, right?" Off she went. Rick and I were left alone. This was the procedure. A guard never stayed in the room with me during the year-and-a-half that I spent inside. We sat adjacent to one another at a table next to the partially open door that contained a small window:

> "Hi, Rick," I smiled, reaching out and shaking his hand. I was slow to ask him what was on my mind. He had been shaking so noticeably in his chair that my reticence was probably just as glaring. Does he have Parkinson's disease?, I wondered about this thin, Jamaican man. He shook as a weathered leaf, fragile and sick. I interrupted my own flow of words about the Education program and the possibility of our working together. I asked him if he needed medication. "If so, I'll call the nurse for you."
>
> "No, not right now. I was shot at a party many years ago as I got up to leave, and the bullet hit my spine."
>
> "And you've been like this ever since?"
>
> "Yeah, and it ain't gettin' any better. It's too damp in here."
>
> I lightly touched his arm in an effort to be upbeat. I refocused the conversation, nervous about more time lapsing. I asked whether he really wanted to do creative writing as one of my specially assigned students. I knew that Sally, my Education Coordinator, must have screened his interests, but her note was atypically vague.

"Yeah, I do. And I'll get started tomorrow. But on what?"

"How about beginning with a journal? That will give us a place to start. You can keep your writing private. We can focus on what kind of writing you'd like to do once you sort through what's on your mind."

"Yeah, great. I was thinking of a diary too."

"That's terrific, Rick." And you know something, I'm going to keep a diary for you, too, starting tomorrow. This process will help me to understand the difficulties you might experience in writing to somebody new. I don't expect you to open up to me if I am not prepared to do the same for you. We might also eventually talk back-and-forth in our diary entries to one another. We could present our two-way conversation as a narrative in a newsletter that features creative writing in the jail. This is something that I'm already actively working towards with other students doing creative writing. We've been cleared to pull our writing together for all of the guys to see. What do you think?"

"Ain't no teacher ever cared enough to write back to me. What's your name again?"

"Carol," I smiled. Taking hurried leave, I added that I wouldn't be able to see him for two weeks. "I'm going to one of the federal pens next week to participate in the inmate-run Addictions group. This is the first of its kind in Canada and I'm excited about the prospect of learning about how inmates function as their own facilitators. Do you have any interest in checking out the program here?," I asked. "If so, just put in a request. Not all of the guys who come out are drug dependent, and yet we relate well to one another' s issues."

Rick shook my hand and looked back at me, with a half-smile, as he was led to his cage (*Prison Journal*, April 6, 1992).

I never saw Rick again. Disappeared. I wasn't permitted to inquire into the whereabouts of Rick and the others, but I often did. The Education Coordinator responded to the casual-sounding query on my teaching sheet that she didn't know herself. Rick and I shared a bright sunny feeling that I often felt with my students. In such moments, something positive split from beige walls, from this manila prison. It was a space that I felt as a connection, a clean, pure spark. They, too, felt a connection. My students would ask me to be their regular teacher. They would feel disappointed whenever they were scheduled to work with another teacher. Some would even become angry, if not impossible, to handle. They made demands of the Education Coordinator whenever they spotted her on their ranges. She would try to attend to their needs while updating her waiting lists; organizing books and other curricular resources; and counting pencils (which were carefully assigned; otherwise, they were used as weapons).

The other teachers and supervisors whom I met also felt connected to their inmate-students, if only to varying degrees. We even felt momentary connections that often taught me how much inmates, and all imprisoned selves value dignity, respect and self-worth. A colleague from the Institute responded to colloquium on the Creative Writing program and stories about developing relationships with inmate-students and professionals in Corrections. She wrote to me about her own experiences as a teacher in a federal penitentiary:

> I remember, on one of those passages that spring, seeing a new prisoner, a big handsome man in his twenties, sitting and waiting in the hallway. His leg was shackled by a heavy chain to a huge iron ball. As I passed our eyes met. I know there was pity in mine, mixed with shame. In his was surprise at first, then shame, then what I think was acceptance of my look, of the small momentary connection between us (Anonymous, excerpt, April 1, 1992).

Eros and Corrections: Men and Women in Confined Spaces

Sally, the Education Coordinator, warned me that Chris would fall aggressively in love with me. While waiting for Chris, we talked about our previous session with Mike. We had both found him slow and almost lifeless, but persevering.

As soon as Chris and I met, he yelled out that he was in love. He declared to Sally that he couldn't thank her enough for sending him the prettiest teacher yet. He cupped his chin in his hands and grinned widely at me. He retained this stance for the next few months that I interacted with him. We worked on vocabulary building; pronunciation of words; and technical uses of a dictionary. Because he was making me feel awkward, I looked at him and said, "This is not the dating game, Chris, so can we get down to serious business, or shall I see the next person on my list?" I was surprised by my own firmness and risk-taking during a training session. Sally later chuckled. It was a good thing, she said, that I had clarified my own position and the intent of the meeting:

He kept accusing me of trying to sweet-talk him in front of Sally. Sally would just laugh at him. He was a such a contrast to Mike.

Before seeing Chris, I taught a lesson to Mike who had been so quiet and respectful. [This section is included to show how different inmates can be from one another in terms of personality alone. I also want to provide a portrait of the range of challenges I experienced in a day's work in my fieldsite.] It was up to me to pick up from his last teacher with very little input from Sally who sat, watched and took notes. She was throwing me to the lions! Mike was a black Bahamian in the middle of a lesson in his basic level English course. He read his answer to a question on Japanese-Canadians and when I asked him if he had any problems with it, he said "No."

We finished the second answer together. The point of the lesson seemed to be that everyone in Canada is Canadian in spite of individuals' differences in ethnic origins. I sensed that Mike, who had said very little, was hesitating. When I asked why he said, "You are always your origins no matter what." Although the lesson did not require him to write his personal reflections, I encouraged him to. We did this together. He wrote painfully slowly, erasing his mistakes with the end of his pencil tip. Although conscious of his spelling errors, he created many misspellings at the same time. He was so quiet and withdrawn that it was difficult for me to connect even though he was pleasant enough. Mike became one of my regular, long term students.

Chris was 21 years old and could not write. Sally didn't seem to mind his digressions on a variety of topics. I looked at the teaching schedule that provided spaces for tasks accomplished with each student. What would we put in Chris's space? He talked on and on about cars while interspersing questions about my own teacher training, qualifications, experience and status. He also asked about my ring and whether I was married. He asked several times. During all of these dynamics, I was trying to persuade him to extend a paragraph he had started with Julie, his other teacher.

My heart went out to him when he told us a story. It was about his own struggles to become literate in the company of his "brilliant" cell-mate who is doing his grade 13 "on the inside". Chris said that Ron helps him by being able to read aloud, without stumbling, his letters despite an abundance of errors. Chris concluded, somewhat proudly and defiantly, that this must mean that he himself is not stupid *(Prison Journal*, May 23, 1991).

Later that evening, Sally pulled me over to the locker room area. She is almost 20 years older than me. The guards seemed amused by our mutually high energy and enthusiasm. When asked by them if we were related as family, Sally grinned: "I wish!" I was anticipating her feedback, and she was ready. Her comment was that I had handled the two students really well, helping them to feel comfortable. She also said that I had challenged them by asking questions and thereby building on what they already knew. She was pleased that I had indicated my boundaries with, and expectations of, both Mike and Chris. I had done this differently in each case.

In the way of constructive criticism, she said that I should not have asked the first student whether he had any "problems" comprehending the homework. She pointed out that I had begun the session with a rhetorical question. This strategy corners the inmate-learner, she said. Her tutors typically begin this way, she added, perhaps as a nervous reaction to being in training. Sally's tutor book also provided that explanation, claiming that inmates will say that they understand something in order to avoid appearing "stupid" (her spoken word). It is best to begin with examples, the book states, to both teach and test a new skill in any topic area.

Sally warned me, coming full circle, that I had to really watch Chris once I was alone with him. She said that it would "blow his socks off to have someone with my qualities show intellectual and personal interest in him." She then wondered if my language might be "too sophisticated" for the "fellows." After pausing, she added that they did nevertheless seem to understand everything. She offered that she always simplifies everything and picks up if they are more capable themselves. We are each "getting there" in our own way, she added, winking at me. I winked back.

Having Respect for Inmates: A Fish with Green Horns

The holidays were upon us. It was the evening of December 19, 1990. I hadn't yet begun my work as an institutional volunteer even though I had been cleared to do so. I was chatting at a correctional event with two female professionals. I was eagerly awaiting my new fieldwork experience in the "joint" to connect with its inmates. I later felt this way whenever I was trapped inside the mousetrap of the jail; stalled on its stairways until a guard unlocked the door; delayed in the corridors along with other professionals; or crowded on the elevator with a lawyer whose schedule was always deemed more pressing.

Cindy was an executive board member with the agency that supervised my visits to the jail. Pam was the facilitator of its internal Drug Awareness program. Both Pam and I are in our mid-thirties and have a similarly positive, interactive style. We eventually "hit it off" as friends (a friendship which has since been sustained) after a few challenging experiences drew us close together. The three of us stood around the food table with glasses of wine snugly in hand. This was my first volunteer appreciation event in a series of many funded seminars, conferences and dinner engagements.

Cindy, the executive, told a story about an inmate who was very intelligent and articulate, but who was without literacy or conventional life skills. She described him as an Italian drug dealer with expensive clothes and cars, and gorgeous women "hanging all over him". With such incentive to continue his current life-style, there was no motivation for him to become rehabilitated. Not learning to read or write, let alone to re-evaluate himself, this inmate will live like other repeat offenders. In and out. He will know of life only as a revolving prison door. Cindy paused, responding: "Education is treated as a privilege in the jail system."

Pam, the facilitator, said that it is senseless that the inmates' own rights get revoked. What is the use of us going in and doing our bit if others aren't cooperating? At times inmates' rights are jeopardized whenever guards are "ticked off." "It's far too arbitrary a punishment," Pam added, "and nobody confronts the guards." Fetching a grape, she said with emphasis that the guards are more of a problem in her work than the inmates themselves. Cindy, who works at arms-length from the institution but is aware of its internal workings, nodded.

After more than four years of being exposed to several detention centers, Pam, the facilitator, smiled and calmly added: "It's best just to be straight with the guys if they're giving us a hard time rather than involve the guards. The guards can be cocky and uncompromising."

I chipped in. I felt uneasy because I felt I had nothing to contribute about my own impressions of the jail and its dynamics. I therefore opted for providing feedback on the institutional orientation itself that took place on December 4, 1990. I told my story. The Volunteer Program Coordinator had informed us, a room half-filled with mostly young women and possibly a few male ex-convicts, that "if a security guard asks you to do something totally unreasonable, then do it!" The senior guard had nodded during her platform speech. He then outlined

88   *Imprisoned Selves: An Inquiry into Prisons and Academe*

in some detail the security regulations of the jail. His large, stern form contrasted with her petite and elderly, but frisky one. His message? Do everything that the guards tell us to, but learn to act street-wise around the inmates. I sat feeling puzzled: I wrote, "How could we manage such a 'tall order' as this? How can we possibly become street-wise around inmates if we are supposed to respond, like clock-work, to institutional expectations, rules and regulations? Shouldn't the inmates experience us as thinking for ourselves?" (*Prison Journal*, December 4, 1990).

I wanted to learn to assess situations for myself; to become reasonably independent; and also accountable for my own decisions and actions. How else would any of us shed the label of "fish" that the inmates used for new volunteers and inmates? During a seminar at the agency that week, the speaker, an ex-convict, told the new volunteers that we were a "fishy lot." As fish, we had to be mindful of being manipulated by inmates who would try to get us to do, or say, what they wanted. They might want drugs, cigarettes, outside connections or affection. I wondered about the specifics of what might happen and how one might best proceed. We had been told many times about the mysterious "blue button" that was within reach throughout the institution should an emergency arise. Would a fish know when, and even how, to call for help? As I recorded the field notes on these conversations, I was creating the prison site that I had already been living in concrete, "real" terms. My study has a principal setting and a defined period of investigation, but no temporal bounds.

One month prior to this volunteer appreciation event, I had entered a deserted, old red brick house for our meeting. It was November 1990 and time for me to establish formal ties with corrections. I wanted clearance to begin work in the jail as soon as possible. Paul, the Volunteer Coordinator of this agency, had told me that I could begin in January 1991, but only if I met with his approval. He would need to check to see if I had a criminal record (which I do not). We had already talked over the telephone several times regarding my goals and reasons for wanting to work in a jail. He seemed satisfied with my plan to teach while researching educational issues for my dissertation. I provided him with the draft of my "Statement of purpose" admissions statement to the Institute as I had not yet formally applied for the doctoral program. In it, I had outlined my study interests and intention to carry out research in a jail:

I will need to find a way to:

1. capture inmates' stories both through dialogue and print;
2. explore rehabilitation in the context of education and lifelong learning;
3. analyze acts of storytelling (and writing) as empowering literary experiences; and
4. finally re-tell my own research story (Mullen 1990, excerpt, 1)

I had not anticipated needing to undergo a screening process with this agency in addition to the jail itself. The meeting hadn't yet started. I had a lump in my throat from just saying hello to the young male clients sitting at the picnic table on the front lawn of the agency. What were they thinking as they drew heavily on cigarette butts with their tattooed fingers? Another worker with green horns and a pretty skirt?

I had time to absorb the room, its contents and images, before the others arrived. I moved around the room, taking possession of it. Bienek, the political prisoner, also performed this ritual in his cell (in Davies 1990) even as I did in mine within a prison-amphitheater (Appendix A, July 6, 1991). I absorbed my new culture: in no particular order, an assortment of employment newspapers and notices on life skills, addiction, sexuality and AIDS littered the walls. I picked up copies of *Conquest holiday* magazine, *City college*, *Renters' news*, *Fresh perspective: [name of city] high school* newspaper, and *The employment news*. The telephone directory sat opened and fingered by rushed hands. Next to the "Keep environment clean" sign, and beside the "Believe in Yourself" drug-free poster, was a rustic-looking painting. I sketched it in my open journal book. It was an abstract. In it, a man, woman and child were embracing behind bars. The holy family? Each individual, although segregated within a set of bars, was interlocked. The portraits were framed by a gray brick prison wall and adjoining rustic scene. I wrote this entry, reconstructed here, and the statement that "I needed to figure out how to participate in this paradox: for each and every one of us who knows what it feels like to live behind loving bars, we are not alone" (*Prison Journal*, November 15, 1990).

I was the only new volunteer who wanted to work in the jails. The others wanted to stay on-site to work with ex-convicts in a number of capacities. The organization offered an impressive range of services: one-to-one counseling; drug awareness program (on-site and in the jails); information on halfway houses, treatment centers, welfare, and housing; family and community support; literacy programs; additional support to inmates (referrals to mailbag program; referrals to lawyers; pre-release planning, and information on the above named support systems).

Paul claimed that he had never witnessed any attacks on volunteers by inmates in the jails, only in his agency. Clients who are incarcerated are actually easier to deal with, he offered, because they are more vulnerable and less aggressive. He alluded to a young, cross-addicted inmate who had only just become manageable. Rod was "locked up" for having killed someone during a drunken brawl downtown. He required immediate servicing by one of us. Paul looked around. I caught his eye. No one else did. It was as though the others invested faith in a possible preconception that work in a jail is more dangerous than on-site here. Two months later I recorded the following entry during my first week of training sessions:

> About 5' 9", 135 lbs, slim and attractive, Rod announced that he has a girlfriend with a townhouse (rental) waiting for him once he gets out. He plans on pleading guilty so that he can get the charge knocked down from first degree murder to manslaughter. That way he'll serve 10 years instead of 20 years. On good behavior, though, he expects to serve only three-and-a-half years. This was mostly all that he had to say. But, it was clear that Rod had something of a grasp on the logistics of his life as they unfolded in the criminal justice system and a prison.
>
> Quite alert for someone so "buzzed out" on the prison's prescribed tranquilizers (a handful of different ones). When he goes to see the "shrink" tomorrow, he said, he'll ask to be put on something less potent. He doesn't want to be like the other guys on the psychiatric ward who talk to lampposts, he said. He imitated talking to a lamppost.
>
> We visited Rod because he's an ongoing client of Paul's. Paul says that Rod just likes the company. Rod has a little trick he likes to play on Paul and others: he shakes the person's hand while pretending to pull off his or her gold rings. He apparently always does this to Paul who wears, against the wisdom of the institution, three large, enticing rings. Rod even pulled this trick on me when I was leaving. I felt that his fun and games drew attention to his motives. Rod said that gold jewelry is worth a lot in prison. He repeated his gesture of stealing in jest. Paul was a very good sport, nonchalant, really.

During our visit, Rod sat lopsided on the floor, eyes half closed, drooling slightly. Paul had told Rod that he could tell that he was drugged. Rod said yes, but that he's more alert than he seems.

I had never met a "social outcast" who had also been labeled a "murderer." I had read a fair amount by people who had killed in response to a complex set of circumstances. I understood them to be ordinary human beings with extraordinary stories to both tell and write. The word "murderer" itself is a prison because it classifies people indiscriminately. The interests of dominant power groups become served.

Rod did not describe the murder scene or critical events in his life that may have led to it. He had alluded several times to his girlfriend and future life with her. When I gently commented to Rod later on that he was lucky to have a girlfriend waiting for him, he agreed. Under "straight" circumstances, Rod is probably easy to talk with. Not a lot was exchanged, in one sense. I guess what we basically accomplished was support.

Rod looked at me at one point, the only time he engaged me directly. He asked who I was and what I was doing with Paul's agency. His tone was sincere. It was really funny to me when he shifted his eyes to ask Paul if I was his boss. It might have looked this way because I was quiet but very attentive. I said that I'm a volunteer doing interviews hoping to do some literacy teaching. He said that the teachers who come to visit are 'nice ladies." I smiled, saying that he knew more about the service than I did as I hadn't yet met the popular teachers (*Prison Journal*, January 10, 1991).

This was not my first visit to the jail. I met Rod at the end of my first week of participant-observation. The day before I began visiting the jail with Paul I had dreamt of being sent roses by his agency (Appendix A, January 2, 1991). The card accompanying the roses had the word "referendum" on it. In the dream I sat down to try and figure out what the cryptic message meant. I interpreted this dream to be a vote of confidence in my ability to work independently, probably because I needed this boost to my morale. I understand the dream as anticipating my success in the jail: I moved from being client contact volunteer, to co-facilitator, to teacher, and then to Creative Writing coordinator. These were not static transitions. I became a Creative Writing coordinator during my weekly visits. These visits already included my sharing in drug sessions, teaching courses, and doing upgrading. I intensified my number of actual visits per week, moving from one, to two, and then to three visits in total. I also participated more widely within the field of corrections itself.

In the beginning, I felt confused as to my place. I wanted to perform as a teacher but the politics of the correctional system interfered. Because the agency that supervised my visits to the jail did not sponsor a literacy program on the inside, I was temporarily stuck. I later saw a way of getting around this by getting to know the Education Coordinators who worked directly for the institution itself. I began networking. I met the teachers at a literacy conference, introduced myself, and sat at their table. They were so supportive and fun to be with that I asked, that same night, to be trained as an institutional teacher. We then set up an appointment. By broadening my scope, I circumvented the agency. It had provided me with the opportunities to become only a client contact volunteer and participant in the drug group. But I did continue on with them as a co-facilitator in the drug groups and on-site at their in-house seminars and other events.

When I was a client contact volunteer with this agency, I felt awkward. I required knowledge of clients' requests of services available to them both inside the jail and in the community. I had never worked in correctional services. I therefore lacked awareness of, and sufficient information about, the agencies in the community that serviced inmates. Even the well organized manual for institutional volunteers outlining basic services did not help me much. We were required to memorize this material at home and leave it behind. While I was thankful for its discussion of the concepts and jurisdiction of bail, probation and parole, I was frustrated by the lists of community contacts and agencies. I had to rely on the inmates to inform me as to what they needed and which service was most likely appropriate or best equipped for them.

While I did not feel confident, I did record pertinent information about each case and request on client contact sheets. We were required to outline the result of each contact. In between sessions we recorded the bulk of the information as well as our impressions about the particular client. I had to listen very carefully. One of my colleagues considered me self-effacing in the degree to which I was successful in this respect. Like Cleaver (1968), the autobiographer-inmate, I placed "a great deal of emphasis on people really listening to each other, to what the other person has to say." But, unlike Cleaver, I did not experience listening for the reason that "you very seldom encounter a person who is capable of taking either you or himself seriously" (33).

In the prison site, I learned very quickly that inmates are sensitive to how others both perceive and treat them. In the Drug Awareness program and in the others I experienced, inmates responded positively to respect. To me, volunteers and facilitators who showed respect took the inmates, their plights, and life histories very seriously. We shared our own stories; provided encouragement for positive thinking, action, and team work; and challenged ideas and perceptions when appropriate. Those "outsiders" who showed the greatest degree of respect responded positively to being challenged themselves. The word "respect" is used in *When words are bars* (Paul, 1991). The author writes that volunteers (literacy workers) must attempt to understand the prison culture on its own terms and to "cultivate respect" by "demonstrating a sensitivity to the issues, needs and values that are important to the individual" (16).

I realized that I was probably showing respect whenever I searched for connections among people's stories and offered my own stories at appropriate junctures. Some inmates wanted to know how I could relate to them, given my own lack of experience with substance use and abuse. Pam was sometimes openly attacked on this very point. Our experience was considered marginally relevant until we told our own stories. For instance, we disclosed aspects of our own relationships with addicts. Unlike Pam, my stories included family relationships. I emphasized my role as support and helper concerning my sister and mother. I asserted that I knew what it felt like to be continually resourced by others in distress. I clearly positioned myself, within the group, as someone who has been exposed to some of the inmates' issues, but from the "other side of the fence."

Some professionals appeared extreme to me in their support of our clientele and other, related clientele. I remember June, a coordinator from a street kids program. This program was connected to a board of education. June's seminar had inadvertently taught me about the importance of balance when dealing with inmates. She presented at an on-site literacy conference. I had written that:

> June wants to look and act like a street kid (big sloppy clothes, dirty running shoes, and tangled hair) and yet be recognized as professional. She was in the business of extending support and services to

disadvantaged youth, she said, during her seminar. She lets street kids stay over in her home once she gets to know them. She has only ever experienced one instance of stealing from her home. After she meets the kids in parks and other places, she invests time and energy becoming familiar with them as individuals. Then, if they are reasonable to her, she offers them a place to stay. All of these transitions seem to take place within a very brief period of time.

To the contrary, we do not have the luxury of getting to know our inmates. During their 22 days with us on remand, we sometimes 'squeeze in' one or two visits. I wonder how June would respond to an environment that thrives on restraints and that shrugs in the face of continuity. People need continuity to grow and develop relationships with one another. Continuity can promote new perspectives for inmates involved in the educative process (*Prison Journal*, April 18, 1991).

A second facilitator, another supervisor of mine, was simultaneously respectful and effective in groups. As outstanding as she was in groups, she was stunning one-to-one. I am introducing Rita for the first time. Before I met George, "the cartoon character," I was briefed for one hour about him by Rita. She gave him a very bad review. It was the month of March and we were sitting in the "lounge" area of the jail. Rita informed me that I would have to interview George, as part of my training, regarding his request. He had a reputation for being a violent, tough guy. This ex-boxer was "missing some of his marbles," Rita claimed. He was the most dangerous client that her agency had ever serviced, and he was Rita's special case. George indiscriminately assaulted both women and men, and had recently injured staff at the agency itself. Rita spoke in hushed tones, providing detail upon detail, preparing me for a virtual monster.

When George arrived, Rita drew her seat close to him. I did the same. She smiled and shook his hand. She then explained the nature of her own role and mine. At every step, she showed respect. This bald-headed man in his late fifties apologized for not having his dentures in. Rita asked him about his family. He talked about his mother who was getting permanent dentures. His request? To locate his reading glasses. He had left them in a desk when he was arrested. As I recorded the details of his request and other relevant information, Rita indicated that his desk had already been checked. His glasses had not been found. He appeared annoyed. As he talked incessantly about the other places they could be found, he repeated himself. He politely asked me to itemize all of the possible places to be checked for his glasses.

Rita asked George about his wife and kids who lived in another province. She gently encouraged him to commit to drug counseling before joining his family. She obviously knew the details of his personal family history. He looked on edge. Rita asked him why. George said that his children had witnessed him "shoot up" narcotics; "pop" pills; and "get plastered drunk." "This is no way," he emphasized, "for kids to be raised." He did not want to drink and become mean anymore, he said. On the way out we "de-briefed" (that is, we exchanged our views on the session). I told Rita that I was surprised at how mild George seemed given her character profile of him. She looked intently at me: "Carol, one simply cannot predict. As counselors we artificially create situations for ourselves and our clients that allow us to make progress. But, everything depends on the individual client, his temperament and issues, and stage of recovery. We can talk sense to them only if they are 'drying out,' and ready to listen and make changes" (*Prison Journal*, March 12, 1991).

Over a two-month period as client contact volunteer, I learned something interesting about inmates' seemingly objective requests. Inmates could turn information gathering sessions into complex situations. Such situations involved self-analysis, analysis, support and disclosure. Bob, for instance, was seeking support for his substance abuse recovery. While outlining his pre-release request, he took me into his life as a cocaine addict; feelings of loneliness and desperation; and yearning to have people trust him again. He asked me to help him with his résumé for his job search, linking this effort to his desire to be trusted again in the workplace. My years as a college-level instructor had been put to the test: We felt challenged to present the five year gap in his work history as creatively as possible.

Enterprising selves: Establishing the Creative Writing program

Sometimes the Education Coordinators would pop in and say "hi" while I was working with my students. By then I had gotten beyond all the training. They always frolicked in the corridors, even on the ranges, and were adored by staff and inmates alike. I admired Sally and Anna whom I thought of as "Raggedy Anne and Andy" because of their Halloween disguises and performances.

While I waited for inmates, Sally grappled with my inquiries. She told me, during my training period with her in March 1991, not to discuss with students their criminal offenses, record and legal status. She insisted that I could be subpoenaed to testify as a witness in court if I knew something of value about an inmate's case. Also, we are not counselors, she warned. Others in the system, who are designated counselors, social workers, and discharge planners, know how to deal with these complex human issues. We simply "do education" to the best of our ability.

She spoke to me in whispers as her confidante, not as a teacher-in-training. As on other occasions, she shifted focus, referring with interest to my experience of graduate studies; formalities involving proposal applications for funding; personal and interactive quality of my research style; and to what appeared to her to be my professionalism coupled with youthfulness. (She'd say: "You can go anywhere you want, Kid. The world's your oyster.") In turn, I would speak admiringly of her success and popularity in a challenging place; happy-go-lucky personality and wonderful sense of humor; high standards for teachers and inmate-students; positive and straightforward ways of connecting with everyone; wisdom of life and kindness towards all; trusting marriage and family life; and sense of peace.

These intimate levels of talk emerged over time. For example, I took it for granted that Sally knew that I felt her to be very committed to the success of the Education/Literacy program. But perhaps I should have told her so. Underneath her interpersonal charms was a great deal of intensity. We openly and consistently applauded one another in our work and life-endeavors. Several guards would smile at the two of us, referring to her as my "older sister." Sally would inevitably grin and blurt out, "If only! Come now, does this mean that you need glasses too?!"

I participated in Sally and Anna's literacy and education seminars, conferences and events during the length of my fieldwork study. One day I visited their office to broach the subject of the "personal" in our work. I said that I was trying to understand why the institution prevented us from learning about the inmates' personal lives. I also wanted to learn more about our own perception of our work with the inmates. The reality was that we were engaging them on a personal level. One of our educational tools promoted this kind of connection, I said. We tutors were encouraged to use the Language Experience Approach to teach reading and writing. With this method, the text is to be both created and learned by the student himself. Students disclose aspects of their life-and-prison experiences whenever they are encouraged to generate their own materials. I pointed out that Sally's own Volunteer tutor hand guide outlines this method and promotes the idea that inmates who are guided in this way will be more highly motivated.

I gave an example of a client whom we all knew, someone from the drug group who was being transferred to a federal penitentiary. He had not been a student of mine, but he had asked if he could be my pen-pal. My idea was to provide him with support while gaining material for my own writing. I wanted to develop a more in-depth case analysis of a single inmate's life. Sally stuck to her point: His best bet was to be handled by a trained counselor. One of them, whom I knew to be popular and effective, had apparently been working with him during this transition, but in a clinical fashion. Later, when some of my students did write me from their new locations, their material was processed by Sally. I was the only teacher in the system, other than she, who received letters from our students and who corresponded with them. Since she had read all of my letters (to them and from them), we openly discussed issues that were forming in sensitive areas. These issues would become amplified in the Creative Writing program. Inmates' need for contact was evident but their talents, circumstances and motives varied. Cleaver's (1968) own creative spirit in isolation came to mind whenever I opened yet another letter:

> My mistress at the time of my arrest, the beautiful and lonely wife of a serviceman stationed overseas, died unexpectedly three weeks after I entered prison; and the rigid, dehumanized rules governing correspondence between prisoners and free people prevented me from corresponding with other young ladies I knew. It left me *without any contact with females* except those in my family (my emphasis, 20).

In chapter 4, I discuss the kinds of relationships that inmates form with females in the penal system. I also explore the special qualities that women bring to their relationships in corrections including our need to know how to draw boundaries.

Sammy figured prominently in my learning about boundaries in my letter writing relationships with inmates. Sammy, my hardworking Native American student, had become emotionally dependent on me. Eventually, Sally and I decided that Sammy was pushing too hard and making me feel uncomfortable. Sally was worried about my safety. We reacted by terminating this writing relationship.

Our official story was that we, as teachers, attempted to avoid conflicts and problems with inmates. We also told stories in public to the effect that we believed it necessary to accommodate inmates and their particular needs and circumstances. We also made it clear that we were restricted to the system and its own cycles and rhythms. During a literacy conference on May 26, 1991, Sally and Anna told stories to the group of social workers and me. Their summary point was that: "We try not to be judgmental. It helps not knowing about the guys' personal lives. The guys think that we have the perfect lives because they only see us from the outside. We don't have perfect lives, but in comparison we certainly seem to!"

I responded. I addressed the concepts of judgment, personal knowledge and storytelling in our work. I asked: "Do you think we make judgments of the inmates by virtue of restricting their personal knowledge and our personal knowledge of them?" I said that my students were storytellers, probably out of their need to connect and to be heard. I therefore could not prevent myself from learning about them as people. They told stories during sessions and wanted us to tell stories too. They also seemed to be understanding the lessons themselves as vehicles for writing and exchanging stories. The institutional procedures and programmatic objectives restrict exchanges to specific agenda items. Yet, the inmates find ways of turning these regulated moments into authentic, two-way connections. Inmates respond creatively to the codification and accountability of talk, as I do. In my sessions, the boundary separating legitimate talk from dangerous story-telling practices is not always clear.

I offered a solution: We could use our energies differently by helping the inmates to accomplish their ends. Although their personal writings can be accessed by the authorities and even other inmates, our students can learn to write anonymously and in the third-person for safety reasons. Could we find a way to entertain their creative thinking and personal ideas without compromising anyone? We could permit them to write in a structured Creative Writing program and to present their ideas publicly, but also anonymously. We could, in establishing this, satisfy our own needs in the process. I asked if we could offer creative writing as a programmatic development in order to both formalize and extend what inmates were already doing alone and with teachers.

That night I re-read Ted Hughes's poem called "Pibroch." It is, to me, about a lack of relationships among sea, wind and stone. All three are imprisoned in an isolated, meaningless existence. The vision is bleak as nothing evolves. The sea that cries with its "meaningless voice" . . . "without sleep/Without purpose, without self-deception" is not alone. Below, I provide excerpts of this poem:

> Stone likewise. A pebble is imprisoned
> Like nothing in the Universe.
> Created for black sleep. Or growing
> Conscious of the sun's red spot occasionally,
> Then dreaming it is the foetus of God.
> Over the stone rushes the wind
> Able to mingle with nothing.
> Like the hearing of the blind stone itself.
> Or turns, as if the stone's mind came feeling
> A fantasy of directions . . .
> Unprepared for these conditions.
> She hangs on, because her mind's gone completely.
> Minute after minute, aeon after aeon,
> Nothing lets up or develops . . .

This dismal vision did not typify my interpersonal experiences in the jail. Just as sea, wind and stone must interrelate meaningfully and with purpose, so too might inmate, teacher and supervisor. As Paul (1991), a prison literacy researcher, writes, people in jail are imprisoned twice: "First, there are the cells, bars, walls and guards. Then, there is the other kind of prison, less tangible, but just as confining, with bars made of words" (41).

I expected to be "bumped back" the next day or disciplined in some manner. Instead, Sally enthusiastically took charge. She kindly assisted me in setting up my own Creative Writing program. She did this without superimposing any stringent formalities on me. On the contrary. Sally initiated the formalities of the program without even notifying me which actually presented some confusion in the beginning. Both teachers were so dynamic, well known and trusted in the system that interested students were easily screened by them and handed over to me. My own image of "mind-forg'd manacles" (Blake, in "London," from "Songs of Experience") shifted. I had been associating this image of restraint with the Education/Literacy program whenever it interfered with my students' creative impulses and my own. I no longer felt handcuffed knowing that I could utilize my best qualities. I also felt especially dignified in the process.

Imprisoned Selves: Living on a Carousel

Sear Robinson and I sat reading over his poetry for the newsletter one afternoon. After the Creative Writing program got underway, I felt inspired to create our own in-house collection of writings. A few other penal institutions had done this. Sear was asking about his musical lyrics. He had written for his rock band and reviewed his lyrics for our purposes. We read them over together, but were continually interrupted by inmates from his range. Dozens of inmates looked into our interview room. The guards were not visible to me.

I have already told this story in chapter 1 where I emphasized having felt threatened by the inmates as a group. Here I am elaborating its significance. Knowing that people generally act according to whatever the "pack" demands, and that "nearly everyone in such situations behaves automatically" (Lessing 1986, 24), I felt nervous. My mind had drifted to the engineering students at McMaster University in Ontario who had, several years ago, simulated the rape of a woman using a doll. I also knew that Sear had been labeled within the prison hierarchy as an "undesirable" because of his assault on a woman. And yet, he and the others in protective custody were themselves vulnerable. They were at risk from the general population of inmates. Protective custody inmates therefore remained stationary: they were not accommodated in interview rooms on other floors (except in closed group sessions).

In *Bingo!*, Roger Caron (1985), autobiographer and convict, tells the story of the Kingston riot in the early 70s. He described the brutal treatment of the "undesirables" by the general population of inmates. The riotous militants forced inmates to join a circle of chairs. These inmates had been segregated, as is the practice, for their offenses against women and children. They were labeled then as they are now as "rats," "diddlers" and "undesirables." In the circle, they were abused and slowly beaten to death. At least 16 men had their knees broken and skulls cracked open with iron bars. They endured slow and brutal death. I felt empathy for these protective custody victims. I sat up, smiled, and began my work with Sear. I refused to feel vulnerable. I ignored the others and asked Sear to do the same. I then reviewed his productivity level; disclosed personal feelings regarding my safety; and returned full circle to his poetry:

"What's that, Sear?" Did you say that you've composed between 700 and 1,000 poems over the span of your relatively short life?" I asked, noticeably impressed.

"That's right!" he exclaimed, gesturing proudly with his tattooed hands. I will get copies of whatever I can to you," he said. "It's been kind of hard lately with the sentencing, relocating and stuff. You understand, don't ya?"

I sat blushing while we were continually interrupted. I quickly calculated that the guards were being detained in some kind of scrap on the ranges. I took a risk. I told Sear, my musician-student, that I was nervous about the inmates' behavior towards me. He agreed, calling their behavior "offensive," saying that he also takes exception to it. I privately wondered if he felt his well-being was in jeopardy unless he "played along" with the others.

He said the inmates act primitively because the "screws" treat them poorly. The authorities should just put up a sign reading, "Don't feed the animals," he said, "because the general perception is that all inmates are inhuman." We continued to talk about poetry. He shared one of his lyrical poems, or songs. In it, written before "doing time," he imagines himself as a "frozen pony on a carousel in mid-gallop." He related this image of the carousel to being an object on a merry-go-round in prison, consequently putting into words how I felt. Did he know how I felt? It was Sear's image of imprisonment that connected me to myself and to him as we sat in that stuffy room. We had been abandoned as two frozen ponies on a carousel halted in mid-gallop, and yet I felt relatively safe with him.

We were distracted by a stretcher that raced by containing an inmate who had been badly injured. Blood smeared the floor. Red. Another color for my canvas.

Sear talked eloquently about his new commitment to a drug-free lifestyle. When I asked him about the nature of his contribution to our newsletter, he elaborated. He said that he was once "jonesing" for cocaine, but now he's "jonesing" for freedom. When he was using drugs, he said, he felt that an evil person was knocking at his door. He was "jonesing" for drugs in the sense that he was craving a fix. He wanted to promote drug awareness by awakening users to their reality. Sear was vocal about the need for personal change. His poetry tells a powerful, but sinister, story of addiction as a "frozen carousel" "halted in mid gallop."

Mr. Jones, a personified image of a drug lord, imprisoned him in full-blown addiction to coke. He wanted to end his own horror and the horror that knocks at all drug users' doors. Although he hated being in segregation, he appreciated the time to "dry-out," and to reflect on his experiences and write about them (*Prison Journal*, March 27, 1992).

I was fascinated by Sear's profound use of discourse (writing and song) to re-examine his life as a substance abuser. One of the primary aims of the penal system should be to encourage inmates to re-educate themselves (Foucault 1977), but in personally meaningful ways. Sear was unusual in that he had managed to situate himself as an educator while in protective custody and within a wider community that was hostile to him. I looked at him as the author of his own knowledge, story, and actions. I was not prepared for the powerful drama that he had created of the addict in the poem below. The addict, locked inside his own static mythology, is not even struggling to be free. In this portrait, he can only hope to live without pain through numbness. The cocaine that numbs him is simultaneously his prison-carousel in "Mr. Jones (to the moon)" (also in Appendix B)::

> Halted in mid gallop, a frozen carousel,
> charging forth without proceeding,
> on my painted pony bound for hell.
> A shadow dancing on the walls, come to bid
> farewell, make claims on my soul,
> someone I've never heard the name a thousand times,
> I can't believe what's happening here,
> Mr. Jones has brought me to my knees.
> Mr. Jones, knocking at the door,
> here he comes, making me want more,
> the tightness comes, it curls around me,
> making me insane.
> The brightness lights the dust in the spoon.
> To the moon! I am high again.
> I can't feel the pain now, I've been lifted

to new heights.
I can tell it won't be long now,
till I refill the pipe. (oh, n-nnnnn-no).
It's all coming down around me,
my sky is falling in.
And now Mr. Jones is knocking.
I don't want to, but I know I'll let him in,
he's going to win.
Mr. Jones is knocking at my door,
and here I am, just another sniveling whore.
He's here to curl his arms around me,
making me insane. Oh my head!
The whiteness made from dust in my spoon.
To the moon, I'm high again.
To the moon! Good-bye! I'm dead.

As short, blond-haired, tattooed Sear sang, a recorded dream of mine surfaced. I was remembering that:

> I'm in a room containing a bed and desk teaching literacy to a short, blond-haired youth. To my surprise, he already seems literate. I feel some confusion as to how to "teach" literacy to him. He is scribbling sentences on yellow foolscap with a pencil. The problem is that his pencil is so dull that his writing is getting bigger and bigger, and harder and harder to decipher. I jump to a meta-level construct: I'm learning, from this prisoner of a high caliber, the irony of being in the position of teaching literacy to a competent reader and writer. I turn and ask to have the bed removed from the room as it is distracting from our professional relationship (Appendix A, April 4, 1990).

I had had this dream not only before I met Sear, but also seven months prior to my initial visit to the jail. I had learned to resource my dreams to re-educate myself. I was learning about my preconceived notions and stereotypes of the inmates as well as of my initial impressions and feelings. I was surprised by the high level of literacy and creativity that some of them revealed in their work. I was pleased that I was learning so much from them about how I might re-educate myself about the realities of imprisoned selves. Selves can be contained physically, emotionally and spiritually. We all struggled to be free in the drug, literacy and writing programs by reconstructing our personal knowledge about who we are. The real test concerned whether we would live, with relative success, our newly inspired stories.

Prolific Participants: Writing Addicts

Black Hawk's long black hair somehow formed a barrier between him and the rest of us. His despondency made me wonder why he even bothered joining us in the drug group. What was he up to? Other inmates had talked openly about how they were "chalking up brownie points" to obtain early parole. After a few months, Black Hawk approached me and, unlike some of the others, his intentions were genuine. With a long side-glance, he mumbled that he would like me to take a look at his poetry. I advised him to put in a request to see me through the Education Coordinator, adding that she preferred not to connect inmates with teachers known to them in other programs. I had inferred that this was a security measure intended to protect volunteers from harassment. I remembered Sally's story about an inmate who knew some of her daily movements and rhythms from having observed her vehicle from his cell-window.

Later, Black Hawk and I spent several intense sessions reading through his thick and mostly typed file of poetry. My goal became to organize his poetry for publication in the creative writing newsletter. Like my other five participant-contributors, he kindly signed my letter of consent. This letter had already been cleared by the Superintendent through Sally. Black Hawk complained about the letter that he had received from me, ahead of time. The vocabulary was too difficult. He and his cell-mate had apparently "spent the evening trying to get a grip on what the words meant" (*Prison Journal*, December 22, 1991). In the same session, he shone with pride, baptizing himself "Black Hawk" for his publications in the newsletter. Everyone, including the inmates and Prison Arts Foundation, had given him supportive feedback. He did not need mine.

Black Hawk told me stories about his drug and needle use. I found them more shocking than Sear's. His goal to become published did not include recovery from drug use. Black Hawk raised his elbows, demonstrating how he had recently strolled through a park with a book under one arm and a needle in the other. He wrote (excerpts only):

Mother of myself and soul
I've never met your blessed soul
I've poisoned myself over the years
Before I go I'd like to see you smile.
I'm wasting away. I drink and smoke
Inside my mind things do hurt
Day, night what is the same
Mother of mystery come and see your boy.

This poem, "Unknown Kin," was censored by the Education Coordinator. It was considered too negative. Black Hawk provided insight into his personal prison as well as the phenomenon of prison itself. For instance, he alluded to self-abuse ("poison[ing]," "wasting away," "drink and smoke") and unfulfilled dreams. Censorship is a defining attribute of prison. The 1989 issue of *Prison Journal* explored censorship for prisoners as not only imposed, as one would expect, but also self-imposed. In order to survive in a prison milieu, inmates refused to publish along with former guards; protective custody inmates; and "skinners" who have been convicted of sex crimes (Paul, 1991).

On a separate occasion, Black Hawk alluded to his partner and child as having fallen down an elevator shaft. He stirred restlessly. It was the missing details that gave me a jolt. If he could, he had said, he'd stick a needle in his arm, right then, during our session.

"You feel that needy?" I asked.

"Yep, and it ain't goin' away," he replied.

"Can't you write about yourself only as a vicarious user? If you are abstaining from drugs in here, then aren't you learning ways of staying clean for your release?"

"Nope," he said, "It's not what I want. It's hard for you to grasp, eh?"

On September 19, 1992, nine months later, I had completed my fieldwork when I dreamt about needle use (see Appendix A, "Street Researcher"). In the dream I was the vicarious needle user. This brought me closer to the inmates than any other experience I have had to date. During the study I created distance in order to interpret the inmates' experiences. Yet, the more deeply immersed I became in narrative modes of interpretation, the closer I came to the human lives I was studying. The dream was one of the most disturbing experiences

I had had while researching inmates' lives. In the dream I am on the side of the law but the image of myself is that of a vicarious junkie. In my complex role, I view knowledge as "first-hand, concrete and immediate, and sensory." My own "drug" is metaphorical. It takes the form of "a deep appreciation for every aspect of the whole experience;" a credible performance as a vicarious knower, and a sensory feeling "of pin-pricks in my arms." This image of myself as the vicarious but knowing drug user provides a dramatic metaphor for writing.

In another dream of mine I also experienced the "quality of the fabulous" (Sacks 1985). As a prisoner, I was forcibly confined in an attic along with my two siblings. I began my master's thesis (1990) with this June 1988 recording. In it, we are literally pushed and shut away from my parents' custody. I clearly felt abandoned in the dream which was based on a real-life event. I recorded my dream, both interpreting and reconstructing it, as a researcher. Black Hawk, too, wrote of the prison house beyond his youth. As an orphaned child, he grew up in a foster home, but then left. He took to the streets and began recording his experiences. I am also striving to understand the story of tragic lives, but as a narrative about schooling, curriculum and the self.

Black Hawk and I connected as two writers, and yet I pressed him for a poem of hope. All that he had asked of me was my time and acknowledgment of copyright. He wanted to be the author of his own voice, and yet I had been positioned as his gatekeeper. I knew that the Education Coordinators would not authorize poetry that promoted destructive and abusive self-images. I therefore felt that I was the implicit disciplinarian of his mind. Contributions belonging to two other inmate-writers had already been returned to me in censored form. This was a difficult situation.

Adrian Sands, short story writer, had been convicted of the murder of his commonlaw partner. He had been sentenced while we worked together. I had read about his case in the newspapers. As one of my more conspicuously medicated storytellers, he asked me, "How can you represent our lives if you are censoring them according to what's comfortable for the teachers?" This was the point. He pushed to know whose reality I was ultimately accommodating in our newsletter. It was clearly an ethical dilemma that has implications for teacher education and research. Adrian had made intelligent inquiries upon learning that, while one of his stories had been rejected, the other accepted. The one that emphasized an "all too common experience" around early childhood abuse was favored. The story that had been returned was a first-person, angry account about a whipped and abandoned child.

The Education Coordinators served as gatekeepers and friends. My loyalities, which were both to them and my students, were sometimes split. Sally pursued clearance, from her authorities, to publish our newsletter. She got the approval we required, but the process itself was not explained to me. It remains an untold story. The inmate-writers were sandwiched between layers of authorities that controlled even their representation of their own experiences. I felt uncomfortable, yet persuaded my inmate-writers that they should conform to acceptable writing themes and notions of storytelling. Even so, the dignity we teachers felt in our hearts for these storytellers was reflected in the final product. Inmates' writings, that were constructed from and through experience, include a series of raw and powerful images. The following themes were illustrated in our joint publication (see Appendix B): abandonment, "Anger for unwanted child"; imprisonment and death, "Locked within a sleeping tomb"; cocaine addiction and insanity, "sniveling whore" and "Mr. Jones has brought me to my knees"; despair and misery, "Entombed within a world of pain"; global plagues and insanity, "Mindless wars and bloodshed/cannot be restrained"; and loneliness and emptiness, "I pray your heart I'll find."

Multiple Imprisonment of the Self: Dirty Socks and Velvet Drapes

Peter came to our first session with his zipper undone. In the logic of prison society, he was an outcast because of his depraved status as a child molester or "diddler." Whenever I met with this elderly man, I cringed. As a beginning novelist, he wanted to pursue creative writing in my program. He briefly sketched his plans, aiming to write a humanizing account about the penal system as it evolved over the decades during his incarceration. I was intermittently thanked for my time and complimented on being "sincere" and "sweet". This rational and humanizing discourse was in conflict with the unfastened zipper. It marked the boundary between his cover story and the real story. The former was shot through with his references to girls being molested in ice rinks; his presence in such places; and the parents' accusations of his offenses. While asserting his innocence, he alluded to charges that pre-dated the abolition of capital punishment in Canada in 1961. Many agencies that work with criminals are described as "advocates." Like my agency, I oppose capital punishment as a deterrent to crime and applaud constructive alternatives.

I attempted to focus on Peter's idea for his book, but my effort proved fruitless. He continued exploiting his cover story of innocence and I reacted by growing distant. Our sessions stirred phantom memories for me. As I looked through the window pane to catch the guard's attention, I felt the pull of my younger self towards the second-story window of the loft in my grandmother's house. The window had a view to a contained but overgrown garden. Lilies were caged. I drifted, behind me, to the puzzle that covered the large, plummeting hole to the kitchen. The puzzle cover depicted mountains, blue sky and pine trees. Yet, all I could smell were the dirty socks.

It was 1969 when my father found out. His "spray of bullets fill[ed] the air as bombs were dropped away" (Appendix B, Phillip Dalley, inmate-writer, "Searching for a place of sanity"):

> Dad punched my Uncle against his 7Up truck parked outside our friend's house in Halifax. Dad had given me money to go to the store. He didn't know that I had sat on the nearby curb. I watched, gripping my striped rubber ball. Unlike my Dad for whom the logic was self-evident, I had mixed feelings about seeing one person's fist smashing another's face. My Uncle bled profusely as he whined for mercy. After his subsequent hospitalization, he roamed for years. Even though we had reported him upon learning that he had been indecently assaulting also his own daughters in a wooden shack, he was never picked up. I remember later seeing his big girls sitting on a couch in the dark. The newspaper article that my Mom shared with me years later sketched the incident of my Uncle's arrest for the bodily assault of a stranger. My Mom had already disowned both this brother and her youngest one years earlier. Where are they today in the system? Have they received any psychiatric treatment? (*Daily Reflections Journal*, July 2, 1991).

Prison waiting lists (or whatever it is in reality) prevent child molesters from re-educating themselves. Gordon Henry Taylor actively sought help but did not get it. He was murdered, at 40, inside Kingston Penitentiary by the "goon squad". His story, as told on the television show, *Fifth Estate!* inspired me to think of the multiple imprisonment of the self: Taylor, an adult trapped inside the mental age of an 11 year old, was himself a boy imprisoned. He was also physically caged inside our penal system. It typically takes eight to ten years for an inmate to even begin to receive psychiatric treatment. In 1978, when he was released, he molested a four-year old girl. I believe that I have a sense of her from my dream world. In it, I reconstruct images of captivity from my real life-experiences and public stories as represented by the media. These three sources, dream-world, life-experiences and public stories, impact on one another. The process is a dynamic, interactive one. It produces images of captivity that represent "shades of the prison-house" to me (Wordsworth, "Ode: Imitations of immortality" 1965, 154). Here is the young girl whom I have invented in dream from multiple sources:

> I asked Sally, my professor-friend, if I could take her little girl for a walk. I stressed that we would only be 15 minutes and implied that there was no need for alarm. Her little girl looked so pretty in her blue dress. Sally, hesitatingly sweet, smiled and then nodded. I added over my shoulder that, if we were any longer than 20 minutes, that she should come looking for us. Sally looked very pretty herself with her shiny golden hair.
>
> The little girl, who was treating me as her playmate, grabbed my hand. We twirled about in the name of short-lived fun and adventure. "The child's world is my own," I thought in a blink as we entered the gym. The heavy wine-colored velvet drapes deeply breathed "No enter" as we skipped lightly and sang boldly in and out of the folds and contours of the dusty old drapes.
>
> I'm not sure at what point exactly, but the little girl suddenly disappeared. How had I lost track of her? I searched the curtains and stage high and low feeling increasingly panicky with each passing minute. Alarmed, I felt exasperated.
>
> Sally entered the scene. Unmusical chords stuck in my throat as my heaving chest grinded them through my broken accordion. We both instinctively knew that the sweet child had been stolen. We stood staring at one another, too shocked to know what to do (Appendix A, September 28, 1991).

Scott (1982), prison psychiatrist, provides detailed case interviews and profiles of federal inmates. Unlike him, I had to rely almost solely on my impressions of inmates gained more fleetingly and intuitively. My multi-faceted narrative extends inward, into my dream world, and outward, into public stories. I develop connections among particulars to accentuate their small, cell-like structures. Conversely, by accentuating their cell-like structures I broaden the scope of relationships among unlikely phenomena. I discuss my introspective processes and relate them to tools of reflection in chapter 4.

Cover Stories: Guns and Chicken Fingers

Pam had been doing institutional work involving substance abuse, recovery and relapse all over the province. Because we were functioning well as colleagues, she welcomed me to join her. I was the only volunteer whom she had linked up with in this way and so intensively. She knew that I wanted as much exposure as possible to inmates who were reflecting on their lives, and I knew that she wanted support and feedback. I responded eagerly to the opportunity to visit other detention centers.

It was September 9, 1991, my first visit, in a series, to this other detention center. It looked like a recreational center both inside and outside. On this day we were interacting with four young offenders in the chapel. The Native American inmate spoke first. He said that he was "sick and tired of all the shit." It sounded to me as though he was ready to make changes in his life. A young, blond-haired fellow blurted out something to the effect that he loved weapons and knew how to "manhandle" the best of them. His response did not logically follow on the first inmate's disclosure. Pam interrupted his enthusiastic monologue. She encouraged all of us to reflect honestly on our feelings. She asked that each of us work from the inside-out in order to connect on a meaningful level.

This same inmate did not hear Pam. He continued bragging, this time about how guns gave him power on the outside and now his armed assault charges, on the inside. It struck me that he could not openly admit to feeling fear in prison. None of the inmates ever admitted to fear, but some of their stories revealed to me that they were feeling frightened, threatened and lonely. Young, attractive inmates especially had much to fear from bodily attacks. It made sense to me that the vulnerable might conjure up powerful images of themselves. The Native American told this young person that, contrary to his impression, the other "guys" (prisoners) were not impressed with him. He added that guns are only an "illusion" of power; that "real" power comes from within; and that weaponry personally "scares the bejesus" out of him. He then told a story about the people in his own home who were out of control. They use the "pieces" (guns) and he "gets the time" for their craziness. Pam responded, asking everyone to avoid using the word "power". When people use this word, she said, they compete by telling "war stories" (which are cover stories) about who is the toughest in the group. Such exchanges only serve to promote dishonest talk. We need to talk honestly in order to make constructive changes.

I had been quiet and so had one other group member. Bob interrupted the discussion to ask me what I had been learning from my work with inmates. I was surprised. This had happened once before, but then it was an older inmate who had attempted to control the group dynamics. I searched for a response. This seemed odd on my part, given that I had been discussing this same question with colleagues for months. I told Bob that my perception of the "guys" in the drug group was that some of their talk promotes the cycle of addiction. Exchanges focused almost exclusively on drug highs; drugs-of-choice; places and people; and street life itself. Such talk seemed to further institutionalize inmates since it precluded reflection on more meaningful issues. (This may be why Pam tended to discourage, and even censor, such exchanges.) Such talk also overshadowed the stories of recovery and renewal that some inmates were ready to exchange.

The videos we showed in sessions may have compounded these processes. In some instances, drug use was actually demonstrated in them to portray the trauma of the addict's life. The "guys" needed to distance themselves from such images of "using," or learn to monitor their private associations. We therefore required feedback on the sessions themselves as well as on the most effective approaches to storytelling. This was my response to Bob.

Privately, I believed that Pam used a storytelling approach to counseling inmates. She encouraged others to reflect on their stories of recovery and relapse in their past, present and future lives. She often asked people directly about their past family situations and present situations with loved ones. It is my sense that she understood addiction to be a multi-faceted phenomenon including self, family and community that is unique to each person. Pam was promoting a narrative perspective on the educational stories of her clients. She also advocated our personal knowledge orientation to them: "Everyone's story is different and needs to be told and heard" (*Prison Journal*, March 25, 1991). Such statements, which may be courageous in academic seminars at the Institute, are life-threatening with and among inmates, especially those for whom confidentiality is essential.

Bob nodded, looking pensive. I had just made the point that we required feedback from inmates on our sessions. Bob asked if he could meet with me. He said that he wanted to discuss my ideas or to correspond with me about them. I wanted to agree, but Pam had cut him off. She said that my work was too "general" for him to be involved in it. I felt that she had interpreted my research interests narrowly. I view my research as an ongoing, fluid part of my inquiry and relations with others.

Bob and I sat looking awkward. He hunched over and I blushed. I thought of the eerie "concrete slabs," from my dream about communication within a prison dome (Appendix A, July 6, 1991). This image, which I am reconstructing in context, implies that we only hear, see and feel within our limited scope. This scope ensures that only the gatekeepers within the Panopticon exercise constant visibility; the prisoner who is confined to his or her cell is denied the same privilege (Foucault 1977). The image of concrete slabs also separates offenders, allocating them to the lower ranks of society. In narrative terms, the prisoner is socially constructed. S/he constitutes a lesser form of life, one that is thwarted and cut short. Like women's lives that are "miraculous in their unapplauded achievement" (Heilbrun 1988), the narratives of inmates need to be discovered, written and shared, but within community.

When Bob raised the subject a second time, Pam got up and replied over her shoulder. She was feeding *The other prison* into the VCR. It is an inmate's story of his transformation to becoming literate inside a federal penitentiary. "Carol is a volunteer only, not a researcher," she added. That was all she said. I became worried. I could detect no hint of any possible change in my status. Had she been informed before me about the institution's decision regarding my correctional proposal and request? Pam was one of my teachers, yet I felt trapped inside her implicit view of me. I felt that she did not see me as a researcher. I also felt at odds with her impression of research as unlived, distant and institutionalized. Bob's silence and disbelief told me that he, too, felt marginalized. What about Pam? She looked awkward. Had I been too open about the other drug group and my impression of it? Or, worse yet, had my analysis dominated and even misrepresented her own?

I was confused. At the bus stop I asked for clarification. I asked Pam how she thought I might best represent myself to the group. She said that I was a volunteer who should remain distant from my research goal. Even if the authorities cleared me, I would receive instructions as how to proceed in the jail. In the meantime, I needed to be careful in this respect. I had to avoid creating the impression that I was recording people's testimonies for a public, but as yet undisclosed, purpose. Again, this was another ethical lesson learned. I gained insight from this exchange. After that, I did not volunteer information that changed the dynamics of the group or indicated my research interests. I was yet to learn, from Sally, the Education Coordinator, that I should not have been introducing myself as a teacher in the drug group either. Apparently she had been approached by a number of inmates who requested that I become their teacher. This included inmates not affiliated with the Education/Literacy program.

After our private discussion, Pam and I became friends. Over chicken fingers and Greek salad, she asked me what I thought of her two college students/volunteers. We agreed that the male, an ex-convict, related well, but that the female, still young, did not. As the weeks passed, we consulted openly about our perceptions of these students; the other group facilitators, guards, and staff; and various incidences that occurred in our sessions. One disturbance resulted from an inmate's verbal attack on the three women in the room. Two of his "buddies" backed him up as he systematically degraded each of us for being too inexperienced to relate to "hard-core druggies. " I felt threatened and so did the other women. Pam was noticeably shaken. She stood up and gestured to the guards. She then dissolved the session for that day. After consulting with several decision makers, she barred the entire federal range from drug group sessions. Pam had anticipated a further hostile reaction from the inmates. We did not consider how they had given voice to their own marginality.

In another session Pam had arrived distraught and tense. She glanced my way and I moved to sit beside her. As it turned out, she was upset about a former boyfriend who had been stalking her for months. He had been sitting in his vehicle outside her home. Now he was following her to work and waiting for her. I offered my place for her to stay; rides with my partner at the time; and emotional support.

We later celebrated her engagement to someone else. She, in turn, was supportive in my recovery from the two relationships spanning the length of my formal study.

Our team-spirit eventually brought us to the Drug Awareness group at a federal penitentiary. The inmates in our drug group at the jail who had been transferred and wished to continue their treatment, initiated this first and only inmate-run group in Canada. We wanted to experience their session first-hand. We felt proud of them. My insider knowledge of some of these inmates helped soften the appearance of this federal prison for me. It was foreboding in its cover story: isolated outside city limits, the grounds of this fortress/dungeon were patrolled and studded with gun towers. It was grim inside the building itself.

This visit coincided with the worse blizzard of the season. The "fellows" warmly acknowledged our effort. Then we were greeted with a great deal of ceremony and pre-planning: a panel set-up (that only we, the visitors, comprised!); tea and snacks; a presentation of their format; and stories of hope, strength and renewal. One inmate showed me pictures of his family. He was very proud of his daughters, but I wondered how much he knew of them. His photos were old and tattered. Numerous inmates we spoke to displayed mottoes borrowed from the twelve-step programs of addiction and recovery. Sam, the soft-spoken "lifer" whom I had had contact with as a volunteer, told a story of recovery, as did a few others. As panel members, we did not exchange our personal stories of recovery, nor were we invited to. A hierarchy had been established wherein disclosure was required of the inmates students only. Disclosure by status has a parallel in classrooms, and in teacher education and research.

Struggling for Clearance in Corrections: Stolen Manuscripts

I had a dream in October 1991 that pre-dated the clearance of my proposal the next month. The dream is about a manuscript that is written by one party and is stolen by another. I now read this dream to mean that a script about others' lives must be shaped interactively. There is a negative undercurrent or warning: The more powerful party—the biographer (or researcher)—can rob another—the biographed (or researchee)—of ownership over his or her own life. The paradox, of course, was that I had been feeling like the biographed in the hands of the jail and its related agency. The dream raised ethical issues regarding who is telling whose story, and whether someone can "own," or steal, another's life-story:

> The manuscript he seized upon dashing through the doors of the bus was mine. I watched with dismay as a large black torso jaunted with athletic precision down a nearby residential street. Wait right there!, I shouted silently, miming the horror I felt as I watched my stolen manuscript vanishing in the distance. No! No! No! I must get it back immediately! I jumped off the bus and, in high heels, pursued my attacker who, with fleeting piracy, remained at a safe distance ahead of me. How dare he? How dare he steal my manuscript, my story, my life? I cried out (Appendix A, October 25, 1991).

In this dream, the biographer and biographed physically struggle over a manuscript. It describes the dilemma of the biographed who takes action to reclaim his rights and voice. The writer-biographer acts similarly. She pursues her attacker in order to recover the text that is her own and that represents her own voice. After this dream, I began implementing the first Creative Writing program in the institution, even though key parties were reluctant. I wanted the opportunity to respond to the inmates who asked for feedback on their writing. I also wanted to "give back" something to the inmates who had so generously shared their stories and time with me. In doing so, I had permitted a dream of mine to inspire me to action. I did not want to be that character on the bus in my dream. The manuscript this character was clutching could have been a reconstructed version of others' life stories. It had become hers by virtue of her own "fleeting piracy" and attempt to "remain at a safe distance ahead of [her participants]". Dreams are instructive to teaching and research.

After preparing my proposal for corrections, I sought its clearance on September 13, 1991. Initially, I did not seek connection with the authorities in my jail setting. Instead I consulted with Kim, the Executive of the agency that supervised my visits to the jail. After submitting my proposal, I had made an appointment with her (the first of several). I wanted to discuss her impression of my proposal. I also wanted to learn what my next step might involve in my becoming an official researcher.

Kim was upfront: She told me not to attempt to seek approval to do my study through the Ministry of Corrections. She was certain that my study would be considered too peripheral and tangential to be of interest. This meant that I should not deal with the authorities in my fieldsite, only her. She thought that my knowledge of the educational literature seemed sufficient, but that my knowledge of the correctional literature itself was not. My knowledge of the correctional literature had been based on my reading of autobiographies and biographies, as well as related academic writing. This was not her focus or interest. She functioned at a remove from the inmates, and their lives, both within her own agency and at the jail itself.

I prepared a second proposal: I read more within my own area of interest in corrections; talked with her researcher-on-site and other professionals; learned about their extensive work in the area of AIDS and condom distribution in prison sites; and re-worked my own perspective. Several weeks later, I forwarded my re-write to Kim. I was informed that my proposal did not fit with her own research directions. Her feedback was vague. I became intensely worried. I wondered if I had somehow misdirected myself in my view of the jail as a school site; in my metaphorical and literal links between teacher education and corrections; and in my narrative inquiry orientation to the jail. Something serious was amiss. I wondered, too, whether there were any untapped and empathetic individuals who would recognize the value of a research study that remains open to discovery. Feeling enclosed without options and no room to grow, I wrote:

> For weeks I have been feeling the weight of anxiety, pressure, and turbulence in learning that I may not get the approval that I require to function as a fully recognized researcher. . . . My perspective on the jail both as an educational site and as a deeply significant metaphor for teacher-learning relationships was considered unimportant. My perspective on convicts' educative autobiographies was also so devalued (Mullen, "Spaces of inquiry," 1991b).

I re-read my proposal: I had included field notes of my recorded visits with inmates in the literacy and drug sessions. The rest of the proposal builds on these stories of experience and links them to both teacher education and corrections; specific methodologies for working with inmates and within the institution itself; and educational findings and outcomes (Appendix B, 1991). I had used topics that covered my professional background and orientation; purpose of the study; ethical orientation and procedures; ethical issues and methods of protection; perspectives of insiders; sources of data and sample writing; and educational and social significance. I had outlined my orientation to the jail as a school environment which fostered teaching-learning relationships within its rehabilitative programs. My emphasis was on inmates' understandings that would provide insight into the educative relationship; wider schooling practices; and the professional development of teachers and educators.

This time I decided to shape my proposal more deliberately to the regulations and expectations of my decision-makers. I had decided to "try my luck" with corrections itself. I submitted my proposal to the Superintendent of the jail through Sally, the Education Coordinator and my informant. I asked Sally my questions, including what I should focus on. She told me all correctional proposals and reports need to attend to ethical considerations. My own would also be read for its ideas regarding the protection of all parties involved: the inmates, teachers and other staff, and the institution itself. She anticipated that the substance of my proposal was a secondary consideration. In my "thank-you" card to Sally, I compared her educated perspective to Pinar's (1988) point of view. He wrote: "We are not the stories we tell as much as we are the modes of relation to others our stories imply, modes of relation implied by what we delete as much as by what we include" (29). She later left a note for me that placed the onus of the official acceptance of my proposal on me, not on her.

Acceptance of the Proposal: My Fairy God-mother

I submitted my proposal in November 1991 to the Superintendent of the jail. It was read and approved by this senior administrator within the same week. Elizabeth is affiliated with the Ministry of Corrections and university departments of education. For me, she re-scripted the image of "warden" as stern and apathetic, and strictly security-oriented. I met her only after she had cleared my proposal at an on-site event on literacy teaching in corrections. Our other interactions at events and seminars were also casual. She obviously meant more to me than I did to her: Elizabeth was my silent but warm and supportive "educator judge" (Foucault 1977, 304). In a single sweep, she had made a decision that created a turning point in my study and life. I had become official on foreign soil and I had been made legitimate at the Institute.

I discovered that Sally was friendly with Elizabeth. Sally was the one who notified me that my proposal had been accepted. I felt a tremendous sense of relief but also disbelief. I asked for details. I was told that the Superintendent approved my request on three grounds: One, I had been functioning as a highly committed and "outstanding" volunteer for months; two, I gained an understanding of the institution, and its programs and people, before I sought clearance as an official researcher; and three; I revealed compassion and patience in my attitude towards the inmates and in my exposure to a variety of situations. Sally was pleased that I had not adopted the route of placing demands on the institution. Other researchers had done this and then disappeared with their results and findings. The institution no longer accepted researchers on site. I also sent Elizabeth a "thank-you" card, but hers had a fairy god-mother on its cover.

During all of these episodes, I was feeling a mixture of frustration and anxiety, relief and elation. I later realized that I had been feeling like an inmate caught in a prison house. I was learning what it feels like to have one's fate determined by gatekeepers who have no direct experience, in most cases, of people, programs or situational dynamics. Yet, they are responsible for them.

This story of my proposal in Corrections illustrates the various forms of contact and communication that such a process can generate. This story has a broader context in my fieldsite: I was never approached by a bureaucrat who asked me any questions; who engaged me on the topic of my research or of the inmates themselves without my initiation; who monitored my progress beyond training unless asked; or who participated directly in the various programs. The exceptions include the Education Coordinators who always made an honest effort to extend guidance and support; a pop-in session with the senior Administator of Programs; and a temporary visit by the Executive of the agency and her assistant. I had spoken with Pam about some of the difficulties that were arising in the drug group with our new and older authoritarian facilitator, and she reported formally. We therefore experienced several visits during our problematic transition from one group facilitator to another. Although the Executive Director appeared stiff and formal, and generally out of her element, her assistant functioned comfortably.

Going Out

The Drug Group: Cigarettes and Sweet Tea

Leslie, the assistant from the agency, joined us one afternoon with a pack of store-bought cigarettes. The guys reached out for regular cigarettes like hungry wolves. Their rolled up ones carried lesser value. Most of the volunteers and visitors smoked in the group. They passed around a pack or two during sessions. This ritual struck me as odd. I could hear echoes of the Institutional Volunteer. She had insisted at the December 1990 orientation that we should not distribute cigarettes, candy, or gum, or anything for that matter. She said that if we were to give one inmate something, we would then have to offer everyone the same and repeat this ritual every visit.

As we talked about issues regarding drug use, mostly everyone (except for me and Pam, the facilitator), smoked and drank sweet tea. We seemed to have access to tea only during the evening sessions for some reason. Even though everyone considered the tea repulsive, we all drank it. Usually, an inmate would offer me a cup, so after a while I would wait for someone to make this kind gesture. The "fellows" also left the most comfortable (meaning not broken) chairs for the women and made certain that the literature was accessible to us. After a while, I forgot about trying to imagine effective ways of accessing the blue button should an emergency arise in the room. I instead came to focus on how to help inmates reclaim their dignity:

> It was a larger group again, and we had to wait patiently for the guys to be brought up from their ranges. They came in droves. I spotted Tom and he remembered my name. We waited for Sid, the musician, who showed up late again with his usual powerful entry, strong anti-drug, pro-community messages, and inspiring music. The guys seemed even more responsive than last time with Sid. One old Jewish man kept shaking his knees and stamping his feet. One black guy started laughing a lot and the rest of us giggled. The same old man was very supportive of Sid, repeating that he was the best he'd ever heard, and that he should sell cassettes of his message. Sid said that he was working out a video with [a major company] to be taken to South America. This may be the same anti-drug video that he's making for high school kids.

The guys were polite about using up Leslie's cigarettes. Tom drew on one as though he'd been deprived. I whispered to Leslie, who was sitting between me and Tom, that their addictive behaviors really showed up in the way that they smoked and handled the ritual itself. I felt foolish saying this to a smoker. One big, black guy (who liked Sid's expression, "crack is black") was practically destroying the empty package of cigarettes, smelling the foil. It was very interesting to watch a drug addict in action. Tom whispered that this guy was looking for drugs, but he must have meant that he was play-acting.

Sid's message was again about dignity. This was the key word in all of his songs and lectures. He wants the guys to work on regaining their dignity and improving their self-concept. "No excuses," he would interject. You can't simply be part of your environment, he said, looking for the easy way out. You need to have the strength to transcend your environment and its negative influences. This is going to be difficult, though, because you guys are strongly inclined to play the "tough guy image", he said. The guys leaned forward, listening with every nerve open and exposed. He was giving it to them straight and they respected him for it, and even loved it. Even the harder ones with tattooed boundaries and tight faces enjoyed Sid's performances.

Sid did his usual: He breezed through a tidy history of cocaine: the opium for the masses, distributed and/or made widely available to sedate and to be seduced into long working hours. The slave drug trade was going strong in South America, he said, turning blacks into slaves and inmates into slaves too. It's no coincidence that crack is appealing to poor blacks. The guys nodded. Tom, a white guy, also nodded. He was considered a dangerous offender requiring mandatory surveillance, he confided in me after the session. Tom also extended a compliment through me to a parole officer at my agency (no longer there) who had helped him over the years (*Prison Journal*, April 22, 1991).

The inmates in the drug group were typically viewed as learners who were being exposed to various destructive facets of addiction. The above transcript recording conveys this impression. I selected it for its teacher-learner dynamics with Sid, the musician-lecturer. At other times the inmates' first-hand knowledge, life-experience, and expertise were relied upon by people in positions of authority. I remember one such occasion (narrated below). It stands out for me as my first exposure to the drug group. It was also one of my few encounters with an inside-out or inmate-as-knower approach to rehabilitation.

I had met with Pam, the facilitator; John, her assistant and ex-convict; and Brian, researcher on a task force. He represented the Ministry of Corrections. Brian told the group that "he was looking for suggestions on how to bring drug awareness to the community. He asked for advice on how to make communities safe from drug trafficking and offenders involved in crime" (*Prison Journal*, March 18, 1991). As inmates made lively suggestions, he wrote them down. This was, to me, a progressive educator-in-action. Inmates mostly emphasized the need for clinics as places to help drug-users, not jails. One inmate announced that most of them should not have been incarcerated because their criminal offenses were drug-related. Tax-payers' money was being seriously mismanaged, they all agreed. They knew the approximate, total annual cost of adult correctional services in Canada in 1989-90. It was $1,745 million ($847 million at the provincial level; $898 million at the federal level) (Correctional Service of Canada 1991).

At this early stage in my exposure to the inmates, it was paradoxical to me that they seemed productive in their ideas, and as responsible citizens. They stressed the importance of children becoming educated about drugs and street life in their homes and schools. One young man pointed out the difficulties of such an approach: "Too much protection of the young leads to chaos. Kids will always feel drawn to what is going on around them. They end up following the crowd regardless of what they are being taught elsewhere. Peer pressure is the worst culprit. I should know."

Afterwards Ralph, an inmate, approached me. I had been functioning, outside of the program, as his client contact volunteer. I commented that he looked as though he was feeling low. He had been very quiet during the session. He pleaded with me, asking how he could raise his spirits. I suggested appropriate reading material and a self-help program on self-esteem where he could work on bettering himself while on the inside. I picked up this theme from Sid who "really gave the place spirit with his guitar-accompanied songs about the need to take responsibility. He's a punk rock 'n roller with a family of his own. He sang that we each create our own existence and that we need to move away from images of toughness that keep us stuck." I was talking with Ralph and feeling uncomfortable. I was learning to listen differently, yet he wanted me to make viable suggestions for him. I wrote that "I feel as though I'm learning to listen all over again, and it's an exciting feeling. In the meantime, Ralph wanted to listen to me" (*Prison Journal*, March 19, 1991). A few days later I learned that I was not alone in this respect:

> The Minister of Education addressed a large group at the Annual Awards Banquet for volunteers in Corrections. He spoke at great length, profusely thanking us volunteers as everyone does. He told a heart warming story about his beginning work with prisoners. He had felt privileged to listen to an inmate whose tale took one hour to tell. The inmate cried while telling his story of "alienation, deprivation and sorrow". The Minister struggled at a loss as to what to say to comfort him, but at the end the man thanked him very appreciatively for his support. The Minister said that he was surprised and so responded, "What for?" The man said, "for listening to me." The message is that learning how to listen is a gift. He thanked us for offering our gifts to people in great need (*Prison Journal*, March 27, 1991).

I felt special. John, the assistant and ex-convict who participated in our meetings regularly, confided in me. He described his program in social services at a community college; his past alcoholism and drug use for 20 years; and his recent potent fantasy. He had spotted a toilet roll in a washroom. This had set in motion vivid fantasies about drug use. I asked John if I could interview him, and later did. He would help me to see that inmates can live successful lives if they permit themselves to function reflectively. This story is told in chapter 4. In it, I include a narrative account of my interviews with various people in the world of corrections.

The Final Visit: Exiting the Mousetrap

On July 3, 1992 my image exited from the monitor for the last time. I felt that I needed distance in order to write my story of the jail. I met with three of my students that last day and received warm hugs from Sally. We spent the evening chatting in her educational office. She invited me to continue corresponding with inmates and to contact her for any information that I might require. We still keep in touch. Pam and I have become even closer friends.

I will not forget Charlie, the university-educated Philippino, whom I saw during my last visit. He and I typically spent our time together talking. Weeks earlier, I had felt anxious about how nothing "official" could be recorded on my institutional sheets. I sought out Sally's advice. I told her about the personal quality of our discussions. She listened to my story and understood his needs. She agreed that I should continue in this vein with him. I was delighted, given her strong views that teachers are not counselors and that we were accountable for how we used our time. I felt free to improvise beyond the parameters of the prison curriculum. I asked Charlie what he found most frustrating about being in jail. He did not hesitate, referring to the glass wall in the visitors' area. It unnecessarily separated him from his new wife and daughter. He connected his feelings to a theoretical point: that it is misleading for people to think that offenders can undergo a process of re-education without contact and communication with loved ones. He told a story: His young daughter had felt proud to present him with her art work earlier that week. Trying eagerly to give it to him, she pushed, and then shoved, it against the glass. When her attempt failed, she destroyed her gift in frustration. He watched the pieces fall to the floor "like sad snowflakes."

When I asked Charlie what he was learning of value in prison, he responded that he could now better understand people. He told me another story. This one was about a "con" (convict) considered to be the toughest on his range and brutal in the "pens" (federal penitentiaries). This man was "really big," "mean" and "booming." Everyone was afraid of him, including the guards who did not get in his way. Charlie said that, when this fellow came back from his sentencing one day he confided to him. The "fellow" was angry because "they" wouldn't let him hug his own daughter. He was apparently denied familial contact, even after many years.

Charlie drew the moral from his own story for me. He said that people in society do not understand how much love and goodness "cons" carry around in their hearts. Inmates are basically good people, he added, who have "slipped up," "been caught," or "led rough lives". They have a lot of love for their families and close friends. If you treat them well and understand this to be a fundamental principle, he said, then you will see the goodness in each of us and within our own community. We do a lot of talking in jail, he added, and are quick to help one another.

I asked Charlie about his future. He said that he will pay with his life for a crime if he is deported to his home country. He was calm on the surface. Then he asked me about my own future. I could not speak.

I was struck by his dignity and sense of self-worth. He would, no doubt, become one of the disappeared. I would remember him for his sensitive words and for what he had taught me.

On my way out of the jail my favorite guard, an Irishman, stopped me on the stairs. He grinned, asking if I wanted to marry a millionaire. He knew one who looked just like him, he said. Then he told me a joke and laughed so hard at the punch-line that I missed it. I left as my own knowing guide. Strangely enough, a part of me felt as though I was leaving home. Another part of me remained behind. The gargoyles that looked down on me seemed to wink. I winked back, moving towards the street.

Chapter 4

Narrative Methodology:
A Personal Account

In this chapter I summarize and comment on questions of method that appear throughout the book. I view methodology itself as an act of creation and a vehicle for constructing meanings. With respect to a narrative methodology, I am focusing on the constructing and reconstructing of a prison culture and imprisoned lives.

I structured this chapter in three parts: an overview and origins of narrative; creativity and narrative method; and reflections on narrative method. In more detail, I open my discussion of narrative methodology with respect to informants. I then consider how methodology itself can be considered as a topic of inquiry. I discuss my personal practical origins as they relate to narrative inquiry, and narrative itself as inquiry. This is followed by the development of my creative research enterprise in detail. I provide a lengthy discussion of my autobiographical and biographical meaning-based data sources. I include an account of my claims of justification of reliability and trustworthiness in the section on my *Dream Journal*. I then relate methodological issues to the jail itself and its shaping influence. I reflect on complications and limitations of narrative method. I also offer strategies for future researchers. Finally, I discuss my perspective on narrative and ethnography as sister methods.

Overview and Origins of Narrative

Informants in My Study

This discussion of methodology begins with reference to informants as a way of building on the last chapter. People can be seen as inmates both in the sense of being trapped in situations and/or stories of constraint as well as being imprisoned for ostensibly (or actually) committing offenses. From my informants I discovered that society, in certain respects, strives to educate inmates but that it also helps imprison them. As inmates, people become caught like spiders in an intricate pattern of miseducative life-experiences. The prison system itself repeats this pattern. Even some of the strongest of those who seek recovery may be defeated. Defeat for the individual can take the form of a cycle of recovery and relapse; success can take the form of reconstructing the self through storytelling.

John, counselor and ex-convict, acted as one of my informants whose own life bridges prisons, schools and communities. I introduced this assistant of our prison drug group earlier. I had spoken casually with John about his life and the life of the addict over the months. Our rapport gave me the incentive first to consult with Pam, the group's facilitator, and then to interview John formally. Seven months subsequent to my work in the jail, I interviewed John in his home. I outlined the intent of the interview in the context of my aim to learn more about his story, family history and background. I also wanted to learn about how our sessions might impact on inmates who are ready to make changes. But I was essentially open to how John saw his experience and interpreted the experience of others in his world. I began our interview by locating us in the familiar context of the drug group at the jail:

> I have the sense that it takes awhile for the guys to absorb the messages that are generated and longer for them to re-live their lives, let alone to re-think who they are. I think it's important to realize that these repercussions can take a lifetime and so maybe it's sometimes hard for us to know to what extent we're impacting on them. Maybe we're impacting on them a lot more deeply than we think; or, maybe we're impacting on them more superficially than we realize. That's why it would be great to *follow up with each of these individuals.*

Track them in terms of where they go once they get shipped out. Keep in touch with them through letter writing, visits. Pam [addictions counselor] and I want to go out to [a federal penitentiary] in the near future. It would be great if you could participate in an inmate-initiated drug group. I see this planned excursion as a form of tracking.

I'm writing to Mark, an inmate who was in the group for months and who has been at [the federal penitentiary of the drug group] for some time and is about to be shipped out to [a pre-release destination], and that's a form of tracking for me as well. I think that it's important because it helps us to understand their transitions as well. A transition might do something to reinforce the addiction or it might do something to let it go, but it impacts on the addiction, I would think, in some way once their community changes and their lives change.

My being here with you is also a form of tracking. I would like to understand the changes in your life that enabled you to become free of 20 years of addiction to deliver yourself to a new lifestyle that includes substance abuse counseling and formal education in human services.

Finally, I am here to gain insight into my own inquiry. . . it's not the correctional field that I'm trying to learn a whole lot about, even though that certainly comes into it. What I'm trying to understand more fully is my own story as it relates to the correctional field. By my own story I mean my teaching and learning experiences, how they've developed over time, and how I'm developing as a professional. One way of gauging all of this is to put myself in a completely new teaching and learning site dealing with a different culture and a new client base, and so on, because such a setting makes stark and bare my own story (transcript, excerpt, 1991, 5-9).

In my attempt to track inmates to recover their broader and deeper life-stories, I created links to four informants (one ex-convict and two correctional professionals); interviewed a wider array of relevant stakeholders in prison education and inmates' lives; and participated in constructing a context beyond the jail setting. This broader context included another provincial jail; a federal penitentiary; correctional conferences, seminars and lectures; and events within the community-based agency itself. My follow-up also included corresponding with known inmates who had been transferred from our rehabilitative programs. My methodology therefore relates to my work both inside and outside the jail within the scope of corrections. My methodology also features the work and perspective I have been developing for a number of years in the field of narrative studies and teacher education. These three areas (consisting of inside the jail; outside the jail; and my research experience within education) together constitute the methodological scope of my discussion.

Methodology as Inquiry

In the social sciences and even qualitative studies, methodology is made to appear as a tidy, transparent and straightforward procedure. We are required, in our proposals for funding, conferences, dissertations and books, and academic papers, to make unambiguous our ways of approaching inquiry. Our practice, which conceives of methodology as somehow separate from inquiry, is stifling. Our field borrows from scientific inquiry to produce the idea that any mode of inquiry is to be accompanied by a set of procedures, techniques and plans for achieving an end. For me, this constitutes an image of authority that constricts possibility. Our habitual practice requires us to think that the more systematic our inquiries are, the more vital will be our stories of practice. We complete the circle of incarceration in our academic lives if we allow unexamined perspectives and practices to continue. This shackles us.

We disrupt this circle, I believe, by exploring, for the purpose of regeneration, how methodological richness is fostered by inventiveness and personal interpretation. The idea is to go beyond the orderliness and regularity of a rehearsed inquiry. Walker (1992) believes that this very spirit captures the current educational research community: "almost as though [certain writers] had been waiting to be freed from the bonds of a narrow scientism, a new generation of curriculum researchers put to use a profusion of innovative methods, a profusion that continues to the present day" (108). I am identifying my own conception of narrative methodology as an unfolding story about a specific culture that the educational researcher both exposes *and* constructs. I give the aesthetic dimensions of my study and self centrality. In practice, I am "creat[ing] the persons [I] write about, just as they create themselves when they engage in storytelling practices" (Denzin 1989, 82). In theory, I am enacting a constructivist doctrine. Eisner (1985) equates construction with knowledge:

> Knowledge is considered by most in our culture as something that one discovers, not something that one makes. Knowledge is out there waiting to be found, and the most useful tool for finding it is science. If there were greater appreciation for the extent to which knowledge is

constructed—something made—there might be a greater likelihood that its aesthetic dimensions would be appreciated (32).

Frye (1963) equates construction with vision:

> . . . you soon realize that there's a difference between the world you're living in and the world you want to live in. The world you want to live in is a human world, not an objective one: it's not an environment but a home: it's not the world you see but the world you build out of what you see (4).

I am equating construction of my life-story and narrative with both knowledge and vision.

Academics strive for certainties and truths, perpetuating a structure that is not only very powerful and primitive but also imprisoning (Lessing 1986). We can aspire to learn more about the very methodology that brings us to others and returns us, transformed, to ourselves. In other words, methodology can be resourced as itself a potential source of experience. Method is central to inquiry, and inquiry itself is an art form evoked as we engage in what it means to study experience and ourselves in the process. As we engage our own mind and senses, we create an experience that defines what and how we perform: ". . . humans do not simply have experience; they have a hand in its creation, and the quality of their creation depends upon the ways they employ their minds. . . . Education itself is a mind-making process" (Eisner 1993, 5).

A present day commonplace in the educational literature is that the researcher should be aware of the diversity of methodologies available. There is virtue in a variety of approaches. It is, moreover, considered liberating to live in a world that is not imprisoned within a single official version of the world which is known through our experiences (Glesne and Peshkin 1992; Eisner 1991; Walker 1992). I have been exposed to a variety of methodologies in my undergraduate and graduate programs in literature and education, respectively. I have also been exposed to diverse methods in my teaching of educational philosophy, cultural foundations and multiculturalism at the university level and in the United States.

These combined methodologies are intended for understanding people's lives and the nature of knowledge and the inmate condition. These include literary and artistic forms of analyses; talking, interviewing, and writing; and descriptions of educational interactions and phenomena. While it is necessary to understand a diversity of methods, it also makes sense that we orient ourselves among self-selected methodologies. As Glesne and Peshkin write, "people tend to adhere to the methodology that is most consonant with their socialized worldview. . . . We are attracted to and shape research problems that match our personal view of seeing and understanding the world" (1992, 9). I come to my chosen methodology with a history of having grown towards it in my field of teacher development within curriculum studies.

Personal Practical Knowledge Origins

In 1988, after two years of searching at the graduate level for an approach to education that promoted personal *and* professional knowing, I arrived at the Personal Practical Knowledge (PPK) center at the Institute. It had been "just around the corner" from me all along, and has since evolved into the Joint Centre for Teacher Development. I took courses on curriculum-making from 1988 to 1991 in order to learn about various methods and tools for engaging reflection. I practiced them all, learning that some are meant to be employed while working alone (storytelling, journal keeping, autobiography and biography, and letter-writing), while others are meant to be used for working with others (storytelling, letter writing, teacher interviews, participant observation) (Connelly and Clandinin 1988b, 1994). At that time I resourced these tools and became immersed in the theory and practice of personal practical knowledge (PPK). Personal practical knowledge is understood as originating in our need for:

> . . . a language that will permit us to talk about ourselves in situations and that will also let us tell stories of our experience. What language will let us do this? The language we, and others, have developed is a language close to experience, a language of affect, morality, and aesthetics. It is a language of images, personal philosophy, rules, practical principles, rhythms, metaphors, and narrative unity (Connelly and Clandinin 1988b, 59).

I felt comfortable with the idea that both the personal and professional images in teachers' classroom experiences need to be inquired into. The spirit was innovative as we sought new ways to talk about educational experience and curriculum. Most of us tackled our accounts of others' teaching, especially in fieldsites with participants, with a deepening appreciation for stories. But the mood sometimes changed when our personal chronicles and journals, which served to launch fuller accounts of our teaching and broader experiences, were also acknowledged as a valid form of knowing. Students felt varying degrees of trepidation, concern and even anger regarding self-disclosure. I noted that the doctoral students in education seemed more rigid and less able to bring their stories of experience to inquiry. The male students appeared to be especially struggling in this respect.

The doctoral students were, generally speaking, resistant and theory-bound. I remember one student in particular who ground the tip of his pencil into the seminar table. He did this as I shared my autobiographical narrative on the very last day. I had begun with my new poem called "Bargain hunting on [a main] Street." In it, the character's mascara (eyelash thickener) mortifies her. It comes loose and falls onto a can like "a cluster of black things/hudd[ling] together/clinging/clinging steadily to their new home." What does not register for her, among other phenomena, is that the mascara is made from life and is tested on life. I had taken a risk with this seminar group by positioning myself as a streetwalker who is self-conscious but not reflective. My purpose of using this poem was to launch my fuller narrative about the ways in which I was seeking reflection through inquiry. In spite of the tension I felt from the grinding pencil, I had found an academic home.

As I became more personally involved with the personal practical knowledge methodology and community, both transformed for me. I was essentially launching myself in the direction of narrative inquiry. I understand narrative to mean the "study of how humans make meaning of experience by endlessly telling and retelling stories about themselves that both refigure the past and create purpose in the future" (Connelly and Clandinin 1988b, 24). I also understand narrative to mean that the situation, as it unfolds during the course of an inquiry, is the focal point of a study of human experience. I have described *situation* in my research as narratives of imprisoned selves. I view these selves interactively and as situated in a jail setting. Eisner (1991) writes that autobiography is an inevitable part of any situation that is described and in all qualitative inquiries that are undertaken. I believe that my personal story resonates as a strong undercurrent to, and as the thematic structure of, my various portraits. And yet, even as I claim that my personal story is a central part of my text, I do not provide a full account of myself anywhere. If anything, I resource this dimension of story mostly as poetry, dream and vignettes about my autobiographical memory, family background and childhood events.

I intend, then, to distinguish between personal practical knowledge and narrative inquiry along these dimensions. I believe that personal practical knowledge is focused on the other (participant/setting) and emergent forms of biographical meaning-based data. On the other hand, narrative inquiry is focused on the self as the vehicle for interacting with the other (participant/setting). Both personal practical knowledge and narrative inquiry recognize how a necessary interaction of both self and other contributes significantly to understanding situations. Once these qualitative researchers have focused on the meaning of various situations personally encountered, then they have essentially configured what is important to know and to share. Both self and situation, then, are understood in relation to one another. Connelly and Clandinin conduct narrative inquiries into the character of teachers' experiences as revealed through their personal accounts (Eisner 1991) of community, collaboration and curriculum-making.

Narrative as Inquiry

Narrative inquiry is a process that respects people and their stories and which uses context to shape and re-shape who we are in relation to others. Narrative inquiry, too, has the potential to imprison us inside our story while we work desperately to create a new story of self to tell and to live. The trend towards theoretical treatments of self, experience and story may turn into a prison in educational research. Narratology is an abstract form of story which "decomposes" or "dehydrates" the very life it strives to capture (communication with Patrick Diamond, November 23, 1993). This is exemplified in the abstractions which are often used of narrative argument and narratology that threaten to nullify story.

Britton (1990) addresses this danger by describing the typical narrative as "diagnostic" and "technically worded." He writes that "the power of narrative had been rediscovered in recent years [and] . . . has sometimes been presented under cover of the term 'narratology' which seems to indicate that a non-narrative, analytic undertaking must be brought in to justify treating story-telling as a serious occupation" (4). Acknowledging that the term *narrative* is sometimes associated with explicit control of the inquiry process at the near expense of the story-line, I think of my text as closer to story. Yet, I intend the term *narrative inquiry* to mean something specific and so to honor it. I defined this term earlier but continue to re-visit and reconstruct it in new writing situations. To me, narrative is a form of inquiry into story, and story itself is potentially a self-reflexive tool of inquiry. Engagement of a storytelling milieu, regardless of whether the context is graduate studies, schools or prisons, takes patience. It also takes a willingness to risk exposure. In my involvement with story, dreams and narrative inquiry, I deal with a "data base" that is slippery, fleeting and fragile. This challenge in my data base is compounded in my fieldsite. It, too, reinforces discontinuity and fragmentation of programs and professional relationships.

I promote the significance of the researcher's own person in curriculum. Connections can be generated to bridge the distance between metaphorical worlds; education and imprisonment; stories of us and them; and theory and practice (Feuerverger and Mullen 1995; Mullen 1994; Mullen and Dalton 1996). Through self-reflexive writing, researchers discover the personal images, metaphors and myths that direct their own research and determine its content. By reconstructing their own telling as part of the research story they are studying and writing about, researchers take the next step in launching deeper, more subjective, and ultimately intersubjective narratives. I elaborate in a following sub-section called, "Telling your own story." As an example, I initially constructed a dream in 1988 as an outgrowth of my journal writing and as a critical educational experience in my childhood. Later I reconstructed this dream. It stood as an account of my incarceration as a child. I incorporated this account of my attic experience into a poem called "Imprisoned selves" (see chapter 3). Reconstructing such accounts draws attention to the phenomenon of experience itself; to the *ever-changing present* (Allport 1965); and to the intellectual activity and growth involved in reconstructing raw experiences (events, desires, impulses) and accounting for "the form in which they first present themselves" (Dewey 1938, 64).

I have configured narrative to mean story *and* inquiry, and described and illustrated it as a process of self-conscious storytelling. This process evolves in the context of transactional story-lines between self and other(s) where the emphasis can be on the self or other. I have constructed a situational narrative of imprisoned selves in community. I use context-oriented journals; letter-writing exchanges with participants; formal interviews and conversations with correctional professionals and ex-convicts; proposal writing to various institutions, and more. My portrait blends autobiographical and biographical sources of meaning-based data. I wanted to develop strategies for learning about others and myself, but I still needed to improvise. Strategies are useful for responding to teaching-learning situations, but they are enriched by a researcher's personal story, sensibilities and artistry. I will begin the next section with those aspects of my study which I consciously systematized and executed promptly, with a range of results.

Meaning-Making, Evidentiality, and Narrative Method

A Creative Research Enterprise

Connecting realms.

As already indicated in this book, I systematically set out to gain entry into a correctional site in late 1990. I wanted to connect a new realm of education to one that was already familiar to me. I wrote about this possibility: "I want to push my own creativity to the limit in my current thesis pre-writing. Perhaps I can accomplish this by connecting the world of education to the world of corrections, and the world of prison stories to my own personal dream narratology and mythology" (Mullen 1991b, *Spaces of inquiry*).

My creative research enterprise was shaped in several ways: I approached the prison scene as material for a study of education and narrative, autobiographical inquiry; I was intellectually open to viewing inmates as storytellers, writers, and teachers and learners; and, I approached the self (and its reconstruction in context) as a primary way for becoming familiar with a new schooling site. I also used the concepts of education and schooling; classroom and curriculum; teacher and learner; and imprisonment and captivity to grapple with understandings of my study, its participants and myself. Connelly and Clandinin (1988b) view "schooling" as a phenomenon that must be enlarged to account for important or special educational experiences that occur outside of the classroom and in the course of one's life.

I anticipated going beyond the usual interpretations, parameters, and constraints of classroom studies in my own study. Among his definitions of creativity, Bruner (1979) includes the element of "effective surprise" in its various forms including "metaphoric effectiveness" (18-19). To him, while surprise is the "unexpected that strikes one with wonder or astonishment," it is rarely bizarre and is, more often than not, obvious: "Effective surprises, . . . seem rather to have the quality of obviousness about them when they occur, producing a shock of recognition following which there is no longer astonishment" (Bruner 1979, 18). Surprise can be brought about through "metaphoric effectiveness," a phenomenon that makes surprise effective by virtue of "connecting domains of experience" or "diverse experiences by the mediation of symbol and metaphor and image" (19-20). In my earlier bodies of work I connected dream to narrative, and to education more widely. In this book, I connect self to prison, and to education more widely. The surprise is that I have used my own story to focus on teaching and learning in a prison.

My assertion, then, that the jail is a schooling and educational site in both a metaphorical and "real" sense; for, I am studying teacher and learner images that are embedded in concrete phenomena, such as formal course work that is supervised by a board of education. In this sense, I interpret Bruner's notion of metaphoric connectedness as relevant to qualitative inquiry. On a meta-level of my curriculum-making, I join unsuspecting domains of education and experience. Another level of my curriculum focuses on the particulars in my fieldsite. I use Schwab's (1969) notion of the quasi-practical as "curriculum in action [that] treats real things: real acts, real teachers, real children, . . . " (35) to present a cast of characters in a variety of situations. I am also embracing Denzin's (1989) notion that we create the people and the worlds we write about. I believe that this tension, expressed as the attempt to capture reality while constructing it, is mediated by my imagination. I construe relationships among images and qualities; create thematic structures; and generate "models of mind and culture" (Eisner 1991, 186).

Focusing and de-focusing spaces of inquiry.

Eisner (1991) argues that selecting a focus for one's research is a task of storytelling. In a course paper, *Spaces of inquiry* (1991b), I wrote about the importance of developing a focus early on. This is one piece of advice that was often extended to me. As I wrote, however, I considered how the *act of de-focusing* my study kept me open to its many possibilities, living and thinking spaces, rifts and shifts, and feelings of wonder, surprise, and amazement. I discovered that the act of staying de-focused can invite a creative, multifocal process. I am therefore asserting that both focusing and de-focusing one's spaces of inquiry, as a creative strategy, can actually enhance insights into educational phenomena and processes. I also had to learn not to panic whenever my chosen focus had blurred and begun to transform or incorporate tensions at odds with itself. My method of inquiry therefore treats these interdependent phenomena as integral parts of my creativity.

Positioning and re-positioning my focus.

The questions of my study shifted and, by doing so, affected my methodology. This process can be viewed as the "inevitable redefinition of purpose that occurs in experiential studies as new, unexpected, and interesting events and stories are revealed" (Clandinin and Connelly 1992). Initially, I framed my study as an inquiry into inmates' biographies and educational stories. As I wrote about my study of the jail, however, I focused on my own story as the guiding force of inquiry. This emerging focus complemented my work on my autobiographical research over a five-year period. I knew that I had been relating my own story to the inmates' as I shaped my understanding in context. I came to see that we shared, in our stories of experience, images of imprisoned selves.

My own ethic of caring is reflected in this final shift to imprisoned selves. I view narrative as an interactive, storytelling process wherein relations of power become diffused and a shared focus of inquiry emerges. This positionality helped me to connect fundamentally with people whose life-experiences are different from my own. Like Sockett (1992), I argue that a "'narrative' approach to moral development, whereby autobiography contributes to understanding, appears particularly congruent with an ethic of care" (555). Relationship, then, becomes defined as a set of relations that takes the researcher beyond simply analyzing other's lives and situations to feeling with another person. The desire to connect is bound up with the desire for education and to be re-educated (Noddings 1992; Sockett 1992).

Sources of reflection and evidentiality.

In my approach to the jail as a study of curriculum and schooling, I made use of various tools of reflection that contributed to my narrative study and creative writing enterprise. My autobiographical tools of reflection have been developing over a longer period of time than my biographical sources. The following list reveals some of the autobiographical and biographical sources that I drew upon in my study. The sources marked with an asterisk (*) are explained in the discussion to follow:

Autobiographical Sources:
- *three journals—on *Prison, Personal Dreams and Daily Reflections*—plus a journal circulated to creative writing students;
- *portraits of creative writing students and stories of teaching-learning encounters;
- correctional newsletter and publication, *The creative writer*;
- autobiographical poetry and stories;
- academic papers containing experiential writing;
- proposal submissions to corrections and education (three);
- *Prison Media Scrapbook*;
- inmate contact sheets and Literacy/Education materials;
- *letters to and from inmates.

Biographical Sources:
- creative writing including poetry, short stories, letters, drawings and art;
- stories of experience told/written in three programs—Drug Awareness, Education/Literacy and Creative Writing;
- prisoners' own autobiographies and stories (some published);
- academic writings on prisoners relating to themes of writing, imprisonment, various abuses and lives analyzed;
- formal interviews and conversations with correctional professionals and ex-convicts.

Journal accounts provided me with a sense of continuity before, during, and after my study of the jail.

Dream Journal. Before undertaking my study of the correctional scene in November 1990, I kept a *Dream Journal* for two years. I used this journal form as the conceptual and methodological basis for earlier research and writing. For this book, I also organized individual dreams thematically, relating them to my autobiographical narrative.

Why did I include dreams in this book? Like Mishler (1990), I am shifting claims for certainty that focus on objective truth—and include validity, reliability, falsifiability and objectivity—to other realms of possibility. He writes that

> reformulating validation as the social discourse through which trustworthiness is established elides such familiar shibboleths as reliability, falsifiability, and objectivity. These criteria are neither trivial nor irrelevant, but they must be understood as particular ways of warranting validity claims rather than as universal, abstract guarantors of truth. They are rhetorical strategies . . . that fit only one model of science—experimental, hypothesis-testing, and so forth. Used as proof criteria, they serve a deviance-sanctioning function, marking off 'good' from 'bad' scientific practice (420).

Narrativists deal with the "rhetoric of exclusion" belonging to traditional, quantitative discourse by developing different kinds of arguments that exhibit their own evidential quality. Bruner (1985, 1986) and Mishler (1990) both formulate ways of knowing that are central to methodological issues involved in qualitative inquiry. Bruner (1985) claims that narrative research "establishes not truth but truth-likeness or verisimilitude" rather than "formal verification procedures and empirical proof" (97). Mishler (1990) asserts that "trustworthiness rather than truth moves us away from objectifying the world to constructing it through our discourse and actions" (420). Other qualitative thinkers (Eisner 1991; Geertz 1988) consider the "question of signature" as a significant criterion of trustworthiness in a writer's identity. As Eisner (1991) writes:

> . . . each person's history, and hence world, is unlike anyone else's. This means that the way in which we see and respond to a situation, and how we interpret what we see, will bear our own signature. This unique signature is not a liability but a way of providing individual insight into a situation (34).

This does not mean that narrativists avoid trying to give accounts for what we assert and how we interpret. On the contrary. For the question of signature involves reflexivity and accountability:

> This appreciation for personal insight as a source of meaning does not provide a license for freedom. Educational critics must provide evidence and reasons. But they reject the assumption that unique interpretation is a conceptual liability in understanding, and they see the insights secured from multiple views as more attractive than the

comforts provided by a belief in a single right one (Eisner 1991, 34-35).

Anderson (1989) asserts that critical ethnographers have attempted to break out of the quantitative paradigm and its methodology. Even so, he believes that they still need to write on "how to systematize reflexivity" "when doing controversial research" (263). Fenstermacher (1994) writes strongly that if sound reasons are systematically and coherently set forth in narrative arguments, then especially useful forms of justification can be made available.

Here I will respond to Fenstermacher's (1994) question, "How do we go about justifying or warranting the claims we make regarding the practical knowledge of teachers?" My concern is with the educational stories of inmates, other participants, and myself. I have systematized my reflexivity into story and provided narrative accounts that carry the mark of my own signature. My personal story has been brought forward and interwoven throughout the entire text. My intersubjective writing enterprise drew upon both my own creative practices as well as the inmates'. I also asked myself what I was feeling in the various situations that I depicted. I took risks in the way that I presented myself. I included the blunders and mistakes that I made in my fieldsite that were a central part of my learning. I exposed myself.

I also provided a central argument that hinged on my understanding of selves as imprisoned both literally and metaphorically, and in both education and prison. I asserted that inmates are inside-out knowers as well as inspiring storytellers and, in some cases, gifted writers. I provided evidence in a variety of forms to establish the credibility of my claim and of my own signature and trustworthiness. Most importantly, I presented inmates' own writings, sharings and discourse in my text. My interpretations of people, events and situations hinge on this meaning-based data. By providing the evidence for my argument, I have given room to my readers to consider my interpretations for themselves.

Meanings have been re-visited which accounts for recurring issues and situations, and an overall cyclic structure. Similarly, I shared and sometimes revised my personal meanings and perceptions with others in corrections and teacher education. I developed relationships with experienced informants at all levels, and interviewed them both formally and informally. Others taught me about the jail and its internal workings as well as about my inmate participants and others.

In summary, my response to Fenstermacher's question involves the following elements:

- internally coherent signature and mark of my organizing consciousness;
- corroboration of my meanings with experienced informants;
- provision of evidence to ground claims in multiple sources;
- reconstruction of meaning in the form of recurring issues and situations, and overall cyclic structure;
- use of my own creative research practice (dream discourse, poetry, journal writing, storytelling) to engage others' writings and meanings;
- context-bound questions that are determined by the inquiry;
- and, participation in three rehabilitative programs over 18-months to gather insights into inmates' stories to yield knowledge that is "context sensitive and particular" (Bruner 1985, 97).

These are the elements that contribute to what I personally mean by the "trustworthiness" of my interpretations. They fit with the portrayal of qualitative inquiry in Glesne and Peshkin's text (1992). These researchers outline ways of demonstrating the trustworthiness of one's "data" and claims. They conclude that, while "both researcher and researched may grow in their interpretations of the phenomena around them," the researcher is limited by certain circumstances and partial states of knowing in social research (147).

My fieldsite has been interpreted through pursuing possibilities, constructing links among them, and by illuminating some of what may exist below the surface. I include illumination, selectivity and relevance as aspects useful to the construction of my teacher development text and personal identity. Eisner (1991) uses the visual arts as a metaphor to think about qualitative inquiry. The phenomenon of seeing as requiring an "enlightened eye" is "important in understanding and improving education" (1991, 1). I use my dreams to this end. They aid me in the construction and reconstruction of my understandings of imprisoned lives. My dream text is one level of selection from among my multitude of dreams; contextually embedded dreams suggest a deeper level. I selected from a multitude of images in order to identify and interpret what I experienced in my fieldsite.

I did not anticipate dreaming about the jail in the context of my study. Perhaps I turned inward, partly as a way of coping with such serious restrictions on what I could know in the prison. I cooperated with this surprise element by selecting relevant dreams; creating meta-themes; incorporating dreams into my story-line about the jail; and devising a personal dream text (see Appendix A). The meta-themes in my dream text are: education, literacy and writing (cryptic messages; Eros and corrections, and violated manuscripts); marginal-insider (college teacher and street researcher); prisoner as criminal (break-and-enter; abduction of children; violence against women; researcher as prisoner), and storytelling (group counseling). Additional dreams that do not appear in my dream text are featured throughout this book.

Prison Journal. I began this journal during my contact with Roger Caron in 1990. I recorded my process of negotiating entry, with an agency, into an unfamiliar fieldsite. I also recorded my sessions in the jail; ongoing involvement with the community-based agency for ex-convicts; and other related correctional activities. Moreover, I recorded my impressions of and reactions to people, including inmates, guards, administrators, facilitators and teachers, and myself.

My entries were often written in a storied form that was sometimes raw and sensory, and sometimes more fully developed. I did not hesitate to openly record my feelings in the first instance, and anticipated patterns of inquiry for further reflection in the second. Stories constitute the experience people live, create and struggle to tell; it is not enough to think that we simply record our experiences as researchers. The stories we are become invoked in our writing (Mullen et al. 1992c). These stories are multifocal. They originate from multiple sources and are simultaneously focused from inside and out, and from backwards and forwards (Clandinin and Connelly 1994). The image of myself as a teacher with a personal history to share grew and became transformed. As I relived and retold my experiences of the jail, I delved into areas that I recorded in a variety of ways.

Daily Reflections Journal. This journal is a day-by-day account of experiences, events and feelings. It overlaps the two other journals. I felt inspired in a summer institute on "Narrative and Teacher Stories" to keep a daily account. I continue to write about experiences that helped me to understand the connections among my prison study, dream-world and childhood. I recorded my reactions to relevant and inspiring readings, community-based events and drug awareness gatherings. With the intention of stimulating writing, reflection on writing, and in-depth representations of experience with the possibility of joint writings, I circulated entries from this journal. I intended them to be read by creative writers and the senior Education Coordinator herself. None of my student-inmates responded by writing journals in turn, except within the context of letter-writing relationships that my personal journals helped stimulate. (Appendix B contains a letter-writing exchange with an inmate-student).

Portraits evolved within the context of the Creative Writing program in which I was trying to find ways of participating in inmates' lives. These portraits are one of my sources of reflection and evidentiality in my text. I developed creative writing portraits (that appear throughout, especially in chapter 3), as I gained a sense of inmates as curriculum-makers and artists. Although I claim that I discovered creativity in the most unlikely place, a jail, I do acknowledge that I played a role, as did Black Hawk, an inmate, to foster a writing forum for those seeking connections and interactions. These interactions affected my teaching and research practice as I came to view some prisoners as artists.

The prison educational culture means that learning is short, temporary, and even disrupted. Such contact is problematic between inmates and professionals whose experience of schooling has broader implications. I created portraits of inmates with some continuity. In a paper presented at the "Teachers Among Teachers" conference, called *Prisoner as artist: A narrative account of a Creative Writing program* (Mullen 1992b), I featured some of these creative writing portraits, and inmates' own writings, as part of my teacher development story. I included my accounts of Black Hawk, the Native American poet and drug addict; Peter, the mentally challenged and sedated short story writer in protective custody; Lloyd, the romantic, and controlling, native musician and artist; Dan, the Canadian-born black RAP youth; Phillip, the romantic poet-francophone; Joe, the imprisoned journal writer; Sammy, the letter writer and formal course enthusiast in protective custody; and Mark, the federal prisoner, drug addict and letter writer.

The themes that follow relate to my inmate-student portraits and much of the book itself. They resonate in my principal metaphor of multiple imprisoned selves that I am attempting to understand contextually. More specifically, these themes are embedded in my image of teacher as marginal-insider and curriculum-maker. I shaped this metaphor and these images by the story I am telling of myself as a young, white professor in teacher education who was a teacher, researcher, writer, co-facilitator and co-ordinator in an all-male jail. These aspects of my teacher development story help to advance my question about how my experience of the jail has influenced me both personally and professionally.

Prisoners and researchers can be viewed as creative writers and curriculum makers. The self can flourish in spite of imprisonment, institutional control and ownership by others of one's story and life. Liberation of marginalized others, of their voice, perspective, and sense of self, can be enhanced through a process of narrative inquiry. In my letter writing exchanges with Mark, the federal prisoner, I discovered that my caring and his loneliness stimulated him to write his chronicle in detail and to pose unanswered questions for himself. He wondered why, for instance, he could not seem to control his temper, or his fists, around guards who were haughty, self-important and unaccountable. I wanted to know Mark's story, even though the violent/compassionate thrust of it challenged my ability to comprehend and my willingness to trust him. In Mark's case, he was sharing his story with me, someone who only knew the prison culture as an outsider. Moreover, he was marginalized, in the sense of being treated as insignificant, by a decision-maker who facilitated the termination of our writing relationship. While I had been consulted, Mark had not even been offered an explanation of the difficult circumstances and subsequent decision. We shared an experience. Because of my vicarious participation in his world and my own feelings about the situation, I, too, felt like an inmate. I related to Mark as someone whose desire for selfhood was creating difficulties in the system.

Eros and education is a familiar concept in the educational literature. It can also be construed as a source of reflection, evidentiality and trustworthiness in teacher education. Schwab (1954) explores the concept of Eros in classroom situations involving a teacher and learners. He defines Eros as involving not just sensual pleasure but also intellectual activity, and not just an object of desire but also a desire for selfhood. It is in this context that Eros involves the "reciprocity of evocation and response which constitutes a genuine interpersonal relationship" (110). I experienced Eros in my relationship to the complex worlds that I am attempting to bring together in my text. I also experienced Eros, as one of the key felt-dimensions of my study, in my contact with the inmates, teachers, guards, colleagues, and others. I believe that narrative inquiry is a process that responds well to the felt-dimensions of a study and to the sensibilities through which consciousness is reawakened. To establish trustworthiness, researchers can share such interpretive processes. This can in turn help to create genuine relationships with both participants and readers.

In the prison programs, teaching and learning sometimes had a sensual, lively quality. The prison milieu is a raw and stark place but it inspired me to connect with others on a personal level. As I see it, my experience of the jail provided me with material for dreams as educational fantasies and impulses. These in turn helped constitute the dynamics in the jail and the stories of recovery most of us shared. Over time, I shared more personally, lowering the mask I had been wearing. My own social pretensions did not fade altogether, however. I derived comfort from my multiple role-playing, especially as "teacher," and always searched for the most effective and literary way to express myself. I also acted mostly in accordance with the image of myself as a "do-gooder." That was how I was perceived by everyone, especially the inmates.

My own acting may have seemed odd given my lack of experience in corrections, with criminology, and street life. The social pretentions of certain inmates struck me as odd in light of their criminal offenses (often repeated), severe addictions, and socially unacceptable aspirations. It was as though these men intuitively knew the power of efficacy: they shared emotionally in the programs in relation to the displeasure they felt towards themselves and others, but not on the ranges or with one another for the most part. For the longest time I felt that as teachers and facilitators, we set the tone, but I realized that the inmates did as well. They also selected certain stories; told them in a particular fashion; and behaved in certain ways. In this sense, we all functioned as partners in curriculum-making, a process that revealed to me two faces of rehabilitation—sincerity (honest disclosure) and seduction (cover stories).

I have translated the idea of Eros and education into my own terms and voice for my study of education in a correctional setting. Schwab (1954) defines Eros as an integral and inevitable part of the educational process, and as the "stuff" of interpersonal relations in university classrooms. To him, dialogue involves conceptual seduction. To me, Eros is present in my growth in this study of myself as a teacher and curriculum-maker and the inmates as partners in curriculum-making. I talked with a teacher educator about our personal encounters with inmates in correctional institutions. We discussed, in this formal interview in 1990, the primal energies of the inmates. These emerged in male-female encounters. Yet, the men mostly acted kindly and even "gentlemanly" towards women in the system, and the women responded warmly. The men and women seemed to understand that we needed to relate to one another by reaching out and by reciprocating human warmth. Certain rituals, such as hand-shaking; mixed gendered seating arrangements; and polite exchanges including farewells, made sense to me in this context. Eros in corrections involves both imprisonment and education.

Eros, in the sense of conceptual persuasion and shared understanding, is a concept that works well for me in my account of the jail, in my life, and in my writing and journaling. As I experience the pleasure of creating and re-creating ideas for my inventive text, I am reminded of Barthes' (1975) erotics of reading and writing.

Ethics and morality constituted ongoing, pressing concerns for me prior to, during, and since conducting work in the jail. The orientation meetings at the agency and jail itself reinforced my concerns. After I had become familiar with my research site, some of them became intensified while others diminished. Whenever I sought out someone for advice either at the jail or the Institute, I was typically concerned about an ethical issue or dilemma. One of my concerns involves measures best taken to protect the anonymity of inmates and talk about my study. Ethical spin-offs involve the inmates' rights concerning copyright regulations and public representation as well as the correctional institution's rights with respect to public representation and anonymity. I was also concerned about the rights of the researcher. As a young female, I had to be vigilant about my safety. This meant becoming aware of my boundaries with respect to potential verbal assaults, and practices of covert and overt manipulation.

I felt particularly sensitive to violations of my privacy. In several instances, violation began to take the form of physical safety. As an example, I dissolved my writing relationship with Sammy, an inmate-student, in December 1992, several months after he had been shipped to a federal penitentiary. He had become unacceptably personal in his letter-writing, aggressively wanting to know about my own life, and determined to have me visit him. Sammy's boundary of privacy was different from my own. He had been making gains within the Creative Writing program in terms of reconnecting with himself through another. Perhaps for this reason, he continued to write to me even after I became anxious and withdrew. His own learning was probably disrupted by the way in which we, the teachers, handled the emerging issues. Sammy had only been told how to behave. His capacity to build healthy educative relationships may have been jeopardized.

Given the sensitivity of my population, I considered the issue of ethics and morality beyond strictly procedural matters. Ethical issues that preoccupied me during the study emerged as four questions:

1. Is it possible for me to live alongside the inmates in order to construct human portraits of them and their stories without being compromised by various individuals and the institution itself?;

2. What is the role of disclosure in sharing stories and writings with inmates (and professionals in corrections) in an interpersonal context? How much can I and should I safely share of myself? How can I be respecting practices of anonymity if I am disclosing aspects of myself and my own family (history/persons)? How much can and should the inmates safely share of themselves?;

3. How does an ethic of caring function with respect to the researcher's and participant's boundaries? At what point am I or they inviting unnecessary risk? How can I go about ending a relationship with particular inmates, if circumstances should warrant this? Is trust a factor in a prison environment? If so, can one trust, or learn to trust, in such a place and encourage others to do so?; and,

4. What is the role of prescriptive and normative thinking in programs of self-expression, educative growth, and personal freedom (the Creative Writing program)? Conversely, what is the role of creative expression in a prescribed curriculum (the Education/Literacy program)?

The concept of marginalized selves relates to my image of multiple imprisoned selves and to my experience as a marginal-insider and curriculum-maker. This concept is also intended to draw attention to offenders' marginality in society (Pinar 1988) and in jail, while acknowledging them as connected knowers on the inside. In the jail I felt that I was neither strictly an insider nor an outsider, so my status was problematic (as I later discuss in "The shaping influence of the institution"). I also feel that particular actions of mine may have sometimes posed difficulties for people. As an example, I may have inadvertently marginalized a few student-inmates in the Creative Writing program by overriding their concerns with my own agenda and that of the institution's. As I see it, I tried to dissipate inmates' marginality to promote their voices, but may have, at times, reinforced their silencing. I have narrated, in chapter 3, how I sometimes unwittingly connived at my participants' disempowerment in the process of establishing meaningful contact. My creative writing portraits generally provide glimpses into the social and personal marginality of inmates.

On writing to connect.

I reflected on my diary entries over a one-year period from January 1991 to 1992. At that time, I wrote that "connection" was a key word that I had been using in my journal entries, without awareness of its repetition and pattern. As I pondered why this might be, I wondered whether my need to connect with others was operating implicitly in my study of seemingly unrelated phenomena, people, processes and stories. In my notes I wrote about connection as a struggle both conceptually and emotionally. I wrote about my "struggle to relate to the inmates and their own, often raw and unpolished, educative tales" and of my growth as I was "reminded of certain facets, and alternative perspectives on, my own narrative" (*Prison Journal,* January 28, 1992).

I also constructed images of education in corrections as I internalized my new culture:

> . . . feeling struck by the number of times certain words claim space in my writing, words such as struggle, survival, love and compassion, dreams, hope/despair, freedom, addiction/dependency, family and future. These are words that I hear the inmates using and these are the same words that fill my own conversational space, storytelling and narrative (*Prison Journal,* January 28, 1992).

Goffman (1961) had a similar experience in his work with mentally challenged patients. He believes that all groups of people, including mentally challenged patients and prisoners, develop a life that makes sense to outsiders. This life becomes meaningful and even "normal" to outsiders once they become close to it. The key, though, is to become involved in the new culture by "submitting oneself to its way of life" (x). I, too, believed that I would need to become a student of prison and community life in order to experience the social world of inmates and to feel the impact of this on my own development.

I write compulsively as a way of deepening my experience of a correctional site that I am interpreting in educational terms and for which I am using the lenses of autobiographical and biographical inquiry. My three journals (*Daily Reflections, Prison* and *Dream*) help me to keep track of the development of my ideas and images in three correctional programs. My *Daily Reflections Journal* overlapped with the journal that I wrote and circulated to my inmate-students (separately from the letters). This shared writing reflects my ethical position on disclosure. Disclosure, as a two-way interactive process, has its own particular dangers and risks in a prison setting, but so does a one-way, student-to-teacher, process of journaling in regular classrooms. I worked to resolve this conundrum by writing to only a few of my students without identifying my place of residence, study, work, and the people I know. This network of writing relationships was formed within a regulated system of documentation, feedback and input. It was monitored by the senior Education Coordinator.

I expect that I will never really know the prison scene. My intent is not to cage the prison culture for display because it is, like culture itself, a loose, slippery concept. This position has implications for the study of culture in different settings. Van Maanen (1988) writes that

> Culture is neither person nor monolith. Nor, of course, is it tangible. A culture is expressed (or constituted) only by the actions and words of its members and must be interpreted by, not given to, a fieldworker. To portray culture requires the fieldworker to hear, to see, and, most important for our purposes, to write of what was presumably witnessed and understood during a stay in the field. Culture is not itself visible, but is made visible only through its representation (3).

But, as I assert this, I immediately reflect on how much I learned about my educational site from interactions with inmates, guards, facilitators, teachers and coordinators, and administrators. I also derived value from my reading of literature that represents several domains and from my autobiographical writing. And yet, researchers can, at best, only live as marginal-insiders. As insider-outsiders, researchers need to generate as many stories as possible in their schooling sites. Although I may never really know the prison scene, or at least know only certain facets of it, I have proceeded as though I could learn something significant about my site.

I circulated entries, in the form of journal writing, to my Creative Writing students on a regular basis. The only person who responded directly to them was Sally, the Education Coordinator. In one of her notes, she called herself "mother" and wrote that I was devoting a lot of time to letter writing and providing much detail in them. Her concern was that I was going to be disappointed by a typical lack of response from the inmates themselves. In my letters, written as journal entries, I discussed aspects of my life outside corrections. Examples include stories about the struggle of writing on an antiquated computer (since replaced); the joys of Sunday shopping; the power of collegial thinking and bonding with college-level students; and our visit to the inmate-run drug group at a federal penitentiary. My journals are written as a series of upbeat, positive tributes to life in community. This form of writing was a kind of experiment in self-reporting to the prison community of writers.

As a more specific attempt at letter-writing, I corresponded with five inmates. This experiment proved to be more successful, dynamic and educative for us all. Each of my exchanges was unique. Some of these were more impressive than others because of the longer span of time covered and intensity of communication. I begin here with my brief exchanges with a few of the inmate-writers:

Roger. As described in "Go-girl's prelude," my initial contact was with Roger Caron, celebrity writer, from November to December 1990. I wrote him two letters of appreciation about his novels and he telephoned me a number of times.

Adrian. Adrian, my student-inmate, wrote a series of notes, rather than full letters, to me. He focused on his progress with the Creative Writing program. From March to July 1992 he solicited feedback and evaluations on his writing from me. One such note, dated July 16, 1992, reads:

> Dear Carol,
> Hi! I want to take this opportunity to thank the Creative Writing program for allowing me to benefit from participating. I would enjoy hearing about the most recent writing I did in terms of an evaluation by you. So far my ability to be creative and articulate has been greatly enhanced. I'm looking forward to your response.
> Thanks again,
> Adrian

Adrian also wrote me one long note. It conveys a very different picture. It is a startling portrayal of his health problems and power struggles with corrections regarding his physical needs and its lack of compassion. Here is an excerpt:

> I have been clinically disabled for about six years . . . The illness I
> have causes a form of convulsive seizures. For the past 15 months I've
> been at the [jail] as an inmate . . . I was examined by an understudy
> neurologist who did the finger-touch-nose test on me and without
> witnessing one of my seizures decided to concur with the [jail's]
> request to have the oxygen therapy stopped. . . When the seizure starts
> I stagger badly and have slurred speech, so when I'm not recovered I
> still stagger, etc. I need the full 20 minutes of oxygen therapy in order
> to recover otherwise I am stuck on a HCU stretcher or on the floor for
> two to three hours until I recover. The time I spend collapsed can be
> really reduced by the oxygen therapy. . . . Adrian.

I spoke with Sally regarding Adrian's life-threatening condition
and the assistance he needed to manage his illness. She responded
that he was an incessant complainer whose hyperchondriasis had
exhausted the system. Still not satisfied, I requested permission to
have Adrian's letter appear in our Creative Writing newsletter. My
permission was denied. I felt helpless and still do. I remember the
slowness of this man, only in his early thirties, and his pasty white
face and bright red cheeks.

Sear. My third contact was with Sear, the musician and writer of
the poem, "Mr. Jones (to the moon)." He wrote once and I did not
respond. The Education Coordinator had indicated to me that Sear was
without an address. He had been released from his new location
shortly after writing to me that he had been

> . . . writing lyrics constantly since we last spoke, but at the moment
> they are in holding at personals and I can't seem to get them, as soon as
> I do I'll send you a couple I think you'll like. It seems to me that I
> hadn't properly thanked you for what you did for me. Besides the fact
> that seeing a pretty lady in jail is a bonus, you also made me feel good
> about myself at a time when I felt less than perfect. Thank you very
> much!! It has been a very long time since anyone thought that what I
> had to say was worth listening to, let alone printing something I wrote.
> (Thank God they get to see your typed version and not the handwritten
> mess that I'm capable of) . . . I can't think of anything else to say that
> wouldn't be classified as absolute drivel . . . It would be great to see
> you again, so if you're in the area, and have the time . . . Sear.

Sammy. In my book, I have represented my writing relationships with both Sammy and Mark. I have discussed the personal, ethical issues that arose from each of these communications. I have also developed themes that relate to this subject of discussion, such as the politics of story ownership; joint narratives of experience and education; stories of childhood; and termination of correspondence.

To begin: Sammy would hand me notes in class. I indicated that I could not accept these notes until he forwarded them to me through the Education Coordinator. In his first note, dated December 6, 1991, he searched for words and settled on outlining his lessons in progress. He then asked me to write to him about myself. His desire to solicit a personal exchange seemed to be the point of the letter. The rest of it inspired me to establish a formal writing relationship for the purpose of creating a joint narrative. Here is an excerpt from that first letter that encouraged me in this direction:

> I guess I could tell you that I was born in Nova Scotia. I have two sisters, one older than me. I lived in Nova Scotia until I was 19 years old. From there I moved to the west coast and worked out there. I have one little girl. I went back to Nova Scotia about three years ago to visit everyone. I left Nova Scotia to go back to B.C., stopped [here], and look where it got me. I should have kept on going. But then if I did I would never got to meet you . . . I hope to hear from you soon. Sammy.

Our letter writing appeared in *The creative writer* which was one productive outcome of our exchanges over the months. A more subtle outcome, about the personal learning value of the Creative Writing program, had been hinted at by Sammy: "I did learn something about my life when I was a kid after all . . . . Doing this program is helping me to think back and realize that I wasn't alone in my life. I would like to thank you for that" (Appendix B, 1992). The other outcome was less than satisfactory. As already indicated elsewhere, the Education Coordinator and I agreed to terminate my writing relationship with Sammy. Sammy had, we believed, ignored our warnings and persevered in trying to establish intimate, personal contact with me. Our situation was not atypical. Knowing that such complications do exist did not make it any easier for me or any less problematic both conceptually and emotionally.

Sammy and I had deepened our narratives over time by establishing a focus and, through it, common links. We had both thought about how to present ourselves and how to make ourselves relevant to one another. We began by sketching our daily routines. We moved to our family backgrounds. The idea was to use such sketches to arrive at ways of understanding how we had each educated ourselves during the course of our lives. Sammy wrote of his routine that "you can keep yourself very busy here if you put your mind to the programs which include the writing program for me." He then elaborated on other aspects of his routine: "I do homework Monday to Friday from 8:30 a.m. to 3:00 p.m. Then yard until supper at 4:30 p.m. and then gym every night from 6:00 p.m. until 10:30 p.m. On the weekend, the yard is open from 9:00 a.m. until 11:00 a.m. in the morning and from 1:00 p.m. until 5:00 p.m., and then we have the gym at night. I am working out, getting into shape. I don't know what for" (May 7, 1992).

I produced an antiphonal account of our exchanges for the newsletter (Appendix B, "*Sammy Larson, Letter Writer*"). In December 1991, I had suggested that we focus on our formal schooling experiences both inside and outside the classroom. What we accomplished, though, was to resource our imaginations in shaping our stories of our learning in life. In his letters, Sammy wrote about the "fields and woods" of Nova Scotia; the ponies and horses for riding; the "big tree house [built] that summer, way back in the woods" [where] nothing could get us." He asked me, "Have you ever found a place that you could call your own?" While chasing a rabbit, he had found his: "a small little green spot in the middle of trees . . . Whenever I wanted to be alone, what was where I would go."

In writing to Sammy, I responded that I had found a place of my own in an urban landscape, rather than woods, as a young girl. I recalled the "hidden worlds and riches of the red library on wheels that no other children took advantage of on our street" (Appendix B). He had inspired me to look back at what had brought me a sense of peace in my childhood. I told the fuller story to Sammy of which an excerpt appears in the newsletter.

In his stories of formal schooling, Sammy wrote about the hockey team he played on in grade eight. He associated its social rejection, because they had played too roughly against other teams, with personal problems. The team "took the playoffs" and Sammy "won the trophy for best defense man that year," but "troubles and problems were piling up that year." As he explained, "this was the year that our Mom started to get really sick. So I stayed home from school sometimes to help her . . . she had breast cancer . . . and had one breast removed . . .

After that I never could have a long relationship with anyone . . . An old man who lived near us told me one day that you could feel yourself and be anywhere you wanted to be . . . I hope that you understand my feeling of not being alone . . . I am telling you things about me that I have not told anyone before" (letter, June 12, 1991).

Much of my own writing focused on the high value I have always placed on formal schooling. Sammy would often refer to my "bookish" ways, comparing me to his school teachers and one studious sister. But, eventually, I broadened this emphasis beyond my early years to look at the attitude I had developed in my relationships with men. It felt like a confession when I wrote this to Sammy: "I remember [Ron], a disinterested student and boyfriend, whom I dated for about six months. He never showed any interest in me particularly until I broke up with him. I learned the bad habit at an early age to instill drama and independence of mind and spirit in a relationship in order to elicit interest . . . I went through a long five-year relationship in my late teens and earlier twenties before I began to value myself . . . and it was an inner battle that rocked my very foundations" (letter, April 18, 1992). I had already provided the context, over the months, about my achievements in school. I came to see that:

> it was much easier for me to study and do well in high school than to learn to value myself as a person and woman. This has always been the case for me. The curriculum of school omits the most critical education of all—the ability to learn to respect one's own person and values, and how to enact our values most meaningfully in the world (Mullen, April 18, 1992).

Through his prison native brotherhood socials, Sammy may have found a way to travel to that childhood place he called his own. This was the same place that, through his connection to his surroundings, he had never felt alone in. Sammy told me that he was "reliving his past" with the help of our writing exchanges. In fact, he suggested that we convey this quality in the title of the newsletter. He suggested *From the past, The act of growing up,* or *To re-live my past.* I appreciated his suggestions and felt that they were all potentially good titles. However, I did not wish to specify a theme in case our inmate-writers felt restricted, deciding then to re-shape or even withhold material. I therefore opted for *The Creative Writer*.

Mark. I wrote the first letter to Mark on June 4, 1991 in response to Pam's request. After Mark had been transferred to a federal penitentiary to serve a lengthy sentence, Pam approached me. She said that her agency aspired to make successful their mail-bag (pen-pal) option for volunteers and inmates alike. She continued, saying that Mark and I had developed a pleasant rapport in her drug group and that I could function as his support for a period of time. I agreed with enthusiasm as I was looking to establish as many narrative inquiry channels into inmates' lives as possible.

In my letters to Mark, I asked him to describe his educational experiences both inside and outside prison life. I also shared my personal dreams as they helped me to construct my understanding of the prison culture. Both of my orientations proved ethically complex for Pam. I had asked her to be my reader of all letters. One day she phoned to say that my writing was too personal and that she was going to terminate our correspondence. As discussed earlier, I was not given room to negotiate other possibilities.

Before I shared my recorded dreams about prison life with Mark, I had outlined my theoretical view. Here is an excerpt: "I've been dreaming of prison (and other institutionalized) settings. Maybe I can share relevant dreams with you. I view my dreams as texts to be analyzed in the company of others" (June 4, 1991). I had sent Mark, with his written consent, selections of prison dreams from my official dream text, connecting them to educational themes.

Mark responded well to my request to learn about his educational concepts and practices in a jail setting. He first told me about a test that every prisoner is obligated to write upon reception. He said that: "it simply tells what academic level one is at. When I got my results, the teacher told me that I shouldn't be in jail! I'm at a post-secondary level, and he (teacher) said if it hadn't been a fairly new test here, he'd of been certain I'd cheated. The spelling was perfect, and the comprehension was the highest mark anyone has gotten so far!" (letter, June 20, 1991). Mark then spun out the irony of his results: "But! Why do so many good things in life have a 'but' tied to them? Actually, I'm over dramatizing all of this. All that comes of the high marks is that I don't fall into their 'need to' category, so I can't go to school here. All I can do are correspondence courses, which are from the [jail]" (letter, June 20, 1991). Like gifted learners in schools, Mark knew too much to learn at that site.

In this letter and others, Mark used the metaphors of thick fog and red tape to discuss his "search for answers" in a place where "red tape keeps dangling in front of your eyes." Part of his query surrounded the reading/scrutiny of our correspondence by Pam; the photocopying of our contents; and her role in circulating our letters to each other. This was the system of correspondence as it existed for all volunteers and inmates. But Mark protested. He said that his own rights were being violated on the outside, by us, and upheld on the outside, by the prison authorities. As far as he was concerned, I was partly responsible for this mess:

> Let me correct you on one point and the [agency] as well. Correspondence to cons in federal institutions is not to be read unless there is reason to suspect something pertinent may be in the correspondence. This right was granted to us (cons) some years ago, and to my knowledge, has never been taken away, nor altered. Your letter writing is most warmly received by myself, and I truly hope we'll continue to correspond, even under such strict conditions. I just find it ironic that I, a convict in a pen, am in even one way, finding my privacy more protected by my 'prisoner's rights' than the [agency], let alone your rights, a person of the 'Free Society.' I'm really disappointed in you and them!! (letter, June 1991).

Mark taught me that my support had been extended to him through a network of governing parties. My own role as the agency's representative was integral to this administrative machine. He had revealed to me a powerful instance of Foucault's (1977) image of the "Panopticon" as well as Goffman's "total institutions," both of which impact on individual identity. Goffman (1961) writes about the "kinds of loss and mortification" that the inmate must undergo, such as being subjected to admission procedures. Mark provided a moving account of how such losses inpact on the individual inmate. In my fulfillment of all of Pam's requests, I had, in Mark's mind, advocated a system that conflicted with his fundamental rights. I empathized with Mark, and the position he upheld and articulated. I never got to tell Mark that I was also motivated to protect my right to remain anonymous. In this instance, I had involved the presence of a third party.

On reading to connect.
    I became immersed in a diversity of sources of prison literature over a three-year period. I wanted to learn as much as possible about

prisoners' stories of experience from others' perspectives. This included my learning about relevant texts as a form of study. The emphasis in my research story is on the study of people and their imprisoned lives. The texts I have chosen are meant to reflect the meaning-making process that a study of experience, and its representation, inspires. If I had wanted to conduct a social inquiry into prisoners' lives using text only, I would have eliminated the fieldwork phase and probably chosen a different methodology. This is the approach undertaken by Davies (1990), a sociologist who uses theory only "in understanding the forms that prison writing takes, its content and how the prison experience might be read" (3).

On interviewing to connect.

I understand the interview to be a form of conversation that respects how human beings make meaning of their experience. By interpreting their experiences in narrative form from an early age, people both live and produce stories during their lives (Mishler 1986). I view the interview as a metaphor of storytelling that invites both parties, interviewer and interviewee, to communicate meaning. I also view narrative itself as a

> basic metaphor for understanding human experience and behavior . . . Because we all create our own sustained mind fictions, narrative is not just an aesthetic invention used only by artists to control, manipulate and order events in books. Everyone makes up stories about themselves and others in order to live. By constructing our narratives we make sense of our world and our place in it. However, by considering what was and what might be we are then better able to change what is. Through self-narratives we can devise and consider other alternative, possible realities. If we are to control and direct our own thinking and teaching lives, both of which are fictive processes, we must begin by becoming more conscious of them (Diamond 1991, 90).

The flow of conversation is somewhat unpredictable in a narrative inquiry forum where stories are not suppressed or rejected. It is the job of the researcher to utilize her creativity before, during and after the interview itself. Or, better yet, I think that she must be as self-conscious as possible about how interviewing functions as a process, or movement, throughout the research phase. She must become alert to all of life as a potential learning experience which embodies what she wants to know about. I see myself as turning storytelling into inquiry on one level. On another level, I communicate inquiry itself, in this written text, as a form of storytelling. To me, the extent to which the narrativist performs these interpretive processes well is the degree to which she is successful.

The interview can take many forms in qualitative research. At one end of the continuum are the "tightly structured, survey interviews with preset, standardized, normally closed questions. At the other end of the continuum are open-ended, apparently unstructured, anthropological interviews that might be seen . . . as friendly conversations" (Seidman 1991, 9). There are different types of conversation. Paradigms of traditional interviewing practice conflict with conversations that validate people's (especially women's) subjective experiences (Oakley 1981). My own goal, then was not to obtain information by approaching participants as instruments of data collection. Like Mishler (1986), Oakley (1981), and others, I searched for an alternative approach to standard research practice. I used the interview as an opportunity to generate stories about participants' life-experiences in specific contexts. My interest was in how people saw imprisonment and education as somehow linked in their life-experiences.

A general assumption of narrative inquiry is that individuals construct and reconstruct meaning by telling stories, and that profound relationships exist among story and life, experience and education (Connelly and Clandinin 1990; Diamond 1991; Mishler 1986). I am making the assumption that both interviewer and interviewee are to be treated as personalized participants in the research process. This is contrary to the emphasis on detachment, objectivity and hierarchy in the standard paradigm of the social sciences. Such a paradigm is carefully reproduced by Oakley (1981) for the purpose of critical, feminist discussion and transformation. However, even within the same framework of interviewing that views story and narrative as fundamental, differences exist.

Mishler (1986), for example, looks at "interviewee responses as narrative accounts or stories" and at "narrative analysis" as an approach to discourse and meaning. He uses the interview to direct attention to the "linguistic and social rules that structure and guide meaningful talk between speakers" (67). I look at stories as joint narratives. Such stories are generated interactively as the researcher invests her personal identity in the relationship (Oakley 1981). In other words, my focus was not exclusively on the interviewee, but rather on the interactive narrative. I assume, as does Mishler (1986), that stories are constructed, or at least affected, by the company we keep. I also believe that disclosure should not be exclusively required of one party; also, questions and expectations should not be the exclusive domain of the researcher. The ethic of caring is easier to maintain for the researcher if she is requiring of the interviewee what she is prepared to give herself: feelings of empathy and compassion, and gestures of constructive feedback and input.

I did not adopt a single method for interviewing. Instead, I combined various approaches, grounding them situationally and experientially, and inventing them as I went along. At times, I attempted in-depth life-history interviewing; sometimes, I strove to understand participants' life-experiences in specific contexts; at other times, I engaged my participants in friendly, open-ended conversations. Unlike Seidman (1991) who focuses on "in-depth, phenomenologically based interviewing" by using a three-interview series with participants, I functioned, at least theoretically, much more intuitively and spontaneously. I asked questions and offered insights, without their awareness, while engaging in friendly conversations.

Since I had spent 10 months in my fieldsite without clearance as a researcher, I had to learn how to improvise with those around me. I gained insights into people's stories of imprisonment and education by inferring connections. I thought, too, that I might learn about such stories if I approached others to understand what they did; what they saw and felt; and how they had come to be in a prison. I had re-birthed myself as a learner and listener. It seemed to follow that the time I spent in my fieldsite became a kind of open-ended interview.

I conducted numerous interviews with people representing the various facets of my study. From 1990 to 1993 I talked with and, in some cases, taped conversations with various correctional people, staff and professionals: an addictions counselor/ex-convict; anonymous addictions counselor/recovering addict; recidivist/ex-convict; published autobiographer/ex-convict; parole officer; drug awareness facilitator; Education Coordinator; prison AIDS researcher; and, finally, a doctoral student and professor studying organized events in a federal penitentiary (see Figure 2 for a list). I also talked casually, and over a period of time, with correctional officers (guards/screws); visiting teachers; lecturers and seminar leaders; and family members who experienced incarceration either directly or indirectly as support.

I cannot provide numbers to represent my informal interviews, as they were ongoing and unstructured, even as they are today.

I turn now to provide mini-portraits of those whom I formally interviewed in order to add to those few details provided thus far:

John Murray. I opened this chapter (and concluded chapter 3), with references to John. John was one of my interviewees and informants. I was exposed to him in both a personal and professional context as we communicated in his home as well as in the drug group for months. I produced a transcript based on our August 29, 1991 interview. I forwarded a copy to John. He read it and approved of my public use of our material.

My informant lived in a drug-infested community in the downtown core. He met me at the subway and walked me back two hours later. I wrote that "His apartment has much character: a few pictures of a special female friend; a refinished wooden table rescued from the garbage; a set of miniature vintage cars; and a computer" (1). I brought cake and he served coffee.

John was a very thin man, prematurely wrinkled. He looked as though he had barely survived a serious illness. His inner strength revealed itself in his storytelling about his personal changes and insights into human life. For the first while, he painted a general portrait of inmates around issues of intimidation (soft drug users who are intimidated by hard drug users); "conning" (inmates who participate in programs just to "score big" with the courts); and "staying straight" (it is easier for an addict in jail because, without money, drugs are less accessible).

I was ready to hear John tell his personal story. I had heard some of it in the drug group and he had heard from me. I had encouraged him beforehand to use our interview as an opportunity to build on his own story. He began slowly: he referred to the low success rate among addicts and the disappointing number of success stories available. He said that "it's a very very low number. It's hard to say. When I took my life abstinence program at [delete], out of 12 people who went through the program, I'm the only person that has come out of it straight that I know of, and I've kept in touch with four of the guys on a regular basis and they're still using" (5-6). His emphasis was educational. Recovery must be accompanied by growth for the addict, otherwise relapse is more likely: "If you don't change and you just drop the addiction, there's no growth, so other than the fact, odds are hey, you may just replace the addiction with something else. Maybe it's over-eating, maybe it's anything you do in excess. It is not healthy" (transcript, 7). The addiction replacement phenomenon shows that the drug education program is misconceived: it teaches how to get off drugs, not a more holistic curricula of health and care for oneself. This is not healthy.

John told the story of his relationship with his mother. He saw his mother as a recovered addict, but not as an educated person who has made fundamental changes in her life. As he explained, she was someone who had "gotten rid of her addiction but there's a lot of underlying work that hasn't been done to further her growth and, until that happens, I guess that I'll just have to wait" (12). John was referring to how his mother had not returned phone calls even though they had been reunited. They had had no contact for 38 years.

John told his personal story in bits and pieces, and usually in the context of others' lives. He lived for 20 years as a substance abuse addict and "hit bottom" when he faced the reality of needing to steal from his best friend to get high. That was, he said, his catalyst for quitting. The rest of what follows, regarding John's story, is what I have culled from his discussion of situations involving other people.

Following in his mother's footsteps, John carried on the personal family history of addiction. His mother lived in a Canadian city as an alcoholic 40 years ago. John found himself in the same area, in the 60s, but as a heroin addict. His mother had recently become sober; is affiliated with Alcoholics Anonymous; and is re-married. She lives in another city and John lives alone. She had ceased communicating with him again. This surprised John as there was no apparent reason for her withdrawal and, moreover, their "instant bond" had felt mutual. But, he interpreted this sad turn of events as a positive sign of his success in recovery. Over a longer span of time, he had grown by learning how to deal with the low-self esteem that he attributes to rejection by women. He teaches how people can make significant changes in their attitudes toward others and to respect values, actions and decisions that may not coincide with their own:

> That's part of my growth in that before I could never handle rejection because I was rejected by my mother when I was very young. As I got on in the addiction, rejection was really a focal point. I would always push people away from me before they would push me away from them. I would always destroy relationships and I would set out to do that on purpose. It all comes back to being rejected when I was young

and then when I get out of the addictions something changed. Now I want a relationship. If I'm rejected, it's not the end of the world and I can move on or I can grow from it. I have a close friend of mine . . . and it was really hard to let her go . . . my old way would have been either to lash out at her and try and hurt her or to completely drop all contact . . . but I really value her friendship (transcript, 13).

My interviewee/informat even managed to learn and grow from his years spent in the psychiatric wards of hospitals: "I didn't know it at the time, but I would take something away, some knowledge that would help me, some little insight into myself to give me strength" (20). He then told a story of his psychiatrist who, at the time, was 36 years old. He had gone back to school for training at a late age. It had really hit home to John that he could make a change if he wanted to. But, as he said, "at the time I didn't want to—I did, but I didn't, I didn't want to put the effort into it, it was like a wish. And this man and the changes that he made always stuck with me" (20).

John had run away from home in the 60s when he was 14 years old. He came to the big city, got into trouble, and went back to his small home town. When he skipped school, the principal offered him a deal: if he could find a job, he did not need to return to school. He conned the principal, and began robbing stores. At 15 years of age he was re-located to a juvenile residence; became familiar with probation officers and how to manipulate them with impressive cover stories; and ended up doing time, periodically throughout his adult life, in prison. He said that he used his intelligence in prison to make friends with the people in power. He would watch for who "ran the show," which wasn't necessarily obvious to a newcomer, he added. He then sought protection from a gang leader, from the streets, on his range.

Basing his assessment on personal experience, John felt that incarceration is not the answer. He said that the sickness within people is actually a learned behavior, not the exception to who we are in society. We break the cycle, said John, by forgiving and understanding "where it's coming from and working with it, but as long as the prison system, as long as those people are the scum of the prison system, it's not going to be broken . . . it doesn't matter to me where the person is within the system, they're just a person . . . like I've done some shitty things in my time, but that doesn't make me a bad person" (23).

When I asked John if we should continue with prison rehabilitative programs given that the statistic on recovery is low and on recidivism is high, he was encouraging. He said that programs give inmates room to air their personal feelings. It is necessary to expose inmates to more responsible attitudes; to involve them in discussion around messages of recovery, even if they seem resistant or apathetic at the time; to get them off the ranges and away from the "closed society"; and to give them a safe place to be where they can relax somewhat. We agreed that an observer can help to generate alternatives for the inmates by resourcing the inmates themselves. Observers in this interactive setting make distinctions between those who blame the system and those who are willing to take responsibility for their actions. As I said to John, inmates will need to both discover and develop the reflective part of themselves in order to imagine how to better their lives. The following exchange highlights the importance of storytelling as self-affirmation and positive change. This is the sort of exchange that is encouraged in drug groups:

> *John:* I had a friend. He overdosed on heroin and two of us, we walked about 10 hours around the room and just kept walking, get him onto his feet, and brought him out of it. We went out and got something to eat and when we come back he was laying in the corner dead with a needle in his arm. So when he come out of it he just went right back. He killed himself. And I think that you'll start out this way, once you lose your self-esteem then, yeah, you almost have a death wish because life doesn't have any appeal and that's why to druggies and dealers life doesn't mean anything, there's no value on a life other than to use and abuse it and that's why people will rip other people off, their own friends because there's no value.
>
> *Carol:* Some of this may go back to your very early childhood when you were abandoned and rejected, and you perhaps felt that you weren't worth anything to anyone, let alone to yourself. Is that all part of it? So, it's been one life-long curriculum of building your self-esteem and believing in yourself?
>
> *John:* Yeah, and it's all happened over the last six years.
>
> *Carol:* I can't believe how far you've come.
>
> *John:* Yeah, neither can I (8-9, 18).

Jenny Smart. I have already referred, in this chapter, to my interview with this University of Toronto teacher educator. I have decided to use a pseudonym for her as I perceive her to be a deeply private person. Jenny, for example, confided to me that she viewed her inmate-participants' needs to be "based on a real human level" whereas her own were "somewhat abstract" (2). Jenny also commented that it was not her intention to write about her more direct experiences of having been inside a prison, talking with inmates. She said that it had been a conscious choice for her not to expose herself.

The focus here is on my understanding of our conversation about methodology in January 1991. I believe that that conversation brought to light our quite different theoretical and methodological orientations to the prison culture. Conversation also helped me to make sense of how I was thinking about my study at the time and undertaking its possibilities. The following reconstruction is based on the lengthy transcript produced.

While Jenny had felt a moral and ethical obligation to declare herself as a researcher to the inmates, I experienced mixed feelings. On the one hand, I often did declare who I was and what I was doing, especially to my Creative Writing students, but, on the other hand, I was advised not to do so. I had even been advised not to declare myself to be an institutional teacher in the drug group. My roles, in other words, were determined by, and restricted to, the programs I functioned in. My role as official educational researcher was mostly kept private as were my methods of producing stories of experience. It was my letter of consent to writer-inmates that clarified my status as researcher and intention to publicize inmates' sharings and writings.

Jenny and I both agreed that our methodologies had been inspired by our personal journeys that required conceptual framing. My own framing was inextricably connected to my impulse to understand my own learning within an unfamiliar culture. I had taken action, in this direction, by recording my dreams without knowledge of how they might fit with a fuller text. I had also undergone this process with my master's thesis (1990) which had been inspired by my dream of being confined in a family attic. I emphasized to Jenny that:

> I want to follow my impulses, that's all. It's so sweet and simple. But if I have to have the logos of it all figured out ahead of time I will feel imprisoned. I have a sense, for example, that I want to document my own experiences as I go through the prison system, as I meet with inmates and so on. I want some kind of meta-level reflections on the experience to come out of this. And I'm dreaming in the right direction. I'm glad that I'm having these dreams because it's a sign to me that I'm starting to live my inquiry deeply, "starting" is the key word here (Mullen, 8-9).

I explained to Jenny that I was resisting being instrumental and superficial at the beginning of my inquiry. I wanted to open myself to deeply satisfying ways of proceeding in my fieldsite. I was intuiting, during my short two-week exposure to the jail, that the inmates were "natural storytellers" capable of "becoming their own scribes." I talked about how I might help them to become their own scribes, capable of analyzing their own texts that reveal their lives as lived. I emphasized that I wanted to help them to "capture their life in some kind of print form" (9). My belief was that I was not going to be teaching the inmates reading and writing. Rather, I wanted to capitalize on their natural abilities. This orientation to the inmates became the significant part of my methodology. I also wanted to capitalize on experiencing the inmates as human beings by "gain[ing] some kind of sympathetic understanding of men as rapists, as murderers and so on, and try to see them as something more than this" (9). Jenny, a veteran prison researcher, accepted both of these orientations of mine.

As I reflect on this interview, it also fed another part of my methodology, but a more implicit one. I was giving attention to how "this study [might] fit with university life, [and I feel that] the idea exists within me already, it's living within me" (10). I later spun this intuition into my metaphor of imprisoned selves that connects education to corrections, and corrections to education. In simple terms, I imagined that we are all inmates struggling for voice and articulation. People live in a constant stream of learning and becoming in various educational contexts. Rehabilitation can be understood as learning, growing and re-living in an educational context.

Regarding the methodological issues that we raised, I recognize that, like Jenny, I was trying to find ways to reach people. Our methods differed from one another's and we were drawn to different frameworks. But, we were both driven to want to find ways to reach people and to reach out to them. We both wanted to operate beyond the superficial kinds of behaviors that researchers can opt for. Jenny and I, for example, expressed the desire to develop coping skills with regard to a strange place. I also wanted, as Jenny had put it, to pull the deeper meaning of my work out of myself and to recognize that this is a continuous process. On this topic, Jenny advised me to work on revealing my dreams in order to "report" more profoundly on them: "I think you ought to search . . . because I think the clues are all in there" (12). In our talk, I returned to this topic and responded that:

. . . once something starts to be unconscious rather than conscious for me, I feel that I'm really on to something . . . there's a very deep mythology in my dreams as there is in everyone's dreams and I feel that that's part of what's compelling as well. The jail can help to round that out for me . . . the boy-prisoner is another image that I hadn't dreamt before nor predicted . . . I felt that I was held prisoner for the many years of my youth in different ways and continue to, for example, with regard to the narrow frames of educational research that we all carry around (Mullen, 15).

This interview gave me a context to search for ways to understand how my inquiry might unfold. Operating on two levels, we discussed our individual approaches to prison sites as well as our learning from one another. This interview turned out to be an outstanding tool of reflection for me throughout my study. Both Jenny and I talked openly and took risks. I would recommend writers of new topics to consider interviewing an advanced colleague pursuing a similar inquiry or set of concerns. I would also recommend writers to interview their informants, as I did formally in the case of John, and informally in the case of ex-addicts, parole officers, teachers, education coordinators, and others.

Investigating the Jail Site

The shaping influence of the institution.
The institutional climate of the jail impacted on the way in which I conducted research and oriented myself to a new culture as an educational experience. As a marginal-insider in the jail, I explored a correctional institution as a humanly significant site of teaching and learning. My intent, as marginal-insider, was to learn more about curriculum-making, but from a perspective that challenged my own biases about curriculum, schooling, and teaching and learning. My inquiry was both assisted and restricted by the prison system. Its methods, systems and techniques for engaging outsiders shaped my orientation to work in rehabilitative programs, to inmates, and to other educative relationships. My inquiry was also assisted and restricted by my own methods, systems and techniques for generating sources to make sense of a unique schooling site. Since my experience of creating, collecting and analyzing stories of narrative experience covers a wide scope, I used my teacher/learner image to focus my discussion. This image of the teacher as marginal-insider and

curriculum-maker extends my former inquiry into the self as a mythological configuration (Mullen 1990).

I was neither strictly an insider nor an outsider in the jail, so my status as "foreigner" was complex and ambiguous. As researcher-volunteer, my visits never took me to the ranges and cells, only to the interview rooms (classrooms). I inquired several times about gaining access to the ranges in order to see inmates in the cells they call "cages," but was refused. Inmates in the Drug Awareness program referred to staff as "outsiders" and members of the "free society." As marginal-insider, I could only know the inmates peripherally. I sometimes felt this way even when certain inmates exposed their private worlds and thinking to me and to others. Most other professionals and staff, except for several female group facilitators and Education Coordinators, did not seem to want to know the inmates on a personal level.

The correctional officers, or guards, seemed to be weary of the inmates' stories and looked upon "repeaters" who returned with new criminal charges soon after release and who helped carve the reputation of detention centers as "revolving doors" with obvious disdain. In *Asylums* (1961), Goffman claims that institutions, notably prisons, actually stage "differences between two constructed categories of persons—a difference in social quality and moral character, a difference in perceptions of self and other" (111). He names "officials" and "convicts" as exemplifying these critical differences. There are also bridges that connect officials and inmates. For example, I witnessed joking among inmates and guards, and other staff. My favorite officer, a cheery middle-aged Irishman, insisted on "burdening" the inmates with his jokes, quips and songs along with the rest of us. Yates (1993), prison guard, writes that inmates and guards have some of the same social problems that are, in turn, shared with people more generally.

I struggled to relate to the inmates and to the prison itself, but I often felt like a foreigner. As a foreigner, my status, gender, and educational background were different. I also do not have formal training in criminology or psychology. Nor do I have an experiential awareness of drug use, crime, street living or even disillusionment with, and failure in, formal education. I arrived in my fieldsite with an appreciation of others through their stories of life and schooling. I did not adopt a statistical and quantitative approach to distance others through surveys, questionnaires and structured interviews. Instead, I relied on various tools of reflection, such as journal notes, conversations, and creative writings, to gather stories for the purpose of understanding the prison. I felt that I was making progress whenever I learned more about the inmates and the phenomenon of imprisonment itself. Whenever I did attempt to locate statistics, within my own framework, on the inmate population regarding variables such as race/origins/ethnicity, age, and nature of offenses, I was blocked. The Program Coordinator for the jail informed me on several occasions, as did the Education Coordinator, that the statistics were simply not available. When I inquired as to why, they said that they do not keep track of these variables and that even if they did, such information would be kept confidential.

As I struggled to relate to the inmates, I shared some of my own family and social history. I came to better understand how one's own story can be shaped in a group situation, even if the configuration of its members seems to dictate that the "essential" story is very different from one's own. Biographical forms of representation have the power to engage, construct and reconstruct autobiographical forms of representation. For instance, as I encountered these other "orphaned" adults, I remembered my own experiences of abandonment, neglect and periodic abuse (Mullen 1990). I sensed the extent to which most of us are both imprisoned in our stories and in desperate need of a new story. The story of the self as a prisoner, or as an expression of multiple imprisoned selves, is my primary story. My research practice has generated this story-line for me.

Polkinghorne (1988) acknowledges that primary stories inform research practice. In this temporal sense, I recall how an earlier dream that I narrated and analyzed (Mullen 1994) "informed" my prison study. It helped to form my early impressions of the self as incarcerated in family and writing situations. This dream of an attic experience had, in 1988, read as a text of personal family dynamics and developing selfhood. It came later to read as an existential text about forcible confinement and the inmate condition more generally.

The sense I bring to inmates' stories arises from within myself and in relation to the collection of autobiographical sources that helps constitute my self. I continue to record my dream experiences to make sense of myself in a jail and its overlapping communities. I believe that narrative inquiry, which values this ongoing experimentation with self in various educational contexts, can give rise to a life-text that is doing biography at the same time that it is doing autobiography. This may account for why I feel uneasy whenever I am asked whether my study is primarily of the inmates or myself. I am calling forth both images of self and other, to varying and sometimes indecipherable degrees, in everything that I write.

When I shared stories in the jail, I did not feel like a foreigner for long. I felt just the opposite. Many of the inmates and facilitators, like myself, were from "dysfunctional" families. I was "orphaned" at the tender age of 15 and managed to put my energies toward excelling at school and in the workplace, and raising my younger sister. Influences of my early years which play a role in helping me to understand inmates' stories are uncovered, but in the context of my formal study.

In spite of my participation in a shared story my "antennae [were] always out" (Shabatay 1991, 140). Like the stranger, I lived in my "adopted community" with a feeling of "greenhornness" that appeared at times and disappeared at other times, and became less pronounced over time. On the surface, I was struggling to establish my professional reputation in an unfamiliar culture while learning about others' educational perspectives and stories, and contributing to them. I was also writing my story in a new storytelling milieu. I lived as a connected knower just as deeply as I lived as a stranger. Eisner (1991) speaks of a "transactional" perspective of the "process of knowing that allows us to avoid the dualisms—objective and subjective—that have led to so much mischief in the methodology of educational research" (60). Although I am trying to understand inmates through their stories and myself through my own stories, my understandings are often ambiguous. Even when I could not identify with the inmates and their world, I still listened for possibility of connection and wrote in the same spirit. My view was from below the platform of the powerful (Haraway 1988).

The rhythms and cycles of the jail.

The prison system itself had a great impact on the methodological considerations for my study. In my *Prison Journal,* I documented my experience of the rotational system of the jail and my continuous struggle with it. I wanted to understand this system and how best to adapt to it in both practical and emotional terms. My own rhythms and ways of conducting business were seriously determined by the cycles and rhythms of my fieldsite. As I attended to the temporality of the jail, I became more aware of how even its practices of discontinuity, fragmentation and uncertainty could be interpreted in educational terms. Temporality, especially in a prison, can be understood as an enemy of learning.

I described the rotational cycle of the jail in chapter 2. It placed great pressure on the continuity and success of rehabilitative programs and educative relationships. Tyler (1949) believes that successful curriculum and effective teaching need to be linked to "significant changes in the students' patterns of behavior" rather than instructors' classroom activities (44). It was a "tall" order to hope for this in my situation. Prison culture is too unpredictable and even chaotic to allow for Tyler's thinking to be meaningfully connected to my work. In my experience, prison culture has its own vitality—the subtle changes that are continuously sparked as humans bond and work to create meaning. Some of my dreams capture the life that connects imprisonment to education. I have had dreams about the sharing of conversational space in a mutually negotiated physical and mental space. I dream about the human spirit and the expansive and expressive self that is entailed in communication with inmates.

Empowering researcher-practitioner relationships can go beyond the job that needs to be done. Feelings of caring and a sense of equality are key dynamics in people-oriented research. Change, as such, is a feeling of caring, connection and educative growth that emerges when students and their personal experiences count as legitimate. This meant that my desire to respect them was partly inspired by the act of interpreting inmates' range of experiences, including those that are miseducative, as valuable. I am reconstructing the meaning of educative. I include in it the stories that inmates share in community. I re-visited my own understanding of what constitutes an educative experience in order to incorporate its less flattering dimensions.

I also undertook this process in writing for myself. I attempted to represent my own problematic actions in my fieldsite by including, for example, my own blunders and mistakes, and theory/practice tensions (Van Maanen 1988). I have already told the story of publication regarding the creative writing newsletter. I illustrated how my focus on my own agenda and/or that of the institution may have inadvertently disempowered certain inmates and undermined their self-expression. I also told the story of how I had unwittingly created a disturbance in the drug group on several occasions. On one such occasion I had learned that my seemingly innocuous introduction of myself as an institutional teacher had, within the drug group and outside it, created complications. Apparently, inmates who otherwise showed little interest in pursuing formal coursework and upgrading had been taxing the senior Education Coordinator with requests to work specifically with me. Such institutions apparently discourage inmates from specifying preferences of volunteers/staff. Sally informed me that my action could have encouraged problems on several levels: an overtaxing of the shortage of resources by inmates; tensions among inmates, coordinators and officials; harassment of female teachers by inmates; and conflict with the Ministry of Corrections itself.

Reflections on Narrative Method

Complications and Limitations of Narrative Method

I have felt challenged to write this chapter because of the sense that I wanted it to convey. Narrative inquiry is an act of creation that includes method, but it should not be reduced to method. My conception of methodology itself is that it is not a tidy or straightforward matter. I think of the students who are new to narrative inquiry. Their conviction seems to be that problems of narrative inquiry are essentially those of method. When they ask questions about narrative, they often restrict themselves to complex issues regarding the negotiating of entry and closure; establishing links with informants and participants; obtaining letters of consent; knowing when best to observe and to participate in teachers' classrooms; and how to record narratively. Although these are pressing concerns, an inquiry into a culture "is as much created by the writing . . . as it determines the writing itself" (Van Maanen 1988, 6). I struggle with this problematic of representation with respect to culture, setting, self and others. My analysis of my educative relationships in the jail, for example, shifts depending on which question I am asking; what source of story/information I am pulling from; the theoretical context that influences my thinking; and even on my frame of mind that moment or day.

I remember how I had struggled, in my early journal writing, to capture a moment that erupted without warning. In 1986 I had worked with a friend of mine in her classroom. I first represented this experience in a clinical observation account and then in a personal narrative account two years later. The emotional moment that arose, taking both of us by surprise, became the learning experience that altered my consciousness about how to work collaboratively with people. To set the scene: I had asked my teacher-friend to justify her classroom actions. She had presented a verbal contract to her students indicating that she would not intervene in their presentations; however, she interrupted them constantly. I interpreted this action as a self-evident discrepancy between her intentions and practice. I went further, clearly indicating that her action constituted an inappropriate teacher response to me. Several years later I re-visited this situation, and its subsequent report, to write:

> It was during the final conference between us that Paula began to cry after I asked her a question about whether she found her actions inappropriate given the nature of her verbal contract with the class. Of course, I had interpreted her outburst as her emotional reaction to a very uncomfortable, if not disturbing, question. Instead, she began disclosing what was really on her mind. She was far away from the conference and into a world in which she was playing "little girl" outside her mother's home. The actual conference was taking place in Paula's home and the apparent connection between my question and her childhood memory involved the voice of the "mother." More clearly, she remembered playing with her sister at the time and experiencing a conflict over whose leaf was the prettiest. Much kicking and spitting and general nasty behavior erupted. The mother's sudden appearance on the scene put an end to the fighting but also a beginning to deep-seated resentment, therapy groups, and problematic relationships with men.
>
> The point was that my "rational" phrasing of the issue had reminded Paula of her mother's haunting words: "Explain yourself, young lady!", etc. Paula held a card, during our session, which had been recently sent to her from her mother. The association of the clinical question with this unanticipated childhood story makes me re-think the kinds of questions I am asking with respect to unstated biases, interpretations and judgments (Mullen, "Dis-close-her: Under imaginary lock and key," 1988).

My methods of inquiry into Paula's college-level teaching rested significantly with personal issues and feelings. In other words, the methods I had employed had not yielded the control that I had hoped to secure as an inexperienced researcher. If we interpret methodology as inextricably linked to humanistic dimensions such as "mentalistic entities" (Walker 1992), then narrative is salient. The lesson that I learned was not to employ qualitative methods in order to avoid error in human relationships, but rather to promote "many humanly important experiences such as spontaneity, caring, joy, love, and adventure [as well as] openness to surprising events and encouragement to speculate and to rely on one's intuitions" (Walker 1992, 105).

A narrative methodology involves the construction of meaning and interpretation of events. The process of narrative inquiry encourages participants to open up and to disclose aspects of themselves and their worlds. Disclosure is problematic for all narrative inquirers, yet it is essential to the process of constructing meaning. It is perhaps most deeply appreciated by researchers who strive to tell their own story. But, researchers who devote energy to telling the narrative of their lives may also be less sensitive, at times, to others' boundaries. If we have told our own story, then we may press too hard to hear others' stories. Issues of confidentiality, privacy of self and untold stories are often at stake.

The following story of my own illustrates this irony. The senior Education Coordinator decided, without negotiation, to eliminate a contribution of mine. This poem, called "Orphaned motherhood," was first shared with my academic community. Sally said that the poem told her that my personal story was "peaking" beyond the scope of my research. I had disclosed aspects of my mythology as "mother" (in a non-biological, mythological sense), teacher and writer in it. I had poeticized their loving and sensuous dimensions in the context of "creating life, creating books, creating." But this was not the complete picture. I had extended this context to life in prison where "my own belly, flat and unalive/touches the steel, concrete and beige walls/of a masculine prison." This was considered inappropriate material for official discourse in corrections. My personal story had been censored. I better understood the feelings of those inmates who had been experiencing the same.

Because inmates are generally without any contact with females, such volunteers/staff are highly valued and prized. One central problem of my methodology as it took shape in my fieldsite is that I encouraged inmates to open up on personal topics, as did some of the programs themselves (e.g., Drug Awareness). But personal interest and involvement produced a paradox. Inmates were rendered voiceless by rejection, censorship and termination. In several instances, I received notes from Anna, the assistant Education Coordinator. Although she was in charge of the Math and Science curricula, she also became involved with my Creative Writing program whenever her own students showed interest. In one note, she said that Enzo's story had been returned to him. She felt that she could be subpoenaed to go to court if the information given in it were true. She also rejected it having taken "exception to some of the language and the graphic details in it and told him so. If you feel likewise, Carol, lay your cards on the table" (note, April 5, 1992). I never saw Enzo again. He had been transferred to another institution.

Anna also wrote me that she had warned Sammy that he would be removed from the Creative Writing program if he continued to delay submitting math lessons to her. She had withdrawn Phillip Dalley, a prolific francophone-poet, from creative writing because he had "lost all privileges for a specific time frame from this administration. If he behaves himself, he'll be back on your list next week" (April 30, 1992). I saw him only once after this incident occurred. He wanted to submit material to the newsletter. I asked permission for him to return to his cell to obtain his writing. His poems, "Searching for a place of sanity," and "All in a dream," were published (Appendix B).

Regarding the issue of termination of my letter writing relationships with inmates, there is something definitely unresolved about the way in which we teachers executed our decision. Moreover, I personally felt that our collective treatment of Sammy was not only deeply dissatisfying but also fundamentally at odds with what we stood for. I realize that the senior Education Coordinator was primarily motivated by her concern for my well-being, which touched me. However, we should have found a way to include the inmates in our communication about our concerns. We could have negotiated, with them, a clearer understanding of our expectations in writing so that premature closure could have been avoided. In the process, we could have learned how to better deal with such sensitive issues for the future. The inmates themselves would have been given the opportunity to become, upon release, more conscientious and sensitive to their impact on others.

Through all of this, we would have upheld the 1989 revised mandate of the Correctional Service of Canada. Its own progressive view regarding human freedom and public safety links these spheres of national concern to educational issues:

> all offenders . . . must have opportunities to serve their sentences in a meaningful and dignified manner and our programs must provide for personal growth within the institutional setting. . . . The second part of our Mission—control—is best assured through positive interaction between staff and offenders, rather than by relying only on static

measures of security. The degree of control that we exercise must be reasonable to the situation, safe, secure and humane (1991, 7).

The issues it names—growth, dignity and positive interaction—are the very issues that concerned me in my study.

Strategies for Future Researchers

Allowing for adjustments, other researchers might find useful the strategies described throughout this chapter. In this section I provide more detail on those strategies that give meaning to method in narrative ethnographic inquiry. However, no "method" exists in narrative inquiry or qualitative inquiry more generally. As Eisner (1991) writes, "no codified body of procedures . . . will tell someone how to produce a perceptive, insightful, or illuminating study of the educational world. Unfortunately—or fortunately—in qualitative matters cookbooks ensure nothing" (169). Methodological considerations are developed in fieldsites because qualitative inquiry is both idiosyncratic and personal to the researcher and sensitive to context and its emerging configurations.

I am neither an absolutist, who relies heavily on prescriptive codes of method, or a relativist who looks only to the production of creative approaches in situations themselves. Like Glesne and Peshkin (1992) who reflect on such positioning with respect to ethical guidelines, I favor a combination of guidelines and situational responses. The following is a map that suggests broad methodological guidelines with room for improvisation, selection and even omission. It is important to keep an open mind and to become relaxed about the unpredictability of narrative inquiry.

Establishing informants.

Researchers need to select an informant in their field. They can then obtain advice in making decisions and receive assistance whenever necessary (Glesne and Peshkin 1992). Put more strongly, researchers should systematically set out to solicit support and to create networking links with experienced individuals. Such conduits can be sought out both in fieldsites and within academic institutions themselves. The obvious contact in the school system is the person with whom the researcher negotiated entry. Several years ago I had negotiated entry into a secondary school with a principal and teacher to conduct research on teachers' professional knowledge. The teacher herself became my central contact and strongest supporter. If researchers situate themselves mainly as learners, then it makes sense to learn from the situation at hand and to invite constructive feedback whenever necessary.

The researcher will need to understand that a paradox exists in forging productive links with informants. As we come to know our informants, we share knowledge with them. I realized that my feelings, observations and insights could become dangerous, especially in a jail setting, where privacy is fragile and trust is paramount. As a strategy for disclosing to others, I kept the same principles in mind when talking about the inmates as when writing about them. In other words, I considered how issues of trust and power are dealt with during the inquiry process and duplicated these in action. I saw myself as partly defined in relation to my participants. It became a matter of course to want to protect their confidences at every step, to preserve their anonymity, and to uphold their dignity.

Sharing knowledge about participants is unavoidable given the nature of an inquiry into people's lives. I therefore shared knowledge about my participants with Sally, the Education Coordinator, in the following ways: as generally as possible and with respect to the context at hand; parallel to my text that preserves anonymity but welcomes understanding; as crises arose requiring attention and action; in response to informants seeking sensible feedback, input and honest appraisal; and finally, where I was uneasy or where my own personal freedom and safety felt jeopardized.

Researchers, when disclosing, should be mindful that they are interpreting an event and that other points of view are equally valid. One might even suggest to the informant that input from others should be sought. In the final analysis, researchers will need to take responsibility for ethical concerns and practices that are "problematic at best and dangerous at worst" (Glesne and Peshkin 1992, 114). We might, in other words, do well to document such processes as they take shape in action even if they are not a formal part of our inquiries.

Just as researchers are interpreting events in their communications with informants, they are also constructing and reconstructing themselves. My own text is, in part, organized according to a "sequence of encounters with informants" and other participants in my fieldsite (Geertz 1988, 92). The characters who function inside my text are an outgrowth of my "organizing consciousness" (Geertz, 93) as well as my personal identity. I seek to know myself through others.

Creating a cover story.

Researchers need to write their detailed proposals prior to seeking entrance to an institution in order to prepare their cover story. Cover stories are "written or verbal presentations of yourself. Different interactions with your others require different introductions of varying levels of detail. You tell the same basic points to everyone, but what else you tell certain individuals depends on the circumstances" (Glesne and Peshkin 1992, 31-32). I used my proposal in Corrections to address much of what I expected my cover story to accomplish. I also used it to aid me in becoming an official educational researcher and to prepare others to assist me in my work, including programmatic development.

Without realizing it at the time, I provided details in my proposal on most of the suggested areas as outlined by Glesne and Peshkin. These areas include who I am (my professional background and orientation); what I am doing (purpose of my study); the promise of confidentiality and anonymity to participants and institution (ethical orientation and procedures, and ethical issues and methods of protection); requests to record observations and words (sources of data and sample writing), and more.

Resourcing the institution.

I wanted to make my investigation official as soon as possible and to have this confirmed in writing. A proposal should be prepared that tells the *cover story* of the researcher's plans and perspectives, one that is sensitive to the setting itself, and to the issues of protection of identity. As I learned, timing is everything. My institutional proposal was cleared mostly because I had already been actively functioning as a volunteer in the jail. I believe that it is necessary to receive approval in writing. Duplicate copies should be kept for additional, ethical review purposes.

As indicated, informants can be very influential as they have inside knowledge. They might know about the mission statement of the institution. More importantly, they might be familiar with the character and concerns of key decision-makers as well as the expectations and life-habits of the place. As informants, or stakeholders in curriculum-making, are involved, the researcher can solicit aid to produce positive results with respect to proposal writing (and any other requests). Researchers should also learn as much as possible about the hierarchy of decision-makers in case of complication. If one party is not receptive to the request, this does not mean that another will respond in the same way. The researcher should also be ready to make changes in writing.

Finally, it is critical for researchers to discover ways of giving back to the institutions that have kindly accommodated them. For example, one might offer to organize a seminar or conference; establish a newsletter; write a report or article; create a new program; or work with participants beyond the scope of the research. Much is left to opportunism, invention and adventure. I realize that, as Eisner (1991) asserts, duties peripheral to the focus of the research may distract and cause tension. He cites the example of participants (namely teachers) who request that the researcher assist in the classroom. Nonetheless, my feeling is that researchers should find ways of expressing appreciation which are appropriate to the situation at hand and to the researcher's own talents and interests.

Soliciting participants as partners in curriculum-making.

Researchers must treat participants with an attitude of respect, equality, and compassion. This attitude also needs to be manifest in action and in concrete and desirable ways. For example, researchers who are forward-looking will probably obtain participants' permission to, for example, make use of their material in multiple ways and beyond immediate goals. My letter of consent outlined my request to use inmates' writings for three purposes: a creative writing newsletter, dissertation, and book on inmates' educational stories. I covered various ethical issues: the use of pseudonyms and other necessary identity changes; a system involving the senior Education Coordinator to scrutinize my on-site publications; and finally, a formal ethical review process to be undertaken outside corrections in an academic institution.

I circulated this letter of consent to the Education Coordinator, who, in turn, helped elicit clearance from the Superintendent. I then obtained permission from each and every writer-inmate. I was careful not to assume that because my participants are disadvantaged and without voice, I could exploit their resources. Instead, I approached them as intelligent, knowing beings. I obtained their signatures, subsequent to discussion with each inmate, before formalizing their material in print. Signature has another meaning. We "display our signatures" when we make use of "expressive language and the presence of voice in text" to make it clear that "a person, not a machine, was behind the words" (Eisner 1991, 36). In my study, my own signature is present as well as those of the inmates. Sometimes the distinction between our signatures is blurred as I interpret their stories, writings and interviews for my own purposes.

The extent to which I was successful in negotiating my own needs with the needs of the institution was ultimately expressed in my work with the inmates themselves. My participants reacted favorably to being published, in particular, as well as to being portrayed in my own writing. Several inmates also brought key ethical issues to their discussions with me. One of them expressed a concern regarding copyright regulations and personal rights (Black Hawk); another focused on attitudes and practices relating to censorship (Adrian).

Utilizing the texts of experienced fieldworkers.

I found the following texts most useful to the issues involved in conducting qualitative, psychological, narrative and ethnographic inquiry, respectively: *Becoming qualitative researchers: An introduction* (Glesne and Peshkin 1992) and *The enlightened eye: Qualitative inquiry and the enhancement of educational practice* (Eisner 1991); *Teacher education as transformation* (Diamond 1991); *Teachers as curriculum planners: Narratives of experience* (Connelly and Clandinin 1988); and *Tales of the field: On writing ethnography* (Van Maanen 1988).

People and situations, self and story, can be approached as text. Researchers can both document and analyze educational phenomena and processes to create meaning. From this point of view, text can take many forms, such as journals, dream texts, creative writing portraits, and proposal writing. Text represents the researcher's experiences in the field or that of other researchers' experiences.

Telling your own story.

The question I am asking is, "How can researchers and teachers help others to tell their stories if this is something that we have not yet done for ourselves?" If we want to listen to teachers' stories and to work with them as a way of empowering teachers/inmates/graduate students as curriculum-makers, then I imagine that we have created a situation in which our own stories need to be told and written.

Researchers' narratives may need to be written as prerequisites to their work with teachers. Researchers will also want their own stories to emerge in a mutual exchange with teachers. There is a possible danger that researchers might use their own stories to determine the shape of teachers' stories. On the other hand, if researchers wait to tell mutually emerging stories with teachers, then they risk being unable to help the teachers to move forward. They also risk not dealing effectively with teachers' concerns.

I suggest that researchers can make autobiographical or biographical gains by exploiting difficult and fleeting data bases. We make assumptions about our images of self that often shift during inquiry. In an earlier study, I developed configurations of mothering and teaching that have been transformed in this book. I now include, on an explicit level, myself as an inmate who struggles for voice and self-representation in community. Through self-reflexive writing, I have discovered personal images, metaphors and myths that direct my own research and determine its context. Images of marginal-insider, vicarious participant, and street researcher constitute my recent constellation of imprisoned selves. By writing, we not only explore our personal narratives but also research stories and myths of personhood. To extend these ideas, teachers/inmates can gain a better understanding of themselves and their classrooms if they, too, are given the opportunity and time to reflect on what they meaningfully embody and experience. In work with participants as partners in curriculum-making, researchers can use writing as a way of helping others to reach into themselves; to trust in their own images; and to draw on images in the process of understanding classroom cultures.

Writing is a process that invites daily acts of construction and reconstruction in the study of life-experience. We can better our lives when we transform stories of our experiences into text to be interpreted and re-lived in new situations. I have studied images of abandonment and empowerment that I had implicitly held throughout my life but never sufficiently storied, even with the advances journaling and narrative writing had offered me. My stories of education and imprisonment offer an experience in self-discovery and ongoing learning which is perhaps helpful to think about and to use.

Creating a system.

Organizing Files. When I began organizing my files, notes, and papers for the thesis-turned-book, I did not realize the extent to which my system would impact on my evolving narrative. I am suggesting that researchers also develop a system to represent aspects of their inquiry. My filing system is accessible to me only and is secure in my private home. I devised subject areas within the curriculum field; within narrative inquiry; within ethnography; within literature and poetry; and other areas of interest. I also devised an authors' list for key papers in my study. In addition, I collected all of the papers produced by these key authors. Each author, such as Eisner and Peshkin, has a separate folder. I also used different colored folders to represent my various purposes and labels that sometimes change.

I prepared separate folders for my book that contained my proposal; chapters (draft) and chapters (complete); and related writings (publications, reports, comprehensive exams, and correspondence). I had, within reach, dividers for my most frequently used sources of information and text. I also had, within view, a list of my table of contents. I included, as a memory aid on this sheet, computer file designations beside each chapter. I created separate computer files for each chapter that I later merged and repaginated.

To represent the correctional scene and the jail itself, I created folders as they suggested themselves to me. Here is a partial list: agency contact sheets; orientations; Drug Awareness program information; literacy teaching materials; conferences/seminars; community agencies/services; Ministry documents; correspondence; creative writing contributions; prison stories; prison articles; and prison references.

I used different colors for my journal books to distinguish them from one another. I labeled, numbered and dated each volume. I also highlighted key sections in all three journals, sometimes writing questions or comments for follow-up beside them.

Establishing Readers. I chose only a few readers for the early draft of my dissertation. They knew a sufficient amount about my writing and thinking and had been exposed to my work, as I had been to theirs, over the years. They understood the context beyond, and implicit in, my writing. This deeper understanding evolved for us through conversation and analysis, and an ethic of caring. Other writers may choose to participate in an academic circle or in one-on-one writing and reading relationships. I approached my readers as caring agents and active participants in meaning-making and curriculum-making. But then the issue of multiple and even contradictory perspectives on one's work becomes evident over time. I sorted through these perspectives by keeping at the forefront my own research story, intentions and interpretations.

Taking gender into account.

Both male and female professionals, from what I learned, have their own set of realities in a jail setting. The male staff (guards, group facilitators, administrators, teachers) positioned themselves as authority figures. Generally speaking, the inmates did not connect emotionally with these men. Ralph, the facilitator of the Drug Awareness program who replaced Pam, both created and experienced problems. He would insist, for example, that his long spell of alcoholism had prepared him for intimate knowledge of the inmates' own addictions. He also approached the drug group using the twelve-step program of Alcoholics Anonymous and focused on his own stories of recovery as pivotal to discussion. He struggled, as a man in his sixties, to make sense of a culture different from his own. Members simply stopped coming, even though they had, in the process, sacrificed the "edge" this would give them with the courts. I maintained contact with Pam during Ralph's takeover, and she eventually sent in other female addiction counselors for support. But it was too late by then. The group, although it still exists today, essentially lost its appeal for members who had tried to confront Ralph openly and honestly during discussion. The small turn-out alone spoke for itself.

The women whom I witnessed (group facilitators, counselors, discharge planners, teachers, librarians, coordinators, and administrators) used, to varying degrees, a personal approach with the inmates. We mostly listened to their concerns beyond the curricular objectives at hand; encouraged them to reach their potential as students, fathers/family members, and citizens; and treated them as human beings with essential stories to be shared. Sometimes decisions were made by these same professionals that proved problematic though: Inmates could become disillusioned with their treatment within formal educational programs and other programs, not just the practices of the jail itself.

The female guards seemed less involved than the rest of the professional staff. They were trained to follow procedures that distanced them from the inmates and their lives. Female guards also witnessed what most of us did not, that is, the inmates as they live behind bars and on the ranges.   I also heard stories, from the other women, of how poorly the female guards were treated by the inmates. The sense was that the inmates viewed them as pawns of the system to be continually tested and mistreated.   I do not wish to imply, however, that correctional officers do not have a working relationship with inmates.   On the contrary.   The penal system is structured in such a way as to enforce inmates' and guards' dependency on one another. And humane and cordial moments do exist between them: As Yates (1993), the only guard to have written his story to date, tells us, ". . . he and I conversed through long evening shifts about every subject imaginable. . . . We were dismissed as a couple of eggheads talking about academic bullshit . . . " (77).   Yates is himself a professor and poet who found himself in the penal system subsequent to a car accident that temporarily confused his memory.   In the above scenario, he is describing his relationship with a teacher-inmate, from a family of educators, charged with aggravated assault.

It is surprising that such a high percentage of women function in correctional facilities for men only and for strictly male client-based community agencies.   I am suggesting that other female researchers should not hesitate to participate in such settings.   The penal system welcomes women's participation and provides a forum for contribution and academic exploration.   As volunteers, we were warned in training by staff, and one former prisoner too, that women need to be mindful of inmates' manipulative ploys as they seek to exploit us.   Researchers might also be extra careful when developing relations with informants in the system.   Researchers should have someone to "clear the air" with regarding uncomfortable situations and awkward moments. Yet, they should also learn who they can trust disclosing to.

Female researchers might develop a self-inventory in whatever form is comfortable for them (dream recording, journal writing, taped conversations).   This produces a sense as to their personal, and interpersonal, strengths and weaknesses. They might also keep a log of their personal problems, issues, concerns and successes.   This should be done regardless of whether or not such a task fits with one's study, and its methodology and aims.   This log could be circulated to the informant on a regular basis for input in addition to the records of progress with clients.

Female researchers will need to be aware of their own boundaries regarding a population that is, in many respects, desperate and lonely. Researchers   can   document   concerns   as   related   to   their   own boundaries. Examples might include feeling tested emotionally or intellectually; being requested to do something suspicious or counter to policy; being asked to share personal information about themselves in a way which constitutes an invasion of privacy; and feeling exposed, awkward, or uncomfortable in any way. They need to realize that they will draw attention to themselves just by virtue of their gender. After a warm greeting with inmates, the female researcher can begin with the day's agenda and return to it, without hesitation, periodically and especially if her boundaries are being tested. My personal approach was to take control of situations with inmates to the best of my ability; to observe how others interacted with them to resource other possibilities; and to reach out to others for advice and support.

As I discovered, inmates respond well to people who are not pretentious and who are connecting, non-judgmental and non-threatening. This is the area in which inmates are not looking to test a female researcher's boundaries. They simply want her to show interest and compassion. I remember a math teacher who worked well with the inmates. At first I had difficulty understanding why this was so. He was skinny and unathletic, effeminate and homosexual, quite the opposite of the picture many inmates projected of themselves. After a while, I could see that he was not authoritarian or superior in his approach to his students. Rather, he was kind, serious about his work, and generous in spirit.

To elaborate, the male inmate population is openly contemptuous of gays as well as dismissive towards those who are short of being traditionally masculine. Much energy is expended, by the inmates, to build muscle and to brand their workmanship with self-made tattoos. In turn, they generally marginalize those who conflict with their reconstructed selves. And yet, homosexual practices and even gang rapes are not uncommon, among heterosexual men, especially in the federal penitentiaries.

Positionality, with respect to participants, is also an important consideration. I positioned myself mainly as a learner. Eisner (1991) writes that "one way to maintain access is not to forget that on the site, in all interactions, researchers are first and foremost students of the situation" (174). Researchers need also to cope with a paradox. We need to situate ourselves both as learners and empowering agents in our fieldsites. In my case, I saw myself as a curriculum planner; English teacher, co-facilitator and Creative Writing coordinator. I believe that we need to develop positive images of ourselves because we not only shape our own sense of potential, but also others' perceptions of us and the world around us. At the same time, researchers might view their participants as more than learners. This is a conceptual form of "giving back." In my case, I viewed the inmates as partners in curriculum-making, vital storytellers, and some as creative writers.

Developing modes of inquiry.
     Below is a list of the methods of inquiry discussed in this chapter:
1.   developing a rapport with informants that enhances research discoveries but that respects participants' privacy;
2.   treating one's methodology as inquiry-based with respect to the construction and reconstruction of meaning;
3.   focusing and de-focusing spaces of inquiry;
4.   positioning and re-positioning central questions;
5.   resourcing one's personal and professional stories, intellectual history, and family history/background;
6.   developing tools of reflection, such as journal writing, letter-writing, interviewing/conversing; and more;
7.   documenting the various levels (individual, institutional, and social) of inquiry as one level impacts on another;
8.   presenting a cover story;
9.   utilizing the texts of experienced fieldworkers;
10. organizing a system of files to reflect one's inquiry;
11. establishing active readers;
12. developing a self-inventory;
13. interviewing participants;
14. corresponding with participants;
15. and, taking gender into account.

Narrative and Ethnography as Sister Methods

     This book presents a narrative ethnographic study of inmates' lives. "Narrative ethnographic" conveys the progressive qualities that I wish to attribute to such an approach. Rose (1990), an ethnographer, has inspired me to facilitate a subjective view of my own "inquiring self" in the study of a prison culture. Diamond (1991), a teacher educator and narrativist, encourages me to do the same and to go further by promoting a "sensitive transformation" of the "main character in each of our individual stories [which] is the self" (91).

Rose makes the fields of ethnography and narrative inquiry less exclusive and more interdependent. He writes that we need to problematize the concept of the researcher self in the same spirit that we already do for cultural others. For Rose, the logic of inquiry that a traditional ethnographic approach had offered him collapsed in the face of his study of African-Americans. He did not disclose his identity as a researcher. His methods of inquiry therefore changed "given the covertness, lack of explicitness, and lack of the sacred status" (13) in his work. Like some other ethnographers, Rose experimented "until [he] . . . broke with the old categories and inaugurated a new narrative responsiveness to changing world cultural relations" (15). I have renamed his phrase, "new narrative responsiveness" as a "progressive form of ethnography." Either way, what gets promoted is intimacy, stories, possibilities and contingent understandings (Rose 1990).

While Diamond (1992) uses the term "autoethnography," I have coined the expression "narrative ethnography." Autoethnographic practices have transformed the ethnographic research tradition. Such practices place value on teachers' capabilities to construct their own accounts of practice and on researchers' capabilities to collaborate in the reconstruction of such accounts of practice. Ethnographers have, in other words, "joined the post-modern fashion of questioning the seeming transparency of their representations of the experience of others" (Diamond 1992, 69). Narrative inquiry joins researchers and participants in the project of making themselves the subject of their own inquiry. Autoethnography, then, is a process of "self-reflexive analysis" that the self engages through methods of reconstrual and renewal (Diamond 1992). I used autobiographic and biographic methods to construct stories of imprisonment and education. I also suggested strategies for other researchers interested in learning about a narrative ethnographic study.

The traditional methodological practices of doing ethnographies promote distance, models, stabilities, and detachable conclusions (Rose 1990). Geertz is one of those ethnographers who is breaking traditional ethnographic forms to promote literary and interpretive possibilities. He writes on the topic of the inquiring self in his "I-witnessing" account. With its poetic and impressionistic dimensions, the whole of the text reads as a multigenre narrative. As Geertz (1988) writes:

. . . there is a lot more than native life to plunge into if one is to attempt [a] total immersion approach to ethnography. There is the landscape. There is the isolation. . . . And, most shakingly, there is the capriciousness of one's passions, the weakness of one's constitution, and the vagrancies of one's thoughts: that nigrescent thing, the self. It is not a question of going native. . . . It is a question of living a multiplex life: sailing at once in several seas (77).

While the ethnographer constructs cultural accounts, Geertz argues that this is not enough. They must be rendered "credible" through rendering the self credible. Ethnography has become increasingly introspective since the 1920's and 1930's. One's "I-witness" of cultural others, then, is dependent on one's "I." The writer struggles to bring the self into an "intelligible relationship" with the other. Geertz recommends the diary as the best way to ensure that an ethnographic account is not only reliable but also personal. He goes further by problematizing journal writing and by offering examples from others' works. He infers that the "sense of construction" in these diaries is what serves as their "organizing consciousness" (93).

I have re-visited ethnography, during this study, to view its vital links with narrative inquiry. I have sought to reconstruct both fields of inquiry, as others have, but in terms of my own organizing consciousness. My book uses ethnography as a sister methodology, but in the context of a specific culture that reflects my personal history in storytelling, teacher development and curriculum. Narrative can be viewed as a form of critical or self-reflexive ethnography.

The next chapter concludes this book. In it, I re-visit the three central questions listed in chapter 1 that inquire into the lives of imprisoned selves. I also provide a portrait of the writer as it relates to my interdependent themes of education and imprisonment. I discuss how the world of corrections might be re-invented along the lines of writing ventures. I then reflect on how teacher education itself can be re-scripted to invite studies on alternative research sites.

Chapter 5

Significance and Implications: Outside the Manila Prison

In the first section of this chapter, I re-visit my text structure and three central questions: "What are the inmates' stories of experience and imprisonment that offer possibilities in education? What is my teacher development story in the context of the prison site?" And, "What is the experience of captivity and education for imprisoned selves?" I then present a portrait of the narrative writer with respect to self-imprisonment in "Re-writing the Self: A Cell of One's Own." In the next section, "Re-inventing Corrections: The Future," I offer educational possibilities within the penal system. Finally, I reflect on teacher education itself in "Re-scripting Teacher Education Out of the Ashes: The Future." In it, I invite studies on alternative research sites and narrative inquiry approaches.

Re-visiting the Text Structure and its Emerging Questions

The circle of incarceration is now complete. My story of the margins of teacher education and research has become central to my inquiry. In turn, it provides an alternative, narrative ethnographic inquiry into an unconventional site as a study of human experience and education. I have argued that a narrative about imprisoned selves as students and teachers is relevant to such a study. I selected a jail and its inmates as a way of evolving my perspective. Alternative research sites and methods of exploration enhance what we can know about teacher education and research. Narrative inquiry offers a fresh approach to such learning and teaching opportunities.

I began my inquiry with the question, "What are the inmates' stories of experience and imprisonment that offer possibilities in education?" (chapter 1). I wanted my research to tell the story of the personal and cultural lives of inmates. I was influenced, by a published convict's writings, to undertake a study in the world of corrections. As a basis for deriving insights into the inmates' stories of experience and education, I undertook 18 months of fieldwork. I participated in the Drug Awareness, Education/Literacy and Creative Writing programs, designing and teaching the last one myself. I also developed teaching-learning relationships with a few inmates-writers over time, in particular Black Hawk, Sammy, Mark, Sear and Adrian. I worked with a number of others, including Sammy, Chris and Mike, on upgrading and formal coursework for extended periods of time. I met for a single session, or for several meetings, with dozens of others.

Special moments shared with Rick, Rod, Joe and even Peter gave me insight into the inmate condition and possibilities for storytelling. My association was deepened through John, ex-convict and counselor, on-site and in the community. I gained other perspectives on inmates' lives and stories from correctional staff, officials and educators, particularly, Sally, Jenny, Pam and even Anna. Finally, inmates' own texts, and writings about inmates, often presented me with reflexive narratives about what it means to be a prisoner. I attempted to bring stories of 13 co-participants to awareness through my own narrative inquiry, or life-experiences and writing.

In summary, the fore-mentioned influences have helped to shape my personal knowledge of the inmate condition. In response to the first question, I have enumerated some of my insights into inmates' lives and stories. On a meta-level they constitute story-lines more generally about multiple imprisoned selves:

- inmates both represent and offer transformative perspectives on marginal, or devalued and neglected, lives;
- inmates' stories make it possible to imagine different ways to educate ourselves and others, and to engage alternative but humanly significant sites;

- even while in maximum security prisons, inmates seek educational opportunities and interpersonal connections;
- the inmates I worked with wrote, and did coursework, for a variety of reasons. These included: expressing themselves and discovering self-knowledge; achieving imaginative and spiritual freedom; breaking the monotony and routine of prison life; protesting inadequate and even unjust prison conditions; documenting their experiences in order to become acknowledged for making a positive contribution to society; maintaining relationships with loved ones and connecting with newcomers; embarking on a program of self-therapy, renewal and personal image; developing mental capacities to improve literacy skills and to widen options upon re-entry into society; and visiting female teachers and staff;
- inmates reflect on the nature of imprisonment and education in prosaic, poetic and raw forms that *is* "writing from an experience,
- not about it" (Stephen Reid, published ex-convict, in Kucherawy 1990);
- my inmate-writers used the following images in their individual and collective writings: misted catacomb; sleeping tomb; age-old time; mid-gallop, frozen carousel/frozen pony; diminishing reality; Mr. Jones, to the moon; sniveling whore; world of pain; insane war; scattered ruins; and notes from a cell (chapter 3);
- and, the various themes in inmate-students' writings include: the crippling disease of drug addiction; childhood abandonment and abuse; memories of Nature and play; the heartlessness and absurdity of the prison system and its guard(ians); feelings of loss, anger, misery, sorrow and disappointment; dreams and visions of immortality and a better life; the search for a place claimed as one's own (sanity); yearnings for romantic love and intimacy; and the feeling of loneliness connected with the pain of living.

In writing about the lives of inmates, I saw them as knowers, storytellers and writers. I collaborated with them as partners in curriculum-making. I saw the jail itself as a site of teaching and learning where partnerships of co-learning are formed and even negotiated, even if only to a limited extent. As I connected with the inmates and the prison, I became more immersed in my own narrative. I re-visited my story as a form of self-study and educational inquiry. I constructed reflexive narratives by asking about the nature of my teacher development story in the context of imprisoned selves and lives, and institutional rhythms and cycles.

Once having connected education to corrections in my study of the jail, I became engaged in a mostly unfamiliar world. I came to see it as a place where the curriculum-maker can thrive, and where the script of teacher education can be re-written. New scripts produce alternative notions of education, schooling and classroom, and teacher development. In their literal captivity, inmates struggle to be active and self-conscious. This is what I experienced. I learned this not only about others, but also about myself. I, too, felt challenged by the established regulations and procedures of prison life; by its paradigms of correctionalism that affect the ways in which programs and research are carried out and people interact; and by the starkness of the institution itself.

In this book, I told my story in my own terms and in a variety of ways: sometimes I analyzed my experience of a new storytelling milieu; at times I presented and interpreted others' experiences; yet, at other times, I provided detailed accounts of my experiences, encounters and feelings. I treated my self-study as a significant part of the creative research enterprise and qualitative inquiry. When education and research are freed from imprisoning forms of knowledge and discourse, they open to possibility. I built on this story-line with my own feelings and thoughts, writings and images. My images included: the mousetrap, newcomer or "fish", researcher on a carousel, partially closed doors, sandpiper, cover stories, meaningful fragments, captivity and addictive writing. I chose to tell the story that was a living part of me, one that reached into my own childhood past, academic life, and towards anticipated scenarios. I felt compelled to produce a narrative about imprisoned selves that was intimate and personal, rather than academic and distant.

A third shift occurred in my inquiry. I had been gaining insights from the inmates' stories and my own. My perception was that our stories involved a complex interplay of elements of self, institution, cycles and rhythms, writing, dreams and lives. My aim became to reconstruct my portrait of self and others. Although I had been co-constructing a set of meanings in my work with the inmates based on our experiences, I had yet to move to a meta-level question. I realized that the metaphor of imprisoned selves linked our lives and stories, connecting corrections to education. I therefore asked myself, "What is the experience of captivity and education for imprisoned selves?" (chapter 1). My response is that the inmate condition permeates all of life, not just its manifestations in prison and academe. People expand the boundaries of their cells by reaching out to one another through storytelling, writing and sharing:

> The products of narrative schemes are ubiquitous in our lives: they fill our cultural and social environment. We create narrative descriptions for ourselves and for others about our past actions, and we develop storied accounts that give sense to the behavior of others. . . . We are constantly confronted with stories during our conversations and encounters with the written and visual media. . . . At the individual level, people have a narrative of their own lives which enables them to construe what they are and where they are headed. At the cultural level, narratives serve to give cohesion to shared beliefs and to transmit values (Polkinghorne 1988, 14).

Narrative impulses run deep. Even prison guards cannot keep inmates from spending time in one another's cells (Yates 1993). Captivity is an experience of education, and education is an experience of captivity. Key concepts were used in this book to illustrate the dynamic interplay between captivity and education: *rehabilitation* (the miseducative experience that imprisons inmates in correctionalism and its "deadtime," but is also a necessary step towards re-education); *education* (the story of possibility that may return us to ourselves and the world, renewed and perhaps ready to live more meaningfully); and *imprisoned selves* (the educational metaphor that underscores the experience of the inmate condition in institutions and society).

As indicated, I have not exclusively focused on the inmates in this narrative text. Instead, I attempted an interchange among self, other and community to explore wider issues of education and imprisonment, of experience and captivity. A "one-sided focus on the offender then is not a dynamic approach and, therefore, can be viewed as correctionalism" (Maclean and Milovanovic 1991, 2). Even if I were to present an insider's story of inmates in terms that are correctionalist in nature, such as deviant, pathology, and "norm violator" (1991, 2-3), this, too, would be limiting. Such an approach does not treat inmates as individuals nor does it problematize their lives in emergent terms. A correctionalist perspective on inmates upholds "social reaction . . . to the label and not the person. . . . Within this approach self-concept is altered by social reaction to the deviant's behavior so that the deviant's behavior subsequently conforms to the new self-concept" (4). Inmates are imprisoned in social forms of deviance labeling that might serve as self-fulfilling prophecies for them. The self-perceptions that are then internalized confine us more securely than any prison.

Encouraging inmates to write in prison may interrupt this circle of incarceration. We cannot stop inmates from writing, just as we cannot prevent people from telling their stories. If we take away their pencils and paper, then they will use blood on concrete walls, jelly beans on floors, or any other imaginative means to express themselves. I now turn to my own experience of self-imprisonment.

Re-writing the Self: A Cell of One's Own

> Women have sat indoors all these millions of years, so that by this time the very walls are permeated by their creative force, which has, indeed, so overcharged the capacity of bricks and mortar that it must needs harness itself to pens and brushes and business and politics. . . . When I ask you to earn money and have a room of your own, I am asking you to live in the presence of reality, an invigorating life. . . . Shakespeare had a sister. . . . She died young—alas, she never wrote a word. . . . She lives in you and me . . . (Woolf, *A room of one's own*, 1977, 83-84, 107-108).

In order to write this text, I devised a cell of my own and made a prisoner of myself. Caron had made "a prisoner of [him]self" in order to write, even when he was released from prison (Kucherawy 1990, 12). I had become my own "jailer," regimented within a routine that seemed to keep "freedom just beyond reach" (Caron 1978, 159). I approached my task as a serious, full-time commitment and made social sacrifices. I worked days and evenings, and mostly isolated myself in the process. Whenever I was too tired to write, I turned to additional reading, or organizing tasks and issues.

I came to this study after having spent my eighth year (a time-line interrupted by studies and research) community college teaching. The book itself came together after an additional year of teaching, but within the university system and in the United States. My earlier years in programs with community workers and legal students enhanced my knowledge base of the social issues involved in my work. I approached my classes with a personal interpretation of the formal curricula that provided us with opportunities to journal, prepare essays and present. We discussed themes relating to law and society, and offenders' and victims' rights. My former students, most of whom advocate capital punishment, believe that all inmates are serious offenders who deserve to "rot in jail." I often faced this frozen perception during my study. It is one that belongs to a wider social audience over which the media exert power and influence.

Self-imprisonment is a topic that is relevant to inquiry in a teacher development study. As I worked on my text, I confined myself to a writing cell, but it opened to other cells. As in my dream of the honey comb-like prison, I expanded the walls of my own "tightly knitted cells" in real-life (Appendix A). In this dream, I lie on the bed in my cell in order to give the place more scope. I communicate with other prisoners as part of a "beehive of activity." In real-life I isolated myself in my writing cell but I still reached out to others. I had deliberately perpetuated a set of isolating conditions for myself. I reduced my network to just a few people who understood my schedule and my need to remain focused. A great deal of daily concentration and productivity was required of me, yet I could not cut myself off from being connected to others. I care about other people and their lives. Indeed, life itself "got in the way" of my ideal work plan.

I experienced the pain of personal loss and the strength of recovery during my three-year study. I also felt the pain of memory. This study returned me to my childhood and to its sometimes grief. Certain family relatives, as well as several friends' step-fathers, violated young girls when the women were at work or away. I remember my friend with the scratches on her hands and back. She used to blame her rose bushes. My other friend did not seem fearful. Because she always had money, she had a false sense of power. The writing re-surfaced such painful memories, but it was also critical to making inside-out connections. But, more than this, it gave me a higher purpose during those times when I felt overwhelmed by pressures, my own anxieties and flashbacks. As Cleaver (1968) writes: "Once inside my cell, I feel safe" (51), but not always!

As is the case with many writers, I also struggled with issues of life and death. Just as something lives during the writing process, something dies. My mother suffered terribly just before my study concluded in 1994. My mother was heavily medicated during her struggle for life. She had lost a great deal of weight; became confused and distant; and essentially retreated into a shell. But she retained her dignity. She insisted on sitting up for her company; on being well groomed; and on being surrounded by family only. We were told not to have any expectations of her, but we did. We shared the difficulty of losing my mother with her and reached out for comfort. Everyone took turns holding her hands.

I communicated from my shell to my mother's on a regular basis, but the nature of our "cells" was different. Mine was self-chosen and connected to vital opportunities for growth each day. I lived to construct educational experiences through writing. The book weighed heavily on me as I sought better ways of writing and thinking about connections among ideas. My mother also felt a weight. The pain pump that was strapped to her shoulder regulated medication that drained into her system, around the clock. She felt disconnected from the world but could not explain why. My health privileges me. I am able to explain myself.

Although this text did not focus on mothering, I became aware, as I developed new educative relationships in prison, of how much impact "mothering" has had on my life. I now write in part through the memory of having connected differently with my mother, my self. I had confided to my sister that I felt like that little girl who used to wonder why our mother "play acted" being sick with a headache. I used to wonder the same about people who wore glasses or even carried a cane. Why didn't they just open up their eyes to see better, or straighten up to walk properly? Why didn't our mother just wish herself better?

With these final words, I write as though I am located differently, outside the manila prison or that place lived and constructed. But, "shades of the prison-house" (Wordsworth 1965, 154) continue to exist for me in my life, in academe, and in the wider community. With regard to the experience of writing, it was restrictive at times and enlarging at other times. As writers, we narrow our worlds in order to broaden our scope. We suffer this paradox. Other writers (Bell 1991; Conle 1993; Dietrich 1992) have also written about their personal knowledge to invoke reflection on teacher development. They captured images of imprisonment and captivity in their writing without having entered a prison. Like Yates (1993), the prison guard, I had chosen to be there and to explore my own "being" in this context.

Such reflections can take place anywhere, on any soil, in a variety of situations and contexts. Dietrich (1992) wrote that "life came to a halt when I was unable to proceed with the writing of my thesis due to a block in my ability to read critically and develop my review of the literature" (2). Like me, she became a "go-girl" of sorts who experienced "breaking through an embedded facade of resistance, rooted in every facet of my life [that] created a major turning point in my thesis journey on relationship and moved me to another level of awareness" (2). Bell (1991) wrote that part of the struggle for her in writing resulted from the lack of recourse to a "ready made paradigm within which to place my discussion" (326). She did not want to compromise the "personal and narrative quality of the individual experience" in a study of cultural literacy (326). And yet, the struggle is to forge understandings of the narrative mode even though "we know precious little in any formal sense about how to make good stories . . . in contrast to our vast knowledge of how science and logical reasoning proceed" (Bruner 1986, 14). But, we all know how to tell a good story.

Conle (1993) experienced a "restriction of movement in [her] left arm" as a "frozen shoulder." She interpreted this bodily experience as a manifestation of her resentment of "functioning very much 'on the surface' only" in terms of "blandness and academic games" (323). One's frozen shoulder is another's cramped hands, blurred vision or aching back. All of my usual stress-related conditions continued and were even exacerbated. I felt driven to write.

My colleagues have written about themselves as inmates in academe, even if only fleetingly. Images of resistance and break-throughs, restrictive paradigms, and the dysfunctional self configure experiences of the doctoral journey. Doctoral writers (Bell 1991; Conle 1993; Dietrich 1992; and Mullen 1994) have nonetheless experienced the paradox of becoming alive through narrative methodology. Narrative inquiry itself demands openness to contexts, to people and their stories and feelings, and to oneself. In short, "we have to *be* in order to do inquiry" (Conle 1993, 329).

The fore-mentioned writers constructed an implicit story-line about imprisonment and captivity in teacher education and research, and in academe itself. Traditional and mainstream academic paradigms often lack authenticity for narrative writers. We search for personal ways of establishing the knowledge that we claim. Personal, practical knowledge research offers a shelter to writers who want to study people in their settings (Fenstermacher 1994). Narrative inquiry offers the same, but in the form of self-study, or the study of self in context.

I want to continue to study, and interact with, people in their settings. In the future I anticipate working further with narrative inquiry in diverse classroom and research cultures. I wish to assist others in telling their research stories and finding creative ways of linking themselves to educational inquiry. My desire to teach, and to be part of alternative classroom sites and innovative forms of curriculum-making, is a story-line of this text. I have dreamt about teaching, even within the scope of prison life and culture (Appendix A).

My dreams feature a variety of teaching and learning images. However, as the following list indicates, only some are connected to conventional classroom settings: training sessions (images of roses with cryptic messages); competent literacy learners; traditional, bookish tutors; dry intellectual faculties; violated manuscripts of people's (participants' and researchers') life stories; college settings with lecture halls for classrooms; performing impostors (teachers/researchers); churches housing the homeless; vicarious needle use by an undercover officer; break-and-entry of a violator into people's homes and bodies; child-victims (my missing participants) of abduction; researcher-as-prisoner inside a prison-amphitheater and against a beige prison wall; and seminar leaders who are effective to the degree to which they facilitate others' stories.

I continue conducting inquiries into sensitive topics and into issues of sensitivity that arise within the research process (Renzetti and Lee 1993). I enjoy the conceptual, methodological and imaginative challenges that such research demands.

Re-inventing Corrections: The Future

The world of corrections has shown me that many of its educational processes carry the stigma of controversy. For example, I have introduced the following issues: condoms and needle exchange programs in prisons with respect to AIDS education (Anonymous, 1992); the "dynamic inter-relations" which underlie the "crime process: offender, victim, police, . . . and community . . ." (MacLean and Milovanovic 1991, 2-5); the "complex interaction of agents of formal social control, public perception, and the media" (MacLean and Milovanovic 1991, 5); the availability of correctional programs and others, such as computers and Ping-Pong. Who would assign educational worth to the game of Ping-Pong? Yates (1993), the prison guard, tells a gripping story of how:

> recreational ping-pong reached far more trainees than the computer-education program did, and had more far-reaching implications for

their lives. In the end, these kids had learned a lot about skill-development, and about winning strategies that they could apply to any aspect of their lives and any goals they chose to reach for. They learned, often for the first time, that with correct application, rather than physical force, they could achieve just about anything they wanted (273-274).

The focus in my text is not on any of the above. Rather, it is on those prison stories that provide insight into the relationship between captivity and education. Stories are shared, written and even published in corrections, but only in very restrictive contexts. Inmates need to be able to tell their stories more freely and these need to be documented for the public. Just as Roger Caron is recognized by Pierre Berton as an experienced researcher (*Go-Boy!*, 1978), so too are other inmates potential researchers. They have a great deal to write about and to share. Rushton, editor of *Words from inside* (published by the Prison Arts Foundation), reflected on his anthology of prisoners' poetry and prose. He gave reasons as to why inmates should be permitted to write:

> I think the purpose is to allow these people a chance to reach the public and let the public know that there are people in prison who are capable of communicating and who have something to say. . . . These people are speaking from a very direct experience. They are trying to decipher emotions which have become impressed by the stark reality of prison. It is a form of self-expression. Also, we can only understand their motivation by reading what they are writing about. How can we expect to understand the reasons behind their being incarcerated in the first place if we don't read what they have to say about their own personal history? (Kucherawy 1990, 12).

Stephen Reid, former inmate and author, wrote in *Jackrabbit parole* that prison writing is unique because "it is writing that never blinks, never backs off. It moves relentlessly inward, driving straight for the wound" (Kucherawy, 1990). But we cannot assume that the circle of incarceration for inmates is broken once they have written and even published. We need to be able to keep inmates' texts in print. My search for inmates' published writing reinforces the sense that prison writers are not in control of their own voices and perceptions. We keep them in captivity by withdrawing their writings from circulation within the public domain.

We also keep inmates in captivity by losing track of their whereabouts in the prison system. To illustrate, my inmate-participants need to deal with Pam at the agency. In order to receive assistance at various stages in their sentencing and release, they must request services. Examples of services include counseling, housing, employment and financial aid. Pam has not been contacted by my inmate-participants. She does not even know the exact locations of Black Hawk, Sammy, Mark, Sear, Adrian and the others. We can both only speculate. Pam names "security" as the reason for her lack of information. The disappeared are not in control of their own whereabouts. They are lost in the system. The inmate narrative and condition is characterized by withdrawal, captivity and anonymity.

One of the most difficult technical aspects of doing this study was my attempt to locate certain texts. For example, Reid's novel, *Jackrabbit parole,* is out of print. According to the central libraries and bookstores I contacted, even the publishing information on it is not available. I have not been able to read his story. Cleaver's (1968) classic is currently in print, but difficult to locate. The controversy surrounding this book had apparently led to its censorship. MacDonald's (1988) book is also out of print. One of her former parole officers kindly lent me his copy.

Writing opportunities and programs for inmates can take different forms. Inmates can even make progress by themselves with the aid of certain provisions and facilities. The Drug Awareness program, sponsored at the jail, had been carried on at a federal penitentiary by group members. They claim that they are mostly in control of the sessions and we could see this for ourselves when we visited them. Inmates have also met to share their writing: "There are quite a few guys here who write. Seems that every convict wants to. Some of them have managed to sell a piece here and there. They have a writer's workshop which meets in the library under the wing of our librarian" (Cleaver 1968, 53). But exclusion still prevails, even in such a seemingly progressive context: "I've never had a desire to belong to this workshop. . . . members . . . are all white and all sick when it comes to color. . . . Blacks and whites do not fraternize together in comfort here" (53).

There have even been models put into place that seemed to be working better than what Cleaver describes, but they, too, encounter resistance. Brian Fawcett, a liberal arts teacher in prisons in British Columbia, has experienced his own writing program being uprooted for unspecified reasons. His approach to the inmates was "not as criminals in need of punishment or therapeutic rehabilitation, but as students in need of historical data, ideas, models and contexts, and the cognitive tools to evaluate and manipulate them." He says that "if we can fill people's heads with words, . . . they're less impulsive" (Kucherawy 1990). Fawcett's claim is an important one. It is a basis for a study that could carry much weight with correctional decision-makers.

Fawcett reports that the rate of recidivism for his students was only 15% compared with the average, which is between 66 and 75%. Despite its apparent success, this program was "subverted . . . in much the same way all successful experiments are. . . . The system wants to control . . ." (1990). Many of the inmates with whom I worked were recidivists. Sammy, Mark, and Sear held criminal records, and had been young offenders. Roger Caron re-offended within the last year, even after having taken successful steps to become a well-known author and public figure.

All of my inmate-writers either wrote to me about the value of sharing their stories or told me as much in person. I experienced with them the therapeutic value of creation and art. In his foreword to Caron's (1978) book, Pierre Berton writes: "I have called him a loser because that is what he is—or at least was until he started work on the present manuscript, an act of therapy as well as an act of creation. . . . For most of his life Roger Caron has been a loser because he has refused to conform and also because, until recently, he has neglected to learn from experience" (7).

I compiled a newsletter that features inmates' writings (Appendix B) and, although it was approved, certain stories were modified or censored altogether. Images of abuse, violence, negativity and criticism were considered inappropriate because they conflict with the rehabilitative efforts of corrections. Such logic infantalizes the very people they say that they are trying to rehabilitate. The newsletter project has been carried on within the context of this surveillant community. Despite censorship practices being actively at work, inmates can find ways to write. Narrative identity is the "unity of a person's life as it is experienced and articulated in stories that express this experience" (Widdershoven 1993, 7). The problem is that the "narrative identity" of inmates is being significantly altered to fit a pattern that constitutes an intelligible way of life within corrections.

Instead of functioning in isolated instances, a writers' forum could be established within and across prisons. A team of inmates and teachers could head such an enterprise locally, nationally and internationally. A formal connection could be made between corrections and teacher education to involve schools in such an activity. At least one Canadian board of education already participates in both worlds. Affiliated with the jail, it appoints teachers, like Sally and Anna, as on-site markers and provides inmates with structured courses.

Prisoners should be encouraged to write their stories as a means of self-expression and of discovering self-knowledge. The less idealistic, utilitarian view is that writing can be a means of rehabilitation. Even this view may not yet be accepted. Corrections apparently views rehabilitative programs as only "gravy." Security is the top priority (Sally, Education Coordinator, personal communication, April 18, 1991). It has always been controversial for inmates to write their stories, regardless of the context and intent. Cleaver's (1968) autobiography created a stir with its re-issue because it "challenge(s) the current bleaching out of the black influence on the cultural and political climate of the Sixties. This book is a classic because it is not merely a book about that decade, regarded as demonic by some and by others as the most thrilling and humanistic of this century, *Soul on Ice* is the sixties" (Ishmael Reed 1968, xx). Reid (1990), author and ex-convict, concludes that "society . . . resents a writer from prison. We can't stomach someone coming out a better person. We want them to be humbled" (Kucherawy, 13).

Rehabilitative programs focus on step-by-step, formulaic understandings of story, self and recovery. Pam's narrative approach to inmates' stories in the drug group was overridden by correctional, mainstream approaches. As a society, we can, and do, derive educational value from inmates' stories, but we still need to find ways of enhancing their efforts. We now accept someone like Roger Caron writing his story. Even though he has made money through his contracts with the publishing world, and was paroled earlier than expected in 1978 with the publication of *Go-Boy!*, he was still a bank robber.

Our perceptions may shift once again when we imagine a Clifford Olson in action. Crimes against humanity conjure up a powerful set of emotions. Olson was imprisoned 10 years ago for killing 11 children and teens. He has embarked on writing his story behind bars, entitling it *Clifford Olson: Portrait of a serial killer* (Cheney 1991). Even if we believe, as I do, that inmates should be permitted to write their stories, we must grapple with the serious ethical issues involved. Olson, for example, could offer valuable insights into the mind of a serial killer whose socialization occurred within familiar micro-worlds. According to Cheney, a journalist, Olson portrays himself as someone who is flawed and troubled, compassionate and remorseful: "the work comes across as a ham-fisted diatribe aimed at convincing the reader that there is hope for Clifford Olson—a calculated, revisionist work [whose] long-range plan [is] to convince the courts that he should some day be allowed to go free" (Cheney 1991). Olson is not unique in this respect.

Jack Henry Abbott (1981) wrote that his story was without personal motive and that it was about the "experience of life" inside prison (22). Lovitt (1992) claims that "many confessing murderers" (though he mentions Abbott, his focus is on Pierre Riviere) aim to get "readers to view them in a particular light [which] often takes precedence as a motive for confessing" (24). On the other hand, Reid (1990), author and ex-convict, points out that: "many people, especially victims of crime, are angered that prisoners should profit from their writing. Even though they realize that outlaws and criminals have fascinating stories, they wonder why publishers should encourage and support these convicts" (Kucherawy 1990).

Who owns Olson's story? Is it Olson, or corrections, or the families of victims, or society itself? Should he be allowed to tell his story and to fashion it as he chooses? What if others, even as few as one or two readers, feel inspired to re-enact his crimes? As a writer and teacher educator, I believe that everyone has the fundamental right to tell his or her story. But, my missing participants, and "the disappeared" within the prison system more generally, have been denied this. I have made this point with the use of particular situations involving Mark, Sammy and Adrian. We need to keep searching for ways to communicate about the ethical issues that arise out of storytelling practices. At one end of the continuum we have inmates like Olson who write. At this same end, there is Andrei Chikatilo, a former school-teacher. He is considered the "world's worst serial killer." He has been charged in relation to 53 killings in Russia ("Onlookers swoon at court gore," 1992). How would we react to someone like this who is probably also fully capable of telling his horrific story?

As I see it, when we use Olson as our test case for discussing whether those in captivity should be permitted to write their autobiographies, we are restricting ourselves. He exists only at the extreme end of the continuum. We might also locate here the men I experienced who were placed in protective custody for their persecution of women and children. Yet, they too have valuable insights to share about a variety of issues, including their reflections on our systems and communities, as well as their personal histories. Adrian Sands, for example, wanted to publish a critique of the medical practice within corrections. His story was rejected, but I included aspects of it throughout this book.

At the other end of the continuum, there are the valorized inmate-writers who enjoy their celebrity status as heroes. They are heralded for their great courage in personal transcendence over unjust treatment within police states. Political (Grossman 1990; Sharansky 1988) inmates, and literary (Dostoevsky 1965; Wilde 1986) writers, tell their own stories of imprisonment within seriously inhumane contexts. They also reveal the untold stories of the powerful and disadvantaged, from the now defunct Soviet Union through War World II Hungary to Milwaukee. Furthermore, these writers are recognized as researchers who can provide insights into the conditions of our international prison systems. As Sharansky (1988) realized, the aim of his interrogator was to "separate [him] from everything and everybody [he] cared about, to deprive [his] life of its meaning, and to leave [him] without dignity or hope" (14). Dostoevsky (1965) wrote that he was unable to tell another inmate "what [he] needed to know, and could not even understand why [he himself] was so interested in the characters of the prisoners around [them], especially those nearest to them. . . . Evidently [he] must find out for [him]self and not ask questions" (100).

Ordinary people who struggle to tell their story of besieged innocence (Callwood 1990; Harris 1986; Radish (with Laurie "Bambi" Bembenek) 1992) are, I reason, situated close to political and literary writers. Their acts of murder arose out of complex life circumstances. Only the autobiographical form can yield insight into their experiences. The middle of the continuum reflects the writings of inmates, such as Caron and some of my students, whose crimes were committed mostly against themselves.

I experienced censorship myself. For example, my poem, "Orphaned Motherhood," was rejected for publication in my own newsletter. I was told that my poem was too powerful and touching. However, it was also a personal account that storied my mythology as a marginal-insider. This level of intimacy had made the officials feel uncomfortable. They may know that compassion is potentially geared towards action, and to the healing impulses within ourselves. In studies of marginalized others, we may re-live aspects of their suffering, especially if we bring personal histories to our work.

I was surprised to have met so many women working inside the prison system. Most were empathetic and hard-working on behalf of the inmates. They were also afraid to confront the established codes. The inmates responded in the same manner. But, together we created an environment in which we strove to transform the story of suffering and punishment into one of healing and hope. For my own part, I functioned interactively, not at a distance. I attempted to give back to the people and the institution itself. I looked for ways to connect not only in a day's visit and over the longer stretch of my research, but also beyond its formal closure.

There are others who have had much more experience within corrections than I have. They offer various alternatives and solutions. These are deserving of study. For example, Scott (1982), prison psychiatrist and author, devised a detailed plan called "Reward city: A new penal environment" (195). To me, it reveals not a vision of communal surveillance or those "mechanisms of power" used "for measuring, supervising and correcting the abnormal" (Foucault 1977, 199), but of an anti-Panopticon or place of community. In this self-sufficient, enclosed city, inmates could live with their families. This would prepare them for re-entry into society. They would work for a living and make use of the usual facilities that are typical of cities. This lay-out is a modification of "farm, industrial and work camp environments" (200). It is an example of what might function to improve the inmate condition, promoting re-education to better lives. This model needs to incorporate writing opportunities and other fora. A library is also necessary. This is not a minor point. As Abbott (1981), published author and convict, writes:

> Books are dangerous. . . . I've served time just for requesting books. . . . No federal penitentiary . . . has a prison library. The authorities say we 'misuse' our knowledge if allowed to educate ourselves according to our natural impulses. . . . That is why they now have 'education programs' in prison, i.e., so we learn *only* what they want us to learn. *I pride myself on the fact that I've never been in a prison school* (20).

Plans for rehabilitation ideally allow for input from the inmates themselves. For example, a reward city requires on-site addiction treatment clinics. Such clinics are high on the inmates' own list needed for personal recovery and change. Such a plan of restructuring could be undertaken to revitalize the old English system that gave rise to such Canadian federal penitentiaries as Millhaven and Kingston (Scott 1982). We need to re-educate in cost-efficient ways by generating progressive alternatives to the existing system. At present, we maintain "warehouses for cons" (Yates 1993, 26) which reduce their own humanity—and ours.

Change will need to come about within the public world itself in order for corrections to become launched in a new direction: "Prison programs that work, that save the taxpayer millions of dollars in the long term, just aren't what the public want to read, see on television, or hear debated on talk radio" (Yates 1993, 307). The media shape what the public experiences. They also perpetuate stereotypical views of inmates and prisons. As Yates (1993) wrote: "My experience in corrections had given me a very different view of media than I had had when I worked in the field. Countless times I and others had called journalists to persuade them to do stories on interesting programs we had cooked up. Nothing. . . . They showed up only to report escapes, riots, or allegations of 'excessive force' by staff" (306). My *Prison Media Scrapbook* is filled with such anecdotes that sensationalize the restrictive, if not damaging, aspects of inmates' lives and the prison culture. We are imprisoned in distorted perceptions that we can confront only by becoming insiders. We need, in other words, to take a look for ourselves.

Imagine a scenario: If either the Minister of Correctional Services (provincial) or Solicitor General of Canada (federal) were to ask me about what I learned from my prison research that could help them to guide policy, I would say: the public does not believe the rhetoric of rehabilitation. They are fed stories about convicted murderers with missing front teeth who sit rolling cigarettes beneath posters of a skull with the inscription: "Bad to the bone" (Cheney 1991). My research supports educational gains of rehabilitation, but not necessarily those regimented, formulaic approaches to transformed lives. Inmates want to learn and teach. Writing, reading and sharing are means of achieving personal empowerment for them. They teach us that their own transformation is possible as well as our own, and that hope and hard-work are the catalysts for such promise. The inmates and teachers taught me that my own humanity is my most precious gift. I positioned myself to relate empathetically. I identified with my participants' problems, worries, joys, dreams and successes that are the collective human lot.

The world of corrections is evolving. It, too, opens doors. The experience of rehabilitation for inmates, although under strain, is in the process of renewal. One of the pieces of the story that is missing is the value of an interactive narrative approach. My research promotes this perspective on the inmates and their educational stories. We educators presume to know too much about them or wish to know too little.

In talking with the Minister and Solicitor, I would refer to the Minister of Education himself. He had addressed the volunteers in corrections during a conference. He told us a story. In it, he had engaged an inmate and the inmates' experiences of "alienation, deprivation, and sorrow" (chapter 3). The Minister struggled at a loss as to how to listen, respond and comfort the inmate. In the process, the Minister seems to have re-discovered his own humanity. I would then tell the Minister and Solicitor the story of how the prison system had educated me in terms of my own humanity. I came to have intimate knowledge of being monitored and regulated, humiliated and even censored. I had also experienced my own dignity once I insisted on it and was given a degree of self-responsibility, recognition and control.

Those inmates who experienced feeling dignified were fortunate and probably the exception: they would thank us for taking the time to listen to them; for treating their ideas, writing and aspirations seriously; and for publishing their work. I witnessed them, against all odds, finding ways to better promote their own re-education. Some inmates are searching for acceptance and for productive ways of giving. Imprisoned selves are worth saving. My perception of inmates as capable learners and teachers is part of the new story that is not yet in place. Stories that promote suffering and punishment, exclusion and ridicule, and even blame and apathy, will not do. The Ministers could make gains by functioning interactively, not at a distance, in order to take a look for themselves. By doing so, they can help to evolve a new story of imprisoned selves.

Inmates themselves should be considered a crucial link in negotiating forms of re-education and curriculum-making. They are inside-out knowers. Scott's plan for a re-envisioned penal system may be an ideal model for assisting inmates towards transformation. However, writing opportunities and other fora could be incorporated into the existing system along with other improvements.   As Yates notes, we also need to help the public to evolve new perspectives on inmates and corrections itself. Those of us who have been inside know that such trustworthy accounts can be generated and shared.

Re-scripting Teacher Education Out of the Ashes: The Future

I undertook research in a difficult-to-access educational site. My meaning-based data sources were multiple, experiential and sometimes fleeting.   Why am I suggesting that other researchers can make narrative gains by also exploiting unconventional research sites and elusive data bases? The aim of many qualitative researchers is "to sensitize rather than generalize" about human phenomena involved in the experience and development of the self (Wiener and Rosenwald 1993, 33).   We need to get into those places to learn about how "human beings can destroy not only their own form but also that of others. We can be deprived of our identity against our will. It is our duty to understand that and how it can happen, and to rescue as many life stories—identities or, if you wish, narratives—as we can out of the ashes" (Funkenstein 1993, 29). By rescuing untold stories of teaching and learning, we can begin to re-script teacher education itself.

My study of multiple imprisoned selves has given me the opportunity to study the rich human resources that are sadly wasted in prison.   My personal and professional stories of conversation and writing, encounters and dreams, offer researchers an experience in self-discovery and ongoing learning that they too can think about and use.   While I am not suggesting that others will identify with the composition of my narrative, I am hoping that others can adopt my starting-point of imprisoned selves to develop the richness of their own stories.   The images of marginal-insider and vicarious participant might also offer positionality and help to yield insights.   I am not necessarily advising my readers to begin work in prisons.   If my readers can find, through another medium, the stories they cannot forget; the stories which propel and shape their inquiry; and the stories which help them to deal honestly with themselves, their values and assumptions, then they, too, can undertake a narrative quest which is personally meaningful.   Such a search, because of the integrity and deep commitment it involves, can lead to a more trustworthy account.

Encounters in correctional facilities have reinforced my sense that narrative is not a static phenomenon. My own portrait, for example, is ongoing, fragmented at times, coherent at other times, but continually shifting and changing. In her use of reflection for a study of teachers' personal practical knowledge, Clandinin (1986) strove to "challenge our assumptions and reconstruct our experience" (167). My research also seeks to contribute to both meaning and knowledge that are experientially-based and practice-oriented. I welcomed being engaged by inmates and others in a process of constructing new perspectives. The significant others with whom I have worked have contributed to the direction of my story, to its very creation, and to my experience of it as transformative.

If an inquiry into imprisoned lives can be looked at in broader, cultural terms, much can be inferred about the role of learning opportunities in education. I ask, "What contribution does my study make to the growing knowledge of storytelling and narrative inquiry in education?" My answer is that, if we want to listen to participants and to work with their stories as a way of empowering them as curriculum-makers (Connelly and Clandinin 1988b; Clandinin and Connelly 1992), then we will have created a mutually satisfying situation. Our own stories need to be told and written, and reconstructed along with participants'. My text also strives to engage more fully the educative process by moving to the margins. By doing so, I enabled myself to re-envision the core of teacher education; classroom and curriculum research; and myself and others.

I intended my study of the jail to make a contribution to educational inquiry, teacher development, and narrative studies. Only a few texts have been written on education in prisons, and fewer have adopted an experiential approach. Davidson (1991), for example, had been a teacher in prison schools, but his focus is not on teacher development or self-story. Rather, his interest is sociological as he attempts to engage those forces which impact on prisons. I could find no other research which has interpreted prison life using the narrative ethnographic construct. A number of North American dissertations have been carried out in the area of correctional education (Angle 1989; Bastion 1987; Clarke 1987; Futrell 1986; Johnson 1987; Ripley 1988). Other studies on prisons have been completed in the areas of clinical psychology (Foreman 1988; Serin 1988); and sociology, criminology and penology (Davidson 1984, 1991; Gallagher 1988; Gardner 1986; McGrory 1991; McMahon 1989).

My aim was to explore a fresh perspective on the worlds of corrections and teacher education. I asked, How could teacher education be re-imagined as the world of corrections, and how could corrections itself be approached educationally? The sub-title of my book, "*An inquiry into prisons and academe*," captures the spirit of my intentions. In terms of application, one could look at the metaphoric use of my ideas in schools and higher education. Just as the prison system regulates, dictates and censors people and their stories, so too do the school system and other formal institutional contexts. A follow-up study could inquire explicitly into educational domains as places of imprisonment. A few others (Foucault 1977; Pinar 1975) have pursued the theme of imprisonment in the context of dehumanizing schooling structures and experiences.

Academe served, in this book, as a backdrop or curtain on the world of corrections. Indeed, the world of corrections could be read as a sustained metaphor of academia, with conceptual adjustments to be made where necessary or desirable. I kept my meanings open or "performable" by the reader, and I did this with respect to metaphoric possibilities: "For with explicitness, the reader's degrees of interpretive freedom are annulled" (Bruner 1986, 25). When implicit ideas are made explicit, the direction of the inquiry itself is altered. I have therefore had to carefully consider how to preserve my story-line while courting other possibilities.

This insider's account provides for an awakening or transformation of perspective. Just as I have learned about myself through others, I hope that others have learned about themselves through this story. My reader can specifically consider how he or she becomes the "main research instrument as he or she observes, asks questions, and interacts with research participants" (Glesne and Peshkin 1992, 6). My readers can also aim to un-cover their own subjugated and submerged voices. Mullen and Diamond (1996) pursue "confinement [as] an epistemological model for studying how knowledge and power, self and others, are intertwined" (Abstract). We study "marginality within both alternative teacher development sites and our own educational narratives. . . . We are scripting and re-scripting teacher education to liberate both students and educators from feelings of exclusion" (1-2).

Future directions of my research take not one but many forms:

- resourcing teacher educators' experiences of imprisonment (e.g, paradigms of research) and their life histories of institutionalization;
- focusing on newcomers (offenders, and beginning professors and researchers) on their orientation to a new culture and experiences of marginality;
- working with prisoners in non-prescribed, open fora on their stories of experience that offer possibilities in re-education;
- discovering teachers' and students' educational meanings of experience and imprisonment within schools;
- interviewing the women who are waiting for men to be released from prisons;
- learning about the lives of prison-teachers;
- tracking inmates both inside the prison system and outside of it;
- pursuing knowledge of the cultural diversity and self-identity representations of inmates in prisons and in academe;
- and, engaging prisoners and in projects of genuine re-education.

My book offers perspectives on the re-education of multiple imprisoned selves as teachers and learners. I also provide insight into the narrative mode of inquiry as linked to teacher development and prison education. The story I tell is intertwined with the inmates' stories. It is about my practice as a researcher whose journey took me to the marginal and oppressed.

Personal encounters with marginalized groups constitute a critical omission in teacher education and in society. I have aimed to treat inmates' lives and stories both narratively and evocatively. In doing so, I offer potential in areas of study which are not yet fully appreciated or un-covered. I also offer an approach to inquiry-oriented questions which is cyclic. The point is that such questions cannot be neatly answered: Insight transcends frameworks. Sensitive topics in education need to be pursued, but we need to de-privilege our academic eye in order to research differently. I now bring my text full circle. I began my inquiry into imprisoned selves with an inmate's own signature. This, too, is how I end it:

> It was my mother who asked, "How can you sit by and let others write about you? It's your life. You lived it." One has little or nothing to say about what is written about you, or by whom, but she was right. . . . There is so much to tell now, such a jumble of caring and thinking and experiencing. . . . But if you are a thoughtful person, and a reasonably

brave person, wanting to live life more fully, you will always be tempted to touch new kinds of fire, and then have to make peace with the person you were before (Harris, 1986, 20, 24).

Appendix A

Personal Dream Text:
Jail-Related Themes (1991-92)

> As I write, the world inside my head becomes more real than the physical world; feelings more real than facts; thoughts more real than spoken words; my unconscious mind more real than my conscious mind; the visionary world of dreams more real than the waking world. . . . I feel as if I've jumped off a cliff and am flapping my arms trying to learn to fly before crashing. . . . At other times I find myself struggling out of a mud hole (Sylvia Fraser, *My father's house*, 1987).

Education, Literacy and Writing

Cryptic Messages

I open up the box of roses sent to me by the [agency that supervises my work in the jail]. The card accompanying the roses has the word "referendum" only on it. I sit with this card in my lap puzzling over the cryptic message. I can't seem to figure out the meaning of the message. (January 2, 1991)

I'm a volunteer in the jail. I watch through a window as handwriting, in the form of a cryptic message, is being scrawled across the sky directly in front of me. I am leaning heavily against an older man who is holding hands with his girlfriend. Many others crowd us. I suddenly realize that the messages are being controlled and directed from within the jail.   Some kind of computerized system is in operation that allows for such an activity to be performed.

After catching on, I sent a message to [a colleague], but it didn't show up on the screen. I reason that the "engineer" can't read his own handwriting.   Just as I surmise that the handwriting across the sky belongs to [a colleague] and that he is sending me a message, his writing becomes so tiny that I squint to decipher the bottom portion of the screen. (The sky had transformed into the computer screen at this point.) Finally his message disappears altogether.

I move throughout one range of the jail with ease talking to inmates, feeling "freer" as days go by. At one point I notice that no one is wearing their identification badge except for me. I reflect on how necessary it is that we identify ourselves as such. We shouldn't become too lax in such matters of grave importance, I'm thinking, as I suddenly register an inmate's warmth towards me. The time is ripe for him. I touch my badge. (January 15, 1991)

Eros and Corrections

I am in a room containing a bed and desk teaching literacy to a short, blond-haired youth. To my surprise, he already seems literate. I feel some confusion as to how to "teach" literacy to him.   He is scribbling sentences on yellow foolscap with a pencil. The problem is that his pencil is so dull that his writing is getting bigger and bigger and harder and harder to decipher. I jump to a meta-level construct: I'm learning, from this prisoner of a high caliber, the irony of being in the position of teaching literacy to a competent reader and writer.

I turn and ask to have the bed removed from the room as it is distracting from our professional relationship. (April 4, 1990)

His tutor was old and rather unattractive—a bookish and dull woman. I watched her as she busily prepared for their meeting which was about to take place in one of the small, overly cluttered and clustered, cubicles. She mentioned that she planned to talk with Sam about Dostoyevsky's (1982) classic novel, *Crime and punishment*. My heart leapt, my temperature shot up, and I grew flustered. I quickly tried to find a way into the conversation that would grab her attention. She seemed so intellectual and in control that it was all I could do to keep my insecurities in check. I blurted out that I had just finished reading Dostoyevsky's novel and that I wished to commend her on her excellent choice. She picked up on this opportunity to develop a teaching angle on the book. First she asked what I thought of the book and what my experience had been of reading it. Then she asked me what I considered to be its most valuable message. I was immediately thrown off-guard and my intellectual faculties felt dry. I searched for something to say and managed to blurt our something that seemed to satisfy the urgency and agony of the moment.

The murmur of voices resonated through me as I listened carefully at a safe distance. With wet hair wrapped in a damp towel, I dashed into their cubicle and, without making direct eye contact, left something for Sam. Had he recognized me? (September 15, 1991)

Violated Manuscripts

The manuscript he seized upon dashing through the doors of the bus was mine. I watched with dismay as a large black torso jaunted with athletic precision down a nearby residential street. Wait right there!, I shouted silently, miming the horror I felt as I watched my stolen manuscript vanishing in the distance. No! No! No! I must get it back immediately! I jumped off the bus and, in high heels, pursued my attacker who, with fleeting piracy, remained at a safe distance ahead of me. How dare he? How dare he steal my manuscript, my story, my life?, I cried out. (October 25, 1991)

Two adolescent lovers lay clutching their manuscript as they watchfully remained hidden from sight. One of their high school peers spotted them but did not expose their hiding place. They looked out at him wide-eyed, afraid as he looked in at them. A crowd milled about in the barn looking for the fugitives. No one thought to explore the semi-secluded area where the lovers lay hiding. The funny thing about the lovers' hiding place is that it was, at least theoretically, transparent because it was nothing more than a flat painted line that exposed open space on both sides. The lovers were literally nuzzled up against this line, and yet the only person who had spotted them was this young boy. (October 30, 1991)

Marginal-Insider

College Teacher

It took me a long time to get to the college where I had to teach a class. I had yet to check with the administrators as to the time and curriculum of the course. I knew that I was arriving late to teach my first course in a new college setting. This reality made me feel very anxious as I rushed towards the building. When I found the appropriate coordinator she didn't seem too unnerved by me. I was equipped with a large, black tape recorder which I carried under my arm to take to class. I wasn't exactly sure how I was going to use the recorder, but it made me feel impressive.

When I looked at the course syllabus for the first time, I was struck by how the course appeared much more involved than I had anticipated. I was aware, too, of not having prepared. I leaned towards the idea of having the students introduce one another and talk fairly generally about what, I wasn't sure. I was also aware that I wouldn't be able to outline my expectations on the first day—this would simply have to wait as I was blanking in this regard.

When I finally found the classroom well into its official starting time, I was shocked to discover that it had been set up as a lecture hall. People were packed into the entire upper floor (balcony) plus the lower floor. Every seat had been taken. Hundreds of eyes suddenly shifted to me! I was feeling that I had no right to be here. I couldn't use my plan and I had no expectations set out either. I felt like an impostor, not a teacher, because teachers always know all of these things. I felt overwhelmed but absorbed the message from my audience that I was supposed to be performing.

I laid down my tape recorder and began to talk, apologizing for being late and thanking everyone for coming. (February 14, 1991)

Street Researcher

I desperately required nourishment from any charity outlet that provided food and sleep. I wandered the streets, arms outstretched. Upon discovering that the cafeteria of a church organization was charging for meals, I felt stunned. I was so hungry that I didn't stop at milk and cereal, but also made my way through honey covered chicken wings and rice. I was pondering whether I'd be able to find my way back home again, and how much time I'd have to spend wandering. (The city was small and quaint, like Quebec, but was unknown to me.) I had stumbled upon this church quite by accident in the first place. I watched the others around me. They were well dressed and generally presentable looking, but ate with the same restraint that I had exhibited. Being in a church wasn't so bad after all, I thought. At least lightning hasn't struck me dead. (August 29, 1992)

He handed me a piece of waxed paper and told me to fold it. I knew what he meant, and I implicitly understood the nature of the "test," but I resisted. I did not know the technicalities of drug-use, but I could use my vicarious knowledge of needle use to distract and confuse him. I had to ultimately "pass" his drug test. In a quick gesture I communicated that I would come back to his request, and successfully satisfy it, once I brought him "inside" my experience of using. The point would then be made that I was a bona fide drug user. My life depended on how credible I was about to perform as a drug user.

My heart raced. I sweated profusely while describing the breaking down of the pill; the release of the powder onto a spoon; the mixture of the powder with a liquid, usually water, but alcohol can substitute; the use of a cotton ball, or something else, to act as a filter through which to draw the liquid into the syringe; the "poking of the needle into a nice fat craving vein." I glowed as I spoke, describing each stage as slowly and vividly as possible, as though I had a deep appreciation for every aspect of the whole experience. I prayed that I wasn't sounding fake, like a doctor who has memorized and is now presenting a medical report (or, even a junkie who was living a double life, such as in the case of the addicted doctor in Morrison's (1989), *The white rabbit*) instead of a drug user whose knowledge is first-hand, concrete and immediate, and sensory. He appeared convinced by my performance.

While quickly briefing another woman who was working for us on the inside (probably as an ex-con turned informant), I said that I had to find a way out of being pressured into "using" by this drug lord. He would be expecting me to need a "hit" any minute. I then told her to tell him that I was trying to quit, that it was really hard-going, and that I had successfully dried out in the past, which was giving me the strength to try again. She *had* to be convincing, I added, because my life was riding on how well she performed. She already knew.

I could feel the sensation of pin-pricks in my arms. I was meditating on this vicarious experience, trying to make it as "real" as possible. This way I could elaborate, in the case of a bind, on the sensation of needle use. I wanted to be able to convince the drug lord of my vulnerability—it was far too early in my "recovery" to appear otherwise. We were ready to pounce on him, and charge him with trafficking, if he tried to stick a needle in my arm for his own satisfaction. (September 19, 1992)

Prisoner as Criminal

Break-and-Enter

I could hear the vicious man trying to break into our house. He was familiar to me. I knew this because I had spotted him in his vehicle with my binoculars. While leaning against the kitchen window, I had carefully observed him rummaging through a box of equipment until he pulled out a large drill. I shook all over while yelling out to my brother to phone the cops right away. I rushed over to Steven (pseudonym) as he looked at me in fear. The "O" line was busy. Try "411"! I yelled. It too was busy.

In a panic I ran out the front door without closing it behind me. I ran towards the nearest phone booth on the corner two long and breathless blocks away. It suddenly struck me that I had overlooked locking the door on the outside! Am I crazy?! Now the murderer will have full access to my brother and sister. I'm going to be sick. I'm praying that they've noticed my mistake. The image of the unlocked door (which was, in reality in the dream, a latch that could only be locked from the inside) loomed before me as I rummaged through my pockets for a quarter.

No quarter! I can't believe this, I thought, as I ran towards the first woman I saw, pleading with her to help me. I briefly indicated our life-threatening circumstances to this young, black woman. She kindly gave me a small stack of quarters while accompanying me to the telephone booth. I continued talking, elaborating in much detail as to who the man was and why he was wanting to hurt us. I even slowed down my pace to ensure that the fuller story was being told and understood. Our energy was friendly as we walked side-by-side. On some level it was registering in my mind that my story-telling impulses were poorly timed if not outright ludicrous, but I couldn't help myself.

While the quarter made contact with the telephone, I rehearsed the message of desperation. I shouted, "Emergency!", followed by "Life-threatening violation at (address)." As I rushed with full-force back to the house, an image of a long drill flashed through my mind. The drill was being used to cut a neat square into the front door. (I'm praying that the killer assumed that the door was locked.) Glass shattered in my mind as the killer reached through the small window panes in the front door to unlatch the lock. The image of two silent and lifeless bodies bolted though me as I neared the quiet and seemingly intact front door. (September 11, 1991)

Abduction of Children

Just a boy. He had been taken away from me against his will by an unknown man. The unknown man became my sole preoccupation as I looked long and hard for the boy. My days were filled with woe and I searched everywhere for this boy to whom I felt so close.

I finally stumbled across his whereabouts in a big house which appeared deserted from the outside. I soon discovered that an alarm system was pervasive throughout the house as well as locks.

After thinking while pacing, I finally decided to knock at the front door in broad daylight, about to pose in what manner I wasn't certain. Placing my hand on the door, I could feel the energy of the boy within. The man answered the door. I talked, and eventually was let in. The boy was immediately visible to me. I wanted to reach out, hold him, and take him back. Controlling my impulses, I took in the scenery. Milling about, I spotted the boy's belongings.

Tucking his belongings inside my long white spring coat, I left, but only temporarily. The boy knew that I would be back for him and I knew that I could count on him to help me. (November 18, 1990)

I asked Sally Heath (pseudonym for professor-friend) if I could take her little girl for a walk. I stressed that we would only be 15 minutes and implied that there was no need for alarm. Her little girl looked so pretty in her blue dress. Sally, hesitatingly sweet, smiled and then nodded. I added over my shoulder that if we were any longer than 20 minutes that she should come looking for us. Sally looked very pretty with her shiny golden hair.

The little girl, suddenly gesturing as if I were her playmate, grabbed my hand. We twirled about having fun and anticipating adventure. "The child's world is my own," I thought in a blink as we entered the gymnasium. The heavy wine-colored velvet drapes deeply breathed "No enter" as we skipped lightly and sang boldly in and out of the folds and contours of the dusty old drapes.

I'm not sure at what point exactly, but the little girl suddenly disappeared. How had I lost track of her? I searched the curtains and stage high and low feeling increasingly panicky with each passing minute. Alarmed, I felt exasperated.

Sally entered the scene. Unmusical chords stuck in my throat as my heaving chest grinded them through my broken accordion. We both instinctively knew that the sweet child had been stolen. We stood staring at one another, too shocked to know what to do. (September 28, 1991)

Violence Against Women

A man, armed, vicious and vindictive, clung to the outside of our speeding car, at the back. He managed to crawl over the back of the car, while we were in motion, and somehow smash the rear window with the end of his rifle. Aiming, he shot me in the leg. (I was relieved that he shot me instead of my sister.) We knew that we were dealing with an escaped lunatic. We also knew that he had been following us. He was drawn to Darlene (pseudonym), my sister, for some reason. It was as though he was going to make an effort to get rid of me—an interfering force!—to fully access her. I grounded myself from within: I would stand in his way.

Earlier in the day we had to pick up our brother and a woman. They did not know the severity of what we had been experiencing. Our brother encouraged the woman, who was busy with her bags, to get ready for something. Darlene and I were trying to hurry them up. Finally, I admitted that we were being followed. Then they hurried things up.

Darlene and I then drove to a house for protection. We knew that it was only a matter of time before the criminal caught up with us. Many people lived in this house. Darlene, or someone who looked like her, approached the house with a rifle in hand. She must have felt fed up with the whole situation. She began shooting at me, or maybe someone else (it was hard to know), but missed. With the last bullet she deliberately shot herself below the waist. She was losing her mind. Maybe she'd been waiting to use the bullets on the criminal. We knew that he was still on our scent . . . It was only a matter of time. (September 2, 1991)

Researcher as Prisoner

As I turned around in the middle of it, I closely observed its tightly knitted cells positioned one on top of the other. The cells looked like bunk beds with concrete slabs separating one from the other. Am I inside a honeycomb, I wondered, or an amphitheater with a roof?

Once in my cell I realized that lying on the bed gave the place more scope. Standing served only to accentuate its small, comb-like size. Contact soon began. Male prisoners yelled to me and sent coded messages my way. I could see the prisoners across on the other side. They began waving and certainly making a point of seeing me. So much activity! Are they going to show me how to live? This wasn't going to be so bad after all! (July 6, 1991)

While leaning against a beige prison wall, dressed in my blue uniform, I'm chatting with the young woman next to me. We are sitting cross-legged. As we busily chat, I'm aware of deserving to be here because of a crime I've committed. This feels like a scene from a high school gym class, I chuckle privately, with the lot of us lined us against the wall, waiting to be "picked" for something. I chat with a male guard who is especially warm and polite, feeling struck by his humanity. It doesn't feel so bad in here after all, I think, as I watch him move down the right-hand side of the corridor.

I need to get to my friend's place. A young girl nonchalantly crosses a bridge by "monkeying" it from one side to the other. (She is moving underneath the bridge, hand-over-hand.) I wonder if I am able to accomplish the same feat as she looks strong. I also monkey it across realizing that I have no choice. I mentally block out the water from below and take it carefully, one step at a time. (July 21, 1991)

Storytelling

Group Counseling

A very good seminar leader led our packed session. She knew how to connect with us in order to "bring out" our stories. I felt comfortable, connected to myself and everyone else.

The next time we were led by a young male counselor. The thirty of us present at the session merely tolerated him as he dictated 'ways of knowing' to us. None of us was pleased. I could feel that I was probably more tolerant than most. I felt sorry for him. He did not seem to value our stories or, if he did, then he did not know how to make something out of them. Also, he seemed oblivious to the friction he was experiencing within the group that was claiming all of my energies of concentration. I had difficulty learning anything from the well prepared, glossy overheads he insisted on showing.

When he moved around afterwards, asking how we were doing, one woman after another tried to speak honestly. But no sooner had a word been uttered than he would scoot off in another direction. When he asked my friend about her impressions, she was really ready to 'give it to him'. She had prepared a ranting harangue, but he once again 'took off', leaving her wheeling and spinning.

He turned to me, without warning, and asked what I had thought. I sat silently. He began acting fidgety. I asked him gently if he wanted to hear the truth or a mockery of the truth. He looked stunned, whispering, "the truth." Searching for euphemisms to translate my thoughts, I told him that I found his style impositional, authoritative and distant. "Your good intentions are covered up by your style," I added. I was taken aback. I couldn't believe that I had spoken so directly and that the world didn't blow up. And, best of all, our male speaker appeared responsive. He slowly moved away. I felt sick and tired of pretending. No more pretending (I was chanting, upon waking). (August 29, 1991)

Appendix B

Correctional Newsletter:
The Creative Writer

Sponsored in 1992 by the Education program, [delete name of institution], Ministry of Correctional Services; [delete address].

Editor's Reflections

The Creative Writer is a collection of creative writings by inmates of [delete institution], one of Canada's adult male correctional facilities. The Department of Education at the jail sponsors and encourages both formal studies and creative writing. The intent of this newsletter, our first edition, is to display some of the talent of our writers and to encourage others to develop and share their own gifts. We are fostering creativity expressed in poetry, short stories, journals and diaries, novelistic segments, drawings and art, and more. The spirit of this project belongs to the inmates themselves who brought, to our attention, their own creative writing needs. We wish to thank our contributors for the help their words can offer others.

This publication was brought to fruition without financial support; it was assisted by the contributions of inmates and a coordinating staff of teachers. The writings in this publication represent most of the contributions to our Creative Writing program thus far. Selections were made in the cases of writers who produced and contributed a lot of material. Congratulations to our writers who persevered in making this project a reality, and their own learning productive, within a challenging environment.

This newsletter tells a coherent story of the writers' contributions; another story might also be told. Many of our writers are involved in works-in-progress either inside the jail or elsewhere. Meaningful fragments of people's lives are waiting to find their expressive form. For instance, one young inmate is serious in his use of RAP music as a vehicle for creating social change. His song-like prose is finding its form as he searches for images to reveal the depths of his world. Another inmate's self-portrait is called "Notes from a cell": in it, he creates an open space in his life in order to cope with imprisonment. Other inmates are putting their "rusty pens" to good use as they experiment with new forms in letter writing exchanges. We are wishing all of our writers the best of luck in making their texts a reality.

Our policy of anonymity protects our contributors; their names have been changed throughout this newsletter.

Carol, teacher

Black Hawk, Poet-Writer

Black Hawk spends many nights alone, asleep inside a misted catacomb. His poetry abounds with cell-like images that express the deep aloneness that is typical of his writing. During our sessions, I often look for signs of hope in his poetry of despair.   Black Hawk, orphaned by society and his own native Indian home as a boy, writes of the timeless child within. In our conversations, he dedicated the following poem to his young daughter. He feels that she plays a significant role in healing his troubled heart. His dedication to her may be the glimmer of hope in a world he otherwise experiences as 'diminishing':

Diminishing Reality
Oh come to me won't you please
Listen to what I feel
Many many nights alone
Locked within a sleeping tomb.
Young flames they burnt in me

A hatred feeling fills me deep
The kin folk watched as I grew weak
So far down they dragged me deep.
Why'd you bother me at all?
False love I felt the wall
Feed your own to the end
What was left you sent it then.
Many nights I left the home
That so far, it set the toll
Anger for unwanted child
Misery, you lied all of the time.
So much pain from hands to sticks
You slashed my sail when you didn't quit
Pain of living with your land
Speak of me and I survive?
Memories of a child in time
The boy still cries inside
Dreamt of many things so grand
You crushed the chance of knowing how
Love was said, false I hate
No one loved a child, it's late
Cast away beyond the reach
pretend to be was made of me.
Silent tears came to me
Memories they are so clear
Hurt the child, mentally
Full life would never come to be.
Bleeding, it hurts to know
Crying, my pain it shows
Lonely in this world so scared
Not knowing where to go, betrayed.
Keep your dreams inside the heart
I know you lost a bigger part
Someday you'll find the missing spot
Someday someone will come to heal your heart.
Once knew the truth of happiness
Instead of falling into madness
I can't forgive nor forget
You played with me, regret it's set.
Time is only just a blink
Just like yesterday's drink
Fight to lose your ugly thoughts
Reality you think I forgot
To me, I fight each day you live
The mistake you made you let me live.

Cell-like images are sometimes related to immortality, dream and magic in the inmates' writings. The image of a "misted catacomb" in the following poem by Black Hawk feels open, historic and reaching:

Dream Duration
Follow me beyond your dreams
To a land of immortality
Shut your eyes, ease your pain
Your thoughts begin to trail.
Further back in time
Feel the grace of the land
Mortal men were dreamt
To which Eve chanced love again.
Walk among Lords and Ladies
Sit to side the King and Queen
Power of the mind from night
Princess in your land tonight.
Wake to feel the wind so cool
Drifting through the misted catacomb
Feel the air of an age-old time,
But forever young within your mind.
Princess of your dreams I feel
Always young within our dreams
Walk with them, you shut your eyes
Remember that time was wise.

Sear Robinson, Musician-Writer

Sear Robinson writes musical lyrics in order to "re-educate" himself and his audience: Sear, a musician-artist who knows the streets, writes about the importance of a committed drug-free lifestyle. His motif is that he was once "jonesing" for cocaine, but now he's "jonesing" for freedom. When he was using drugs, he felt like a frozen pony on a carousel halted in mid-gallop. Even more severe is the image, in his song, of an evil person knocking at his door. He explains: "Jonesing" is an expression used by drug users when they're craving drugs. Sear turns this craving into an evil person called "Mr. Jones." He says that his message is meant to promote drug awareness by awakening users to their reality. He feels strongly that it's time for everyone to *stop* their drug use: this is the only way to put an end to the horror that knocks at their own doors:

Mr. Jones
(to the moon)
Halted in mid gallop, a frozen carousel,
charging forth without proceeding,
on my painted pony bound for hell.
A shadow dancing on the walls, come to bid
farewell, make claims on my soul,
someone I've never met but seem to know so well.
I've heard the name a thousand times
he has spoken in my dreams,
I can't believe what's happening here,
Mr. Jones has brought me to my knees.
Mr. Jones, knocking at the door,
here he comes, making me want more,
the tightness comes, it curls around me,
making me insane.
The brightness lights the dust in the spoon.
To the moon! I am high again.
I can't feel the pain now, I've been lifted
to new heights.
I can tell it won't be long now,
till I refill the pipe. (oh, n-nnnnn-no).
It's all coming down around me,
my sky is falling in.
And now Mr. Jones is knocking.
I don't want to, but I know I'll let him in,
he's going to win.
Mr. Jones is knocking at my door,
and here I am, just another sniveling whore.
He's here to curl his arms around me,
making me insane. Oh my head!
The whiteness made from dust in my spoon.
To the moon, I'm high again.
To the moon! Good-bye! I'm dead.

Phillip Dalley, Poet-Writer

Phillip Dalley, a prolific francophone-poet, writes about the desperate state that the world is in. In our conversations he has stressed how the world's plight is, in part, responsible for the heavy despair that plagues the souls of some people. Some people, he explains, turn to crime and drug use and even addiction in this state of sickness. This poem is about the anarchy of the world as reflected in human lives:

Searching For a Place of Sanity
Entombed within a world of pain,
where any madness reigns.
Mindless wars and bloodshed
cannot be restrained.
This never-ending onslaught
continues night and day.
The spray of bullets fills the air
as bombs are dropped away.
People fearing for their lives,
never knowing what's in store.
Striving for a world of peace,
to end this insane war.
Their cries for peace are only echoes,
in the minds of those who care.
But yet persistence leads them on,
only leading to despair.
Still the bullets leave their scars
as death invades the world.
Nothing left but scattered ruins,
anguish, pain and sorrow.

Phillip also writes love poetry. He explains the value of love as a dream that keeps him going as he lives locked up in jail. Heart-felt dreams of his "pretty lady" inspire poetical thoughts:

All in a Dream
I had a dream of me and you,
a dream I wish were true.
Together hand-in-hand we walked
laughing in the sun.
We danced below the azure sky,
you and I were one.
In this dream of fantasy,
we lay beneath the stars,
ecstatically embraced in love
happiness was ours.
Thinking back, my heart it soars
of the special times we shared
Now all I have are dreams of you,
I hope you know I cared.

Forever will you be with me
in heart in soul in mind
and in my dreams of happiness
I pray your heart I'll find.

Sammy Larson, Letter Writer

Letter writing is a form of creativity that Carol (teacher) and Sammy Larson (formal course enthusiast) are tackling. In her first response letter to Sammy in December 1991, Carol wrote:

I have been giving some thought as to what we might concentrate on in our letters to one another. You asked me to tell you about myself. . . You also told me a little bit about your life in Nova Scotia and elsewhere. Since we were both born and raised in Nova Scotia, why don't we focus on our early life and schooling experiences? Eventually, we can make selections from our letters for the prison/education newsletter.

By the time April arrived, much of the talk about formal schooling experiences during various grade levels turned to talk about family crises and personal learning experiences as youths. What counts as a true educative experience, after all? Read on to see how Sammy and Carol's experiences of the imagination had much do with shaping their learning in life.

Sammy: Sometimes it is hard to go back in time because you really don't think that there was anything there for you to begin with. . . Where I lived down home in Nova Scotia was all fields and woods. Where we lived we were on our own land. We used to ride ponies after supper, when all of the other animals were in the barns or moved into their fields . . . Did you ever ride a horse or do something and pretend that you were someone else? Well, that is what I used to do was pretend that I was Zoro and could hide anywhere I wanted to. We also built a big tree house that summer, way back in the woods. That was our hideout. As long as we got there, nothing could get us.

Have you ever found a place that you could call your own? That summer I found mine. It was a place I came across in the woods one day. It was a small little green spot in the middle of trees. The way I found it was strange because I was running after what to me looked like a rabbit, but I didn't catch it so I didn't find out. But the place had the greenest grass and was so clean. Whenever I wanted to be alone, that was where I would go. I never even told my best friend where it was. A place of my own . . . I guess that I did have time for all of the things I wanted to do along with helping to get things ready for the winter.

I did learn something about my life when I was a kid after all. . . Doing this program is helping me to think back and realize that I wasn't alone in my life. I would like to thank you for that.

Carol: By the time I started high school we were living in Ontario, not Nova Scotia, and so the woods receded in my mine, becoming a fond memory. You asked if I had ever found a place that I could call my own. I've been thinking about this interesting question ever since I read your letter. At first I wanted to answer "no," but as I thought more carefully I recalled the red library on wheels that parked outside our apartment door. I would often table a peanut butter sandwich on my lap and wait for the library on wheels to come to me. There was something strangely exotic about this arrangement. This became my special place to be as no other children on our street took advantage of its hidden worlds and riches. Maybe it was special to me in the way that the green patch in the woods was special to you—you know, the one that you discovered while in pursuit of a rabbit. Although my special place was part of an urban, rather than natural, landscape, it was still "a place of my own," like yours.

Even in high school I never really learned that there was time for play. Your story seems balanced in this respect as you reflect on how the woods symbolized both work and play for you. If you weren't building a tree house for play, then you were chopping and piling wood for winter. Whenever I "played" in high school, it was somehow directly linked with school, my homework and goals . . . .Now I realize, what does it matter what any of us accomplishes if we don't feel loved for who we are as a person?. . . I have learnt from writing to you that the most valuable educative experience in my youth related to the lesson I needed to learn in valuing myself as a person and woman.

Adrian Sands, Short Story Writer

Adrian Sands is trying his hand at writing short stories because this activity is consoling and therapeutic to him. As he writes he works through problems, expressing them in story form. We agree that family unity, and the importance of maintaining good-will within the family, is the theme that enriches these two stories and informs Adrian's concerns in general. He hopes to create change for the better in his personal and social life by writing. Billy Graham's book, *Hope for the troubled heart* (1991), a gift from his mother, is a new source of inspiration for him.

An All Too Common Experience

There we were, John, Herb and myself, all 11 or 12 years old. Boy, did we have our workload set out for us. You see, way out in north British Columbia is a ranch of limitless boundaries. This was a place where many families lived in a communal situation. Children were forced to work weeding many vegetable gardens the size of football fields. Since the kids worked an average of eight hours per day without pay, the temptation to run off and play always existed. We all had to report to Norman who was in charge of supervising the young children's work pattern.

One day, the three of us took off during work time and rode our bicycles out to a big shed where hay, for cattle, was stored and dried. We began rearranging the top bails of hay into tunnels and a nice fort. No sooner had we built our fort than Norman's car came driving our way. He got out and called to the three of us to get down and to come to him immediately! We all did, laughing all the way.

Norman drove us back to his marital home. Since he had five children of his own, you might expect him to know how to treat children. After piling the three of us into a backroom containing no exit, he lined us up side by side. Almost instantly Norman asked John, "What do your parents do all day?!" He said, "Work." *Wham!* Norman slapped him across the face. Next in line, Herb was asked the same question and *wham,* his glasses were knocked off. Then it was my turn. *Smash!* "See to it that you all work from now on!" Norman exclaimed. "But I'm not finished with you yet!," he added, while leaving the room. He returned with two belts. "You can get eight strokes an hour with the skinny belt and ten with the thick belt, so choose!" We thought to go with the skinny belt.

"You will be here for a total of three hours, so make your choice!" Without going into details, we got our first set of lashes right away and then each of our faces was smashed into the corners of the room. We were told to remain facing the corner until the next session.

While crying, after he had left closing the door behind him, we felt confused as to what to do. It never really dawned on us that what he was doing was wrong and that his form of punishment was out of line with our actions. But we did collectively decide to change over to the thick belt. After he finished his second round of the belt and corner routine, he told us that if our parents found out what we did they would beat us as well. Lashing us one final series of welts, he released us. In continuing episodes with Norman we were told to write one thousand lines to the effect that we would be good work boys in future. My respect for authority was diminished greatly as a result of my exposure to Norman and, subsequently, my entire early teens were wracked with learning problems in school.

230 Imprisoned Selves: An Inquiry into Prisons and Academe

Now at 40 years old I haven't heard from Herb or John in many years but I'll bet that they're also having some difficulties coping with life. As it turns out, we really do learn major behavioral patterns while we're young. Wouldn't it be nice if we could just let the past be bygone? From the seeds we plant so shall we reap. This is a reality that I have observed and directly experienced many times in my life. No matter what we experience or cause to happen, good or bad, it all comes back to us, just like Karma. Maybe some of you can relate to this story of early childhood punishment and survival.

Editor's Final Word

The Creative Writer is a newsletter devoted to inmates' creative writing needs and various forms of expression. Much correctional literature stresses the great need for literacy and trades' training in institutional environments. Our contribution extends this continuum of educational needs and opportunities to acknowledge the vital role of creativity in some inmates' lives. In many cases, inmates introduce us to their own curriculum for re-educating themselves as part of a life-long program. One-to-one tutoring provides inmates with the encouragement they may be seeking in order to have their material read and acknowledged. These writers look for avenues to discuss their creative ideas and to elicit feedback on their works-in-progress.

Bibliography

Abbott, J. H. 1981. *In the belly of the beast.* New York: Vintage Books.

Adler, P. A., and P. Adler. 1993. Ethical issues in self-censorship. In *Researching sensitive topics,* C. M. Renzetti and R. M. Lee (eds.), 249-266. London: Sage Publications.

Allport, G. W. 1965. *Letters from Jenny.* New York: Harcourt Brace.

Anderson, G. L. 1989. Critical ethnography in education: Origins, current status, and new directions. *Review of Educational Research* 59 (3): 249-270.

Angle, T. G. 1989. *An examination of the evolution of correctional education in Upper Canada and Ontario: 1835-1900.* Unpublished doctoral dissertation, University of Miami, Florida.

Anonymous. 1992. *Prisoners and aids.*

Banks, J. A. 1993. The canon debate, knowledge construction, and multicultural education. *Educational Researcher* 22 (5): 4-14.

Barone, T. 1992. On the demise of subjectivity in educational inquiry. *Curriculum Inquiry* 22 (1): 25-38.

Barthes, R. 1975. *The pleasure of the text.* New York: Noonday Press.

Barthes, R. 1989. *Mythologies.* London: Paladin Grafton Books.

Bastion, A. 1987. *The right of prisoners to education.* Unpublished doctoral dissertation. University of British Columbia.

Bell, J. S. 1991. *Becoming aware of literacy.* Unpublished doctoral dissertation, University of Toronto, Toronto.

Birney, E. 1966. *The creative writer.* Toronto: Hunter Rose.

Birnie, L. 1990. *A rock and a hard place: Inside Canada's parole board.* Toronto: Macmillan.

Britton, J. 1990. Heads or tales? *English in Education* 24 (1): 3-9.

Bruner, J. 1979. *On knowing: Essays for the left hand.* Cambridge, Massachusetts: Harvard University Press.

Bruner, J. 1985. Narrative and paradigmatic modes of thought. In *Learning and teaching the ways of knowing*, E. Eisner (ed.), 97-115. Eighty-fourth Yearbook of the National Society for the Study of Education. Chicago: University of Chicago press.

Bruner, J. 1986. *Actual minds, possible worlds.* Cambridge: Harvard University Press.

Bruner, J. 1990. *Acts of meaning.* Cambridge, Massachusetts: Harvard University Press.

Bruner, J. 1991. The narrative construction of reality. *Critical Inquiry* 18 (1): 1-21.

Butt, R., D. Raymond, and L. Yamagishi. 1988. Autobiographic praxis: Studying the formation of teachers' knowledge. *Journal of Curriculum Theorizing* 7 (2): 87-164.

Cadieux, P. 1990. *Mission of the Correctional Service of Canada.* Ottawa: Ontario.

Callwood, J. 1990. *The sleepwalker.* Toronto: McClelland-Bantam.

Caron, R. 1978. *Go-Boy!* Toronto: McGraw-Hill Ryerson.

Caron, R. 1985. *Bingo!* Agincourt, Ontario: Methuen.

Carr, D. 1986. *Time, narrative, and history.* Bloomington: Indiana University Press.

Cheney, P. 1991, July 7. In a jail of evil Clifford Olson stands apart. *The Toronto Star:* A7.

Clandinin, J. 1986. *Classroom practice: Teacher images in action.* London: The Falmer Press.

Clandinin, D. J., and F. M. Connelly. 1987. Teachers' personal knowledge: What counts as 'personal' in studies of the personal. *Journal of Curriculum Studies* 19 (6): 487-500.

Clandinin, D. J., and F. M. Connelly. 1989. Personal knowledge in curriculum. In *The international encyclopedia of education, research and studies: Supplementary volume one,* T. Husen and T. N. Postlethwaite (eds.), 577-580. Oxford: Pergamon Press.

Clandinin, D. J., and F. M. Connelly. 1991. Narrative and story in practice and research. In *The reflective turn,* D. Schon (ed.), 258-281. New York: Teachers College Press.

Clandinin, D. J., and F. M. Connelly. 1992. Teacher as curriculum maker. In *The handbook of research on curriculum,* P. Jackson (ed.), 363-401. New York: MacMillan Publishing.

Clandinin, D. J., and F. M. Connelly. (1994). Personal experience methods. In *Handbook of qualitative research,* N. K. Denzin and Y. S. Lincoln (eds.), 413-427. London: Sage Publications.

Clarke, G. S. 1987. *Breaking with tradition: Role development in a prison-based baccalaureate program.* Unpublished doctoral dissertation, University of British Columbia.

Cleaver, E. 1968. *Soul on ice.* New York: Dell Publishing.

Clifford, J. 1988. The predicament of culture. Cambridge, Massachusetts: Harvard University Press.

Coles, R. 1981. Minority dreams: American dreams. *Daedalus: Journal of the American Academy of Arts & Sciences* 110 (2): 29-41.

Conle, C. 1993. *Learning culture and embracing contraries: Narrative inquiry through stories of acculturation.* Unpublished doctoral dissertation, University of Toronto. Toronto.

Connelly, F. M., and D. J. Clandinin. 1985. Personal practical knowledge and the modes of knowing: Relevance for teaching and learning. In *Learning and teaching the ways of knowing,* E. Eisner (ed.), 174-198. Eighty-fourth Yearbook of the National Society for the Study of Education. Chicago: University of Chicago Press.

Connelly, F. M., and D. J. Clandinin. 1986. Rhythms in teaching: The narrative study of teachers' personal practical knowledge of classrooms. *Teaching & Teacher Education* 2 (4): 377-387.

Connelly, F. M., and D. J. Clandinin. 1987. Teachers' personal knowledge: What counts as 'personal' in studies of the personal. *Journal of Curriculum Studies* 19 (6): 487-500.

Connelly, F. M., and D. J. Clandinin, 1988a. Narrative meaning: Focus on teacher education. *Elements* 19 (2): 15-18.

Connelly, F. M., and D. J. Clandinin. 1988b. *Teachers as curriculum planners: Narratives of experience.* New York: Teachers College Press.

Connelly, F. M., and D. J. Clandinin. 1990. Stories of experience and narrative inquiry. *Educational Researcher* 19 (5): 2-14.

Connelly, F. M., and D. J. Clandinin. 1994. Narrative inquiry. In *The international encyclopedia of education,* vol. 7, Second edition, T. Husen and T. N. Postlethwaite (eds.), 4046-4051. Oxford: Pergamon Press.

Correctional Service of Canada. 1983. *Beyond the walls.* Ottawa: The Communications Branch of The Correctional Service of Canada.

Crites, S. 1979. The aesthetics of self-deception. *Soundings* 62: 107-129.

Correctional Service of Canada. 1991. *Facility directory.* Ottawa: Ontario.

Crites, S. 1971. The narrative quality of experience. *American Academy of Religion* 39 (3): 291-311.

Davidson, H. S. 1984. *Kohlberg's moral judgment interview: Dialogue or dictate in the practice of interviewing for moral stage scores.* Unpublished master's thesis, University of Toronto, Toronto.

Davidson, H. S. 1991. *Moral education and social relations: The case of prisoner self-government reform in New York State, 1895-1923.* Unpublished doctoral dissertation, University of Toronto, Toronto.

Davies, I. 1990. *Writers in prison.* Toronto: Between The Lines.

Denzin, N. 1989. *Interpretive biography.* London: Sage Publications.

Dewey, J. 1934. *Art as experience.* New York: Minton, Balch.

Dewey, J. 1938. *Experience and education.* New York: Macmillan Publishing.

Diamond, C. T. P. 1990. Recovering and reconstruing teachers' stories. *International Journal of Personal Construct Psychology* 3: 63-76.

Diamond, C. T. P. 1991. *Teacher education as transformation: A psychological perspective.* Milton keynes: Open University Press.

Diamond, C. T. P. 1992. Accounting for our accounts: Autoethnographic approaches to teacher voice and vision. *Curriculum Inquiry* 22 (1): 67-81.

Diamond, C. T. P. 1993. Gridding a grid: An artist re-views his recent exhibition. *Empirical Studies in the Arts, 11*(2), 167-175.

Diamond, C. T. P., C. A. Mullen, and M. Beattie. 1996. Arts-based educational research: Making music. In *Changing research and practice: Teachers' professionalism, identities, and knowledge,* M. Kompf, R. T. Boak, W. R. Bond and D. H. Dworet (eds.). London: Falmer Press.

Dietrich, C. E. 1992. *Narrative of a nurse educator: The interconnected beginnings of a daughter, a teacher, a friend—family—a personal source of practical knowledge.* Unpublished doctoral dissertation, University of Toronto. Toronto.

Dostoyevsky, F. 1965. *Memoirs from the house of the dead.* New York: Oxford University Press.

Dostoyevsky, F. 1982. *Crime and punishment.* New York: Penguin Books.

Eisner, E. W., and E. Vallance. (eds.). 1974. *Conflicting conceptions of curriculum.* Berkeley, Calif.: McCutchan Publishing.

Eisner, E. W. 1979. Five basic orientations to the curriculum. *The Educational Imagination.* New York: MacMillan.

Eisner, E. W. (ed.). 1985. Modes of knowing. In *Learning and teaching the ways of knowing.* Eighty-fourth Yearbook of the National Society for the Study of Education: Part II. Chicago, Illinois: University of Chicago Press.

Eisner, E. W. 1991. *The enlightened eye: Qualitative inquiry and the enhancement of educational practice.* New York: Macmillan Publishing.

Eisner, E. W. 1993. Forms of understanding and the future of educational research. *Educational Researcher* 22 (7): 5-11.

Feinstein, D., and S. Krippner. 1988. *Personal mythology: The psychology of your evolving self.* Los Angeles: J. P. Tarcher.

Fenstermacher, G. D. 1994. The knower and the known in teacher knowledge research. *Review of Research in Education* 20: 3-56.

Feuerverger, G., and C. A. Mullen. 1995. Portraits of marginalized lives: Stories of literacy and collaboration in school and prison. *Interchange* 26 (3): 221-240.

Fitzgerald, J. 1986. Autobiographical memory: A developmental perspective. In *Autobiographical memory,* D. C. Rubin (ed.), 122-133. Cambridge: Cambridge University Press.

Foreman, M. E. 1988. *Interpersonal assessment of psychopathy.* Unpublished doctoral dissertation, University of British Columbia.

Foucault, M. 1977. *Discipline & punish.* New York: Vintage Books.

Fraser, S. 1987. *My father's house: A memoir of incest and of healing.* New York: Harper & Row.

Frye, N. 1963. *The educated imagination.* Toronto: Hunter Rose.

Funkenstein, A. 1993. The incomprehensible catastrophe: Memory and narrative. In *The narrative study of lives,* R. Josselson and A. Lieblich (eds.), 21-29. London: Sage Publications.

Futrell, M. D. 1986. *Academic and vocational education programs in twelve California Department of Corrections institutions.* Unpublished doctoral dissertation, University of Southern California.

Gallagher, E. M. 1988. *Older men in prison: Emotional, social, and physical health characteristics.* Unpublished doctoral dissertation, Simon Fraser University.

Gardner, J. J. 1986. *Attitudes about rape among inmates and correctional officers (prison, minimum security).* Unpublished doctoral dissertation, University of Northern Colorado.

Geertz, C. 1988. *Works and lives: The anthropologist as author.* Stanford: Stanford University Press.

Glesne, C., and A. Peshkin. 1992. *Becoming qualitative researchers: An introduction.* Longman: University of Vermont.

Godfrey, T. 1992, August 23. Cries in the dark: One neighbourhood's battle with drugs. *The Sunday Sun,* 49-53.

Goffman, E. 1961. *Asylums.* New York: Doubleday.

Grossman, I. 1990. *An ordinary woman in extraordinary times.* Toronto: The Multicultural History Society of Ontario.

Guba, E. 1990. Subjectivity and objectivity. In *Qualitative inquiry in education: The continuing debate,* E. Eisner and A. Peshkin (eds.), 74-91. New York: Teachers College Press.

Grumet, M. 1988. *Bitter milk: Women and teaching.* Amherst: The University of Massachusetts Press.

Hardy, B. 1975. *Tellers and listeners: The narrative imagination.* London: The Atlone Press.

Haraway, D. 1988. Situated knowledges: The science question in feminism and the privilege of partial perspective. *Feminist Studies* 14 (3): 575-599.

Harlow, B. 1987. *Resistance literature.* New York: Methuen.

Harris, J. 1986. *Stranger in two worlds.* New York: Kensington Publishing.

Horsburgh, R. 1969. *From pulpit to prison.* Toronto: Methuen.

Hospital, J. T. 1986. *Dislocations.* Toronto: McClelland and Stewart.

Huxley, A. 1977. *The doors of perception: Heaven and hell.* London: Collins.

Jailhouse author Roger Caron gets eight years for two robberies (1993, June 26). *The Toronto Star,* 9.

Johnson, J. R. 1987. *For any good at all: A comparative study of state penitentiaries in Arizona, Nevada, New Mexico, and Utah from 1900 to 1980.* Unpublished doctoral dissertation, University of New Mexico.

Karpis, A. 1971. *Public enemy number one.* Toronto: McClelland and Stewart.

Katz, G. 1970. *The time gatherers: Writings from prison.* Montreal: Harvest House.

Kirby, S., and McKenna, K. 1989. *Experience research social change: Research from the margins.* Toronto: Garamond press.

Kucherawy, D. 1990, May 26. Writing behind bars. *The Toronto Star,* M12-M13.

Lamberti, R. 1992, August 23. Heroin scooped. *Sunday Sun,* 8.

Lamberti, R., and J. Schmied. 1992, August 24. Killer-grade heroin alert. *The Toronto Sun,* 9.

Lamberti, R., and M. Stewart. 1992, August 26. Pure heroin kills 4. *The Toronto Sun,* 10.

L'Engle, M. 1972. *A circle of quiet.* San Francisco: Harper & Row.

Lessing, D. 1986. *Prisons we choose to live inside.* Toronto: CBC Enterprises.

Livesay, R. 1980. *On the rock: Twenty-five years in Alcatraz.* Don Mills: Musson Book.

Lovitt, C. 1992. The rhetoric of murderers' confessional narratives: The model of Pierre Riviere's memoir. *Journal of Narrative Technique* 22 (1): 23-34.

MacDonald, M. (with Gould). 1988. *The violent years of Maggie MacDonald.* Toronto: McClelland-Bantam.

Macey, D. 1993. *The lives of Michael Foucault.* London: Hutchinson.

MacLean, B. D., and D. Milovanovic. (eds.). (1991). *New directions in critical criminology.* Vancouver: The Collective Press.

Marcus, G., and M. Fischer. 1986. *Anthropology as cultural critique: An experimental moment in the human sciences.* Chicago: University of Chicago Press.

Marken, R. (ed.) 1974. *Don't steal this book.* Prince Albert: Saskatchewan Penitentiary.

McClane, K. 1988. Walls: A journey to Auburn. In *The best American essays,* A. Dillard (ed.), 220-234. New York: Ticknor and Fields.

McGrory, J. J. 1991. *Violent young offenders: An investigation of the overcontrolled/undercontrolled personality typology.* Unpublished doctoral dissertation, University of Toronto, Toronto.

McMahon, M. W. 1989. *Changing penal trends: Imprisonment and alternatives in Ontario, 1951-1984.* Unpublished doctoral dissertation, University of Toronto, Toronto.

Mellody, P. 1989. *Facing codependence.* San Francisco: Harper & Row.

Mishler, E. G. 1986. *Research interviewing: Context and narrative.* London: Harvard University Press.

Mishler, E. G. 1990. Validation in inquiry-guided research: The role of exemplars in narrative studies. *Harvard Education Review* 60 (4): 415-442.

Morrison, M. 1989. *White rabbit.* New York: Berkley Books.

Mullen, C. A. 1990. *The self I dream: A narrative reconstruction of a personal mythology.* Unpublished master's thesis, University of Toronto, Toronto.

Mullen, C. A. (ed.). 1992a, June. *The creative writer.* Toronto: Ministry of Correctional Services (Education Department).

Mullen, C. A. 1992b, June. Prisoner as artist: A narrative account of a Creative Writing program. Symposium conducted at the conference of CSSE, University of Charlottetown, P.E.I.

Mullen, C. A., M. Blake, L. Ford, D. Furlong, L. Xin, and R. Young. (eds.). 1992c. *Stories we are: Narrative enactments of inquiry.* Toronto: JCTD Publishing Press (Among Teachers Community).

Mullen, C. A. 1994. A narrative exploration of the self I dream. *Journal of Curriculum Studies* 26 (3): 253-263.

Mullen, C. A., and J. E. Dalton. 1996. Dancing with sharks: On becoming socialized teacher-educator researchers. *Taboo: The Journal of Culture and Education* I Spring: 55-71.

Mullen, C. A., and Diamond, C. T. P. 1996. Narratives of marginality: From imprisonment to transformation in educational research. Manuscript submitted for publication.

Noddings, N. 1992. Gender and the curriculum. In *Handbook of research on curriculum,* P. W. Jackson (ed.), 659-681. New York: MacMillan Publishing.

Oakley, A. 1981. Interviewing women: A contradiction in terms. In *Doing feminist research,* H. Roberts (ed.), 30-61. London: Routledge & Kegan Paul.

Onlookers swoon at court gore. 1992, April 25. *The Saturday Sun,* 8.

Padel, U., and P. Stevenson. 1988. *Insiders: Women's experience of prison.* London: Virago Press.

Paul, M. 1991. *When words are bars: A guide to literacy programming in correctional institutions.* Kitchener, Ontario: Core Literacy.

Pearson, C. 1989. *The hero within: Six archetypes we live by.* San Francisco: Harper & Row.

Peshkin, A. 1985. Virtuous subjectivity: In the participant-observer's I's. In *Exploring clinical methods for social research,* D. Berg and K. Smith (eds.), 267-282. Beverly Hills, California: Sage Publications.

Peshkin, A. 1988. In search of subjectivity—one's own. *Educational Researcher* 17 (7), 17-22.

Pinar, W. F. (ed.). 1975. *Curriculum theorizing: The reconceptualists.* Berkeley, California: McCutchan Publishing.

Pinar, W. F. 1988. Autobiography and the architecture of self. *Journal of Curriculum Theorizing* 8 (1): 7-35.

Pinar, W. F. 1981. 'Whole, bright, deep with understanding': Issues in qualitative research and autobiographical method. *Journal of Curriculum Studies* 13 (3): 173-188.

Polanyi, M. 1962. *Personal knowledge: Towards a post-critical philosophy.* Chicago: University of Chicago Press.

Polkinghorne, D. 1988. *Narrative knowing and the human sciences.* New York: State University of New York Press.

Radish, K. 1992. *Run, Bambi, run.* Toronto: McClelland-Bantam.

Renzetti, C. M., and R. M. Lee. (eds.). 1993. *Researching sensitive topics.* London: Sage Publications.

Ripley, W. L. 1988. *Prisoners (original stories).* Unpublished doctoral dissertation, University of Utah.

Rose, D. 1990. *Living the ethnographic life,* 23. London: Sage Publications.

Sacks, O. 1985. *The man who mistook his wife for a hat.* New York: Harper & Row.

Samuelson, L., and B. Schissel. 1991. *Criminal justice: Sentencing issues and reform.* Saskatoon: University of Saskatchewan.

Schon, D. 1983. *The reflective practitioner.* New York: Basic Books.

Schon, D. 1987. *Educating the reflective practitioner.* London: Jossey-Bass.

Scott, G. D. 1982. *Inmate: The casebook revelations of a Canadian penitentiary psychiatrist.* Toronto: Optimum.

Schutz, A. 1971. The stranger: An essay in social psychology. In *Collected papers II: Studies in social theory.* The Hague: Martinus, Nijhoff.

Schwab, J. 1954. Eros and education: A discussion of one aspect of discussion. *Journal of General Education* 8, 54-71.

Schwab, J. 1969. The practical: A language for curriculum. *School Review* 78, 1-23.

Schwab, J. 1971. The practical: Arts of eclectic. *School Review* 79 (4): 493-542.

Shabatay, V. 1991. The stranger's story: Who calls and who answers? In *Stories lives tell: Narrative and dialogue in education,* C. Witherell and N. Noddings (eds.), 136-152. New York: Teachers College Press, Columbia University.

Sharansky, N. 1988. *Fear no evil.* Toronto: Random House.

Seidman, I. E. 1991. *Interviewing as qualitative research.* New York: Teachers College press.

Serin, R. C. 1988. *Psychopathy and violence in prisoners.* Unpublished doctoral dissertation, Queen's University, Kingston.

Sockett, H. 1992. The moral aspects of the curriculum. In *Handbook of research on curriculum,* P. W. Jackson (ed.), 543-569. New York: MacMillan Publishing.

Soren, B. 1992. The museum as curricular site. *Journal of Aesthetic*

Education 26 (3), 91-101.

Tyler, R. 1949. *Basic principles of curriculum and instruction.* Chicago: University of Chicago Press.

Van Maanen, J. 1988. *Tales of the field.* Chicago: University of Chicago Press.

Walker, D. F. 1992. Methodological issues in curriculum research. In *Handbook of research on curriculum*, P. W. Jackon (ed.), 98-118. New York: MacMillan Publishing.

Widdershoven, G. A. M. 1993. The story of life: Hermeneutic perspectives on the relationship between narrative and life history. In *The narrative study of lives*, R. Josselson and A. Lieblich (eds.), 1-20. London: Sage Publications.

Wiener, W. J., and G. C. Rosenwald. 1993. A moment's monument: The psychology of keeping a diary. In *The narrative study of lives*, R. Josselson and A. Lieblich (eds.), 30-58. London: Sage Publications.

Wilde, O. 1986. *The Complete illustrated stories, plays & poems of Oscar Wilde.* London: Chancellor Press.

Winterbotham, R. G. 1989. *Self-reports of parasuicidal behaviours and social desirability effects in a correctional setting.* Unpublished doctoral dissertation, Simon Fraser University.

Woolf, V. 1977. *A room of one's own.* London: Grafton.

Wordsworth, W. 1965. *The prelude: Selected poems and sonnets.* Toronto: Holt, Rinehart and Winston.

Yates, J. M. 1993. *Line screw.* Toronto: McClelland & Stewart.

Zerubavel, E. 1981. *Hidden rhythms: Schedules and calendars in social life.* Chicago: University of Chicago Press.

Index

Author's Biographical Sketch

Carol A. Mullen is Research Associate in the Learning Systems Institute at Florida State University. She was a Visiting Assistant Professor in the College of Education, Texas A&M University, from 1995-96. She taught courses in the philosophy of education, cultural foundations and multiculturalism. Carol has published in educational journals on themes related to prisons and academe as well as diversity and artistic methods of research. Her applications of prison contexts and correctional processes to teacher education have been described as innovative and groundbreaking. Carol received her doctorate in curriculum studies and teacher development at the Ontario Institute for Studies in Education, Toronto, Canada.